S0-AXV-986

Donaghy, Thomas

KEYSTONE DEMOCRAT D. Lawrence   Bio

Rules of the
McDonald Free Library

This book may be kept fourteen days. *TEN*

A fine of ~~five~~ *TEN* cents a day (including Sundays and holidays) must be paid on all books kept overtime.

Borrowers must pay for books lost or damaged while charged on their cards.

KEYSTONE DEMOCRAT

David Lawrence Remembered

Thomas J. Donaghy

VANTAGE PRESS
New York / Washington / Atlanta
Los Angeles / Chicago

6-21-88

FIRST EDITION

All rights reserved, including the right of
reproduction in whole or in part in any form.

Copyright © 1986 by Thomas J. Donaghy

Published by Vantage Press, Inc.
516 West 34th Street, New York, New York 10001

Manufactured in the United States of America
ISBN: 0-533-06724-3

Library of Congress Catalog Card No.: 85-90221

For Jerry O' and the three Davids

Contents

Acknowledgments

In his autobiography, Mark Twain wrote: "Biographies are but the clothes and buttons of man—the biography of the man himself cannot be written." In my sartorial pursuit of David Leo Lawrence, I acknowledge with gratitude a multitude of individuals who were touched by Davey. His friends both in and out of public life generously contributed time and memories through personal interviews. Grace Sloan and Anna Mae Lawrence Donahue shared private collections. Patrick Sheekey, F.S.C., Robert Eugene Carlson, Judge Genevieve Blatt, Elizabeth Mason, Joseph O'Grady, Anna Mae Lawrence Donahue, and the late Louis Starr read all or portions of the manuscript and shared enlightened insights. Thomas Warner, F.S.C., was tireless in his interest in the development of the Lawrence segment of La Salle University's Oral History Collection, while La Salle's Board of Trustees generously provided research leave. Walter Giesey and Gerald Lawrence opened many doors of the governor's friends and enemies. Library personnel at the University of Pittsburgh, Columbia University Oral History Collection, La Salle University, the University of Pennsylvania, the Pennsylvania History and Museum Commission, and the Enoch Pratt Library of Baltimore were most cooperative. Judge Genevieve Blatt provided substantial help and encouragement in bringing the work to completion. Finally, a number of friends provided lodging, hospitality, and support in my research travels. The words, along with the errors, are mine. I end the project with the conviction of John Buchan: "Politics is still the greatest and the most honorable adventure."

I
Funeral

On November 21, 1966, at 2:55 P.M., David Leo Lawrence, former governor of Pennsylvania, died in Pittsburgh's Presbyterian-University Hospital, seventeen days after suffering a heart attack while speaking at a Democratic political rally at the city's Syria Mosque. The cause of death, as given by Dr. Campbell Moses, was "brain damage as a result of cardiac arrest."[1] Because of the impending Thanksgiving holiday, the family scheduled the governor's funeral for Friday, November 25.

The Lawrence family gathered at the governor's apartment in Chatham Center on that chilly, damp, gray day. The family then motored to McCabe Brothers Funeral Home in the East End section of Pittsburgh, where the wake for Lawrence had been held three days and nights. There was a short prayer ceremony at the funeral home. As the casket was carried outside, the bells of Sacred Heart Church across the street tolled every four seconds. The coffin was carried by eight city policemen wearing civilian clothes. The procession of twenty limousines moved steadily through the cleared streets, as police officers saluted and business people paused for a final gesture of respect. Gerald Lawrence was reminded of *The Last Hurrah.*[2]

When the cortege arrived at St. Mary of Mercy Church in the Point Section, over 2,000 people had already gathered. Among the throng were some 400 dignitaries who had marched from the conference room of the Bell Telephone Building across from the church. Mayor James H. J. Tate, of Philadelphia, remembered some jockeying for position. Mayor Richard Lee, of New Haven, remarked to Tate, "You know, a lot of these people are very foolish. The only

1

thing important here is the fellow in the casket. He knows you're here and I'm here, and that's enough for me." Jacob Arvey, Illinois Democratic leader, recalled, "I don't mind telling you that an old man like me, I shed tears. It was too bad that a big heart like that had been taken away." Some of the other notables in attendance were Orville Freeman, secretary of agriculture; Stewart Udall, secretary of the interior; Robert Kintner and Marvin Watson, special assistants to Pres. Lyndon B. Johnson; Martin McNamara, special counsel to Vice Pres. Hubert H. Humphrey; Fale Coffeey, Ireland's consul general, and Sen. Robert Kennedy. Also, former governors James H. Duff, Richard J. Hughes, John S. Fine, and William Scranton and Governor-Elect Raymond Shafer were there. Further, Mayor Jerome Cavanaugh, of Detroit; New Jersey attorney-general David Willents; Richardson Dilworth, former mayor of Philadelphia; Matthew McCloskey, former ambassador to Ireland; Congressmen William Green and Fred Rooney; Thomas Minehart, Pennsylvania state chairman; Harvey Taylor, veteran GOP state senator and longtime Republican wheelhorse; George I. Bloom, former GOP state chairman; and Frank Smith, Philadelphia Democratic leader, attended. Finally, John Robin, former executive secretary to Lawrence, made the long journey from Calcutta.[3]

As the flag-draped casket was carried into the church, a light rain fell. There was an irritating delay for the family in the church vestibule, because Bishop John Wright, Roman Catholic bishop of Pittsburgh, celebrant of the Low Pontifical Mass, was late. Finally, John Gabriel, Chief sergeant-at-arms of the state senate, entered the church carrying the state mace, draped in black crepe. The Lawrence family filled the first ten pews, while dignitaries and the press occupied the remaining spaces. The overflow crowd was housed in the church basement and the Diocesan auditorium next door, where T.V. coverage of the ceremonies was provided.[4]

Despite the prevailing custom of not offering eulogies, Bishop Wright spoke glowingly of Lawrence, calling him a great friend of the poor who "never outgrew his initial loyalties" in his rise to political power. Lawrence, according to Wright, saw human life as basic no matter how "poor or stunted or underprivileged it might be." Moreover, Wright reminded the congregation, Lawrence fought for social morality, slum clearance, and fair housing for blacks.

2

Lawrence's concern for humanity extended to every person regardless of "his color, or plight, his background or handicap. . . . to the meanest life, the least promising."

At the end of the mass, Mrs. Lawrence, feeling weak, expressed her desire not to go to the cemetery. She was taken to her apartment by police escort in the company of one of the grandchildren. In the cortege to the cemetery were 120 cars. Upon arrival at Calvary Cemetery, the procession went to a chapel rather than the family plot. There, over 200 people had gathered before the cortege arrived. Bishop John B. McDowell, auxiliary bishop of Pittsburgh, presided at a brief prayer service, and the mourners returned to their respective homes.[5] Pittsburgh, the state, and the nation would never be the same without David Lawrence.

Who was this man whose funeral touched the nation, as witnessed by the presence of so many political luminaries? It is believed President Johnson would have attended if he had not been ill. Paradoxically, Vice-President Humphrey said he would attend, but was countermanded by the president, who wanted Humphrey in Texas for a meeting the vice-president could have certainly missed. Later, almost as a political gimmick, Johnson released to the public a letter that he had sent to the Lawrence family explaining his absence. His rival Robert Kennedy had been there.[6]

Notes

1. *Pittsburgh Post Gazette*, November 22, 1966, p. 1.
2. *The Reminiscences of Gerald Lawrence*, (1976), in the Oral History Collection of La Salle University, hereinafter Gerald Lawrence; *Pittsburgh Press*, November 25, 1966, p. 1.
3. *The Reminiscenses of James H. J. Tate*, (1974), p. 25, in the Oral History Collection of La Salle University, hereinafter Tate; *The Reminiscences of Jacob Arvey*, (1975), p. 3, in the Oral History Collection of La Salle University, hereinafter Arvey; *Pittsburgh Post Gazette*, November 24, 1966, p. 1.
4. *Pittsburgh Press*, November 25, 1966, p. 1.
5. Ibid.
6. Ibid.; Gerald Lawrence, p. 1; *Pittsburgh Post Gazette*, November 26, 1966, p. 1.

II
Pittsburgh

As a young man, Lawrence must have often wondered just how great a legacy he really had in Pittsburgh's Democrats. That William Brennan's law firm proved a significant learning experience for Lawrence is admittedly true. Yet, as a young man starting out in politics, Lawrence certainly must have realized that if political success was to be achieved, it would take every effort he could mount. Perhaps the young visionary saw the void and determined, at his own pace, to fill it. Whatever Lawrence's plans for his future were in early–twentieth-century Pittsburgh, he snapped up every opportunity to move ahead with his education in politics.

As the nation prepared to elect a president in 1912, William Brennan thought perhaps the time had come to test his protégé, David Lawrence. Brennan led Pittsburgh's delegation to the Democratic national convention in Baltimore, where he appointed Lawrence a page. Pittsburgh's delegation included one Joseph Guffey who was a first-time delegate. Lawrence and Guffey, who eventually controlled the Democratic party in Pennsylvania, prophetically ended up on opposite sides at the convention. Guffey joined A. Mitchell Palmer and Vance McCormick in supporting Woodrow Wilson. Brennan, and other Pennsylvania delegates, went with Champ Clark. Lawrence, naturally, worked for the latter group.[1] It was the last time Lawrence supported the losing side at a national convention.

Surely, since Lawrence had no franchise at the convention, this was another learning experience for him. At age twenty-three, he was, interestingly enough, impressed by Wilson even though working for Clark. Decades later, reflecting on his first convention, Law-

4

rence said, "FDR was the greatest when it came to handling people. He knew exactly how to get them to do what he wanted. But Wilson, Wilson was real class." Further, Lawrence's admiration for Wilson was based on Wilson's academic background and experience.[2] This esteem for Wilson, apparently spawned at the 1912 convention, motivated Lawrence into staying with a Pittsburgh Democratic organization that had seemingly little to offer.

Just two years later, in 1914, Lawrence served in his first official political position as a member of the Bipartisan Registration Committee in the city of Pittsburgh. Lawrence secured the spot through the efforts of Joseph Guffey. This was an excellent opportunity for Lawrence politically, as his talents were now exposed to both major Pittsburgh parties. At the time, many took the committee for granted, but Lawrence made his association with it beneficial for Democrats and Republicans alike. His energy, enthusiasm, common sense, and pleasant personality gave the committee a spark that the majority members found difficult to ignore. Moreover, Lawrence learned a great deal about party mechanics on both sides of the fence. Although a minority member, he served well for ten years, analyzed the committee's needs, which in later years he would be in position to correct, and made friends as well as a reputation.[3]

Shortly after World War I, Lawrence's political fortunes, which were intimately connected with Guffey's, took a turn for the better. Since Guffey supported A. Mitchell Palmer at the 1920 Democratic national convention, Guffey was rewarded with a place on the Democratic National Committee. The Allegheny County chairmanship became open, and Lawrence was selected by Guffey. This was an important appointment for Lawrence, even though the Democratic party in Allegheny County was thin. It gave Lawrence the opportunity to lead his newly gained forces to the control of Allegheny County. That such would eventuate was not evident in the *Pittsburgh Post Gazette*'s lackluster comment that Lawrence was "one of the most widely known of the younger members of the Democratic Party in Allegheny County." Beyond that, no one seemed willing to make any predictions about Lawrence's or his party's future in the county.

When Lawrence was appointed chairman in Allegheny County,

5

the rather intense issue of the women's right to vote was under debate in the nation. The press wanted to know how Chairman Lawrence felt about the issue. His forthright answer surprised many of his contemporaries. "I want the women to have the right to vote for all offices, national and state, and I hope the Attorney General will find a way of permitting them to do this."[4] No doubt Lawrence, as his later actions proved, was sincere in supporting the female franchise. At the same time, his position did not harm Allegheny County Democrats. It gave them a broader area of support.

Personally, Lawrence's county chairmanship enhanced his position in national politics. In 1924, Lawrence attended the Democratic National Convention for the first time as a delegate. The tumultuous meeting in New York's Madison Square Garden was the longest in the nation's history, running seventeen days before a compromise candidate, John W. Davis, was selected. During that time, Lawrence voted 103 times for Gov. Alfred E. Smith. In character, Lawrence, a novice delegate, worked behind the scenes with Emma Guffey Miller. A fight had erupted over a platform plank condemning the Ku Klux Klan. Mrs. Miller delivered a speech that Heywood Broun called "the intellectual treat of the convention." Just before her delivery, Miller dictated the speech as Lawrence typed it in the Garden basement. Unhappily, the Smith forces lost their battle for the anti-Ku Klux Klan statement. When this happened, Charles P. Donnelly, Philadelphia's Democratic leader, went home. Before leaving, he said, "I'd like Davey to sit in my place" [on the Smith Strategy Board]. This was, in light of what would transpire in the future, a tremendous opportunity for Lawrence, especially since Franklin D. Roosevelt chaired the meetings.[5] What impression, if any, Lawrence made on FDR in 1924 is not recorded, but in twelve years Roosevelt would be undisputed leader of the national Democratic party and David Lawrence a name known in the White House.

Back home, Allegheny Democrats did not share Lawrence's seeming success. Entrenched Republicans gave little ground, except that required by law. Frank Happ, a Lawrence associate, recalled Lawrence gathering his forces on election night at Democratic headquarters on Fourth Avenue over a Greek restaurant. "With his nails

6

bit back to the quick," Lawrence watched the returns on a tape machine. A minority commissioner position was the only one available to the Democrats. Once Jimmy Hoolihan was elected, the Democrats went to the Hotel Henry to meet the newly elected Republicans.[6] Actually, Lawrence had nothing with which to provide refreshments for party workers after the election. His courtesy call on the Republicans served the dual purpose of a minority faction keeping lines of communication open, while, at the same time, sharing the Republicans' convivial abundance. Some Democrats questioned Lawrence's actions to the extent that he was accused of currying Republican favor. Others felt Lawrence was just making the best of a difficult situation. There is no evidence that Lawrence had Republican leanings, even though he received tempting offers from the other side. According to Lawrence, times were tough but he never had any intention of abandoning the Democrats. He said, "Prior to 1932, just a few old faithfuls stuck by the party. It was a long gap between Wilson and FDR. Before 1932, Democrats always played for the minority places."[7] Realist that he was, Lawrence determined to weather miserable party conditions in Allegheny County, slowly but surely and effectively working for the day when a more powerful national Democratic party with a Democrat in the White House would enable his organization to unplug the Republican machine and allow his dormant forces to engulf Allegheny County. Perhaps 1928 would be the year.

When the Democrats met at Houston in late June 1928, Lawrence was present. He was, for the second time, going to back Gov. Al Smith. This time Lawrence's man was nominated. Guffey, in his biography, suggests that the nomination of Al Smith as the Democratic party's presidential candidate in 1928 was a turning point for the Democrats in Pennsylvania. In 1924, when Smith failed to get the nomination, he had been top choice in Pennsylvania's primary. In backing the Smith candidacy both in 1924 and 1928, Guffey and Lawrence provided a sense of leadership and were thus able to gain control of the Democratic organization in Western Pennsylvania. True, Smith was not elected president, but his campaign ably demonstrated a new movement among voters in urban communities, a force that leaned heavily toward the Democratic party. Republican

7

bastions across Pennsylvania had been breached, particularly in Pittsburgh, Philadelphia, Scranton, and Erie, and Allegheny County Democrats' hopes awakened.[8] Lawrence, strongly backed by Guffey, stood at the crossroads of how far, how fast.

Democrats, however, were not yet out of the woods. Mayor Joseph Barr described the party in 1928 as an "abject minority in the city and county." Barr, whose great-grandfather was Democratic national committeeman from Pennsylvania, was just twenty-one during the 1928 campaign. His father took him to meet Lawrence. "It was going to be my first vote and naturally, getting out of college, I was pretty much interested in politics. And Lawrence was such a dynamic fellow that a young man would immediately look to him."[9] Given the Democrats' situation in Allegheny County, Lawrence and Guffey continued to look to the national party for the strength needed in bolstering party interests at home. Whether or not Guffey saw the brilliance others observed in Lawrence is difficult to say. Guffey's many national connections may have allayed any fears as to a possible challenge from Lawrence. Moreover, it did not appear at the time that Lawrence felt personally strong enough to make any moves against Guffey. So, with the unsuccessful 1928 campaign over, Lawrence remained Allegheny County chairman.

One of the knottier problems for Democrats and Republicans alike in Allegheny County was the division of county and city government. Pittsburgh, along with many other cities, municipalities, boroughs, and townships, rests within the boundaries of Allegheny County. County commissioners controlled one segment of the government, while city fathers ruled others. The city of Pittsburgh had, in effect, two governments, working sometimes at cross-purposes. Civic tangles arising from the situation were one thing, but intraparty squabbles caused grief for both parties. In 1929, during a supposedly bipartisan attempt to establish a countywide charter, Lawrence declared it to be a "patriotic duty to adopt the metropolitan system to enable this great district with its population of a million and a half, to expand its activities and act unitedly to meet the municipal competition of this modern age."[10] Despite the Lawrence view, charter government in Allegheny County was never realized, and once

8

Democrats controlled both Pittsburgh and Allegheny County, Lawrence no longer saw a county charter as "patriotic duty."

It was just two years after Lawrence's charter statement that he decided to test the waters and run for public office. Lawrence became one of the two Democratic nominees for county commissioner in the 1931 primary in Allegheny County. (According to Allegheny County statute, a minority commissioner had to be elected. This was, in the twenties and thirties, usually a Democrat, although an Independent candidate was free to seek the office.) The Republicans were, to some extent, divided at the time. Independent Republican Charles McGovern was joined in the 1931 campaign by C. M. Barr as running mate for county commissioner. Backed by Governor Pinchot, the Independents were challenged by Regular Republican William Mansfield. Mansfield wanted to be chairman of the county commissioners, and if Barr and McGovern were elected, Mansfield would be in the minority spot. Republicans Kline, mayor of Pittsburgh, and State Senator Coyne both stated they would vote straight Republican. However, many Republicans suspected Kline and Coyne were really supporting Mansfield and Democrat Lawrence. One newspaper suggested, "Lawrence, although a Democrat was known as a 'Coyne man,' first and last and would therefore be amiable to suggestions of the Mayor [between Kline and Commissioner Armstrong] probably those of Armstrong as well."[11] This assertion cannot be taken at face value. True, Lawrence and Coyne had been close friends over the years. Lawrence's position on the Bipartisan Registration Commission and his chairmanship of the Democratic party in Allegheny County brought him in frequent contact with Republican leaders. Lawrence was not one to bristle or tighten on such occasions. Rather, he allowed fellowship and professional courtesy to prevail, while, at the same time, learning as much as he could about the opposition in general and political success in particular. For Lawrence in his early political career, the Republicans represented the available example of successful politics in Pittsburgh and Allegheny County. What he learned from his opponents Lawrence eventually used to replace them.

Whether Lawrence actually sought Republican support in the

1931 campaign is another question. There were some who felt Lawrence compromised himself in his appeal for Republican votes. Nine* prominent Allegheny County Democrats made the following statement in the *Pittsburgh Post Gazette* of October 31, 1931. "We believe that his [Lawrence's] election will unquestionably give a vicious Republican organization a continued foothold in the county commissioner's office and will perpetuate the bipartisan machine in which David Lawrence has long assumed an important role." How effective the charge was on election outcomes is hard to say. But it does indicate a sentiment within the Allegheny County Democratic party in opposition to Lawrence and his willingness to cooperate wholeheartedly with the bipartisan county commissioner organization. For Lawrence, a Democratic minority commissionership was far better than nothing, and perhaps, without a stronger national candidate to pull votes for Democrats in the county, Lawrence knew that if they chose to do so, Republicans could have denied Democrats the third spot in favor of an independent candidate. What is more, the evidence seems to point toward Lawrence having allowed the Republicans, Kline and Coyne in particular, to support him. Lawrence did not feel obligated in his 1931 campaign to appeal only to Democrats. He knew this meant certain defeat on registration figures alone. That Lawrence was politically wise enough to appeal to all voters, even though privately he might have known of the Kline-Coyne support, does not make it clear that he sought Republican organization support. If he received such backing, all the more power to him. The pique expressed by his nine Democratic colleagues merely reinforces our picture of a Democratic party and organization in Pittsburgh and Allegheny County in "miserable" straits. Yet, because of Lawrence's work in a political campaign that failed, this same destitute political party was the better for it.

When election results were tallied in 1931, Lawrence had polled over 120,000 votes. Usually Democrats at the time in Allegheny County polled only about 10,000 votes. Moreover, in the city of

*A. M. Thompson, John M. Henry, George H. Stengel, Carl D. Smith, Martin F. Lowley, Thomas H. Hester, Gregg Lewellyn, Barbara M. Sullivan, and Bradley McK. Burns.

10

Pittsburgh, Lawrence garnered more votes than Independent Republican Barr. Lawrence lost the election in the outlying areas of Allegheny County, and despite a Republican victory, the GOP intraparty fights and economic recession served the Democratic party interests in many ways.[12]

Lawrence, a rather sensitive man, was deeply distressed in defeat. As party leader for eleven years, Lawrence blamed himself for the election outcome. Much of his anxiety focused on his personal qualifications and background. Moreover, he was convinced his religious affiliation had something to do with the results. This unfortunate belief would not leave him for many decades and was a potent force in his entire political career. It would be another fourteen years before Lawrence would again attempt to win public office in Allegheny County.

Other unpleasant results of the 1931 disaster awaited the Democrats. Those who questioned Lawrence's candidacy, now calling themselves Independent Democrats, assailed Lawrence and Guffey, charging them with the breakdown of the two-party system; saying thousands of Democrats were leaving the party; and alleging that the county committee had not been called together and had never functioned.[13] A substantial percentage of the charges were political rhetoric, although there were many dyed-in-the-wool, rank-and-file Democrats who were confused by the 1931 campaign. Still, Lawrence and Guffey sat tight and rode out the storm. With the approach of the summer of 1932, Lawrence and Guffey, sensing a changing mood abroad in the nation due to the economic crisis, had high hopes for a renewed Democratic party nationally, which would help them reap the whirlwind of dissatisfaction and economic dejection in severely depressed Allegheny County. This was probably the only time in his political career that David Lawrence thanked God for his 1931 defeat at the polls.

Just fifteen short years later, riding the Democratic party's meteoric rise under Franklin D. Roosevelt, Lawrence found himself on top of the heap in Pittsburgh politics and immediately realized that political success carried with it ever increasing problems. Inaugural festivities in January 1946 had hardly terminated when now Mayor Lawrence faced a serious crisis on the labor front. Before

11

Lawrence had a chance to acquaint himself with the problems associated with city administration, Duquesne Light Company employees threatened a strike that would cut off electric energy in and around the city. Immediately, Lawrence got company and union representatives together. Things did not go well, and at one point, Lawrence kept bargaining sessions going for nineteen and one-half consecutive hours, securing an agreement to postpone the strike. Pittsburgh was spared a midwinter power outage. Lawrence's first month in office was characteristic of his first term in that he seemed "not too concerned with details of public administration," according to Jack Robin, Lawrence's executive secretary. Labor and development occupied much of Lawrence's time during his first term. In reality, routine government operations went much the same as they had under Mayor Scully.[14]

Labor was indeed a challenge for Lawrence in 1946. This friend of labor saw his city plagued by strikes. Cold-storage plants were shut down. A 26–day steel strike, two coal strikes, and a 115–day walkout at Westinghouse Corporation caused untold suffering, unrest, and damage to Pittsburgh's economy. At the same time, city hotels were struck for fifty-three days, several bus companies that served surrounding communities were idled for various periods of time, and eighty-one other work stoppages demanded Lawrence's attention that first year. But worst of all, two power strikes erupted, causing severe inconvenience and suffering in Pittsburgh.[15] Lawrence almost became a full-time negotiator, trying to bring contesting parties together. In some cases, Lawrence was accepted as the mediator. According to Robin, Lawrence, always an excellent judge of character, was not impressed with big names. He demonstrated extraordinary patience in negotiations and was able to use the status of his office wisely. Still, in the power strike Lawrence was exercised to the limits of his ability as mayor, mediator, and negotiator.

From January 1946, when Lawrence secured a promise from Duquesne Light employees not to go on strike, little progress was made in talks between company and union. By late August, Lawrence was back in the middle, mediating the two sides. A strike had been called for midnight, September 10. Lawrence went on the air on the tenth and blamed the company and its independent union

12

for the strike. He accused Duquesne Light of being "psychologically incompetent. It does not know how to deal with human beings." Lawrence then called on county, state, and federal agencies to step in, while, at the same time, he threatened an injunction.[16] When Commissioner Kane got labor leaders to agree to try to stop the walkout, the injunction was dropped. Lawrence proclaimed the end of the strike lifted a burden and averted a disaster. "It proves once again that no one is above the city."[17]

Negotiations continued, but from the union position, no progress was made. As a result, the union was set to strike again at 9:30 A.M., Tuesday, September 24. Lawrence called in the peace authorities of Allegheny and Beaver counties, along with newspaper editors and municipal officials. There he mapped a strategy for dealing with the consequences of the threatened strike. At the same time, Lawrence summoned Leo T. Crowley, president of Standard Gas and Electric Corporation, the parent company of Duquesne Light, and asked him to resubmit proposals before the strike deadline. Disaster plans were initiated. The city borrowed thirty-seven generators from the army for emergency services, city swimming pools were filled with water, and police were put on a twelve-hour day. All last-minute negotiations failed, and Pittsburgh virtually came to a standstill except for emergency services. George L. Mueller, president of the independent union at the power company, was put in jail, sentenced to one year for having defied a court order. Union members surrounded the courthouse, shouting in unison, "Put Lawrence in jail. Put Crowley in jail."[18] Ironically, the majority of the marchers had just put Lawrence in office the preceding November. The strike ended twenty-seven days later, with Lawrence getting most of the credit for bringing both sides together. He skillfully mediated an acceptable agreement. But Lawrence's labor worries were not over, and like most areas of postwar United States, Pittsburgh remained saddled with labor problems through the middle and late forties.

During a jurisdictional labor dispute over breweries in November 1946, a bomb ripped through a tavern in Pittsburgh's Lawrenceville section. Teamsters and CIO United Brewery Workers were fighting for control of brewerymen then represented by the

13

CIO. A jurisdictional dispute was one thing, violence another, for Lawrence. Despite his ties with and political dependence on labor, Lawrence told the police "to go as far as humanly and physically possible" to stop the spreading violence.[19] The dispute was settled quickly, with Lawrence none the worse politically for his strong stand. Still, by year's end, an exhausted Lawrence remarked, "I hope the next three years will not be like this one."[20] As it turned out, 1946 proved to be Lawrence's most difficult year as mayor. It became evident to the people of Pittsburgh that they had an exceptional leader with a capacity for greatness. His efforts in Pittsburgh's labor troubles clearly demonstrated Lawrence's leadership qualities, aptitudes that labor unrest constantly tested.

Lawrence again found himself in labor's spotlight during his second mayoral campaign, in 1949. A threatened nationwide steel strike, which would have had disasterous consequences on Pittsburgh, Allegheny, and surrounding counties, caused Lawrence to move into action. He called on the United States Steel Corporation to accept the recommendations of President Truman's fact-finding board and avert a strike. Lawrence suggested that corporate steel invoke again the "industrial statesmanship that impelled it to recognize the union without a strike in 1937." Lawrence continued, "Nothing could be more hollow than a so-called victory which would plunge the business life of America into a new depression."[21] Lawrence's strong appeal to business interests hardly offended labor in this instance, since he was really asking industry to meet labor's demands, which, in the long run, would benefit the steel industry. As White House advisor, mayor of a large steel-producing center, and powerful political leader, Lawrence's voice was an influential one in helping to avert a strike. The following year, Pittsburgh was hit by a newspaper strike. Lawrence declared it a "calamity" for the community. At a time when state and federal mediation was not as highly developed as it is today, Lawrence immediately offered his services as mediator.[22] In a short time, Pittsburgh's newspapers were back on the streets.

As time passed, the people of Pittsburgh looked to Lawrence when labor difficulties arose, which were not infrequent. For many years he mediated labor disputes involving public welfare. According

14

to Frank Hawkins, for a politician who needed labor's backing for election, this was a delicate, dangerous venture. Yet Lawrence usually retained labor and management's respect and confidence. In the process, one side or the other had to be angered, but Lawrence got away with it.[23] During the 1957 transit strike, Lawrence brought both sides together. During long hours of negotiations, some bargainers played gin rummy with the mayor and small stakes were bet on the games. When the strike concluded, negotiators on both sides purchased a television set for Lawrence and attached a plaque that read: "We admit that at gin rummy you can't be beat, But if in the future we chance to meet, We'd rather not just lose our dough, But turn this on and watch the show."[24] It was not unusual for Lawrence to evoke such sentiments of respect, goodwill, and humor from individuals with whom he worked in tense situations, particularly in labor negotiations.

Even after Lawrence became governor, his reputation as a mediator followed him. During the 1959 steel strike, Lawrence organized a group of governors in an attempt to bring pressure on the Eisenhower administration to move toward a strike settlement. The administration did not react to the governors' suggestion, so Lawrence's role terminated in that strike.[25] It should be understood, however, that Lawrence did not wed himself to labor. He was sympathetic toward labor's aims and was well aware that a major portion of his constituency was labor-oriented. At the same time, Lawrence saw merit in management's view, while understanding clearly just how significant a contribution business interests made toward Pittsburgh's well-being. Lawrence did not hesitate to exercise leadership in both camps, since he was convinced the mayor's office called for total community involvement.

Just before Lawrence was elected mayor for the first time, he confided to a friend, "I expect to be the best mayor Pittsburgh ever had."[26] This from a man who posed as the reluctant nominee! It was Lawrence's great love for his native city that stiffened his determination to be top-notch in the mayor's office. He wanted only the best for Pittsburgh, and as mayor, that is what he tried to give it. His administrations absorbed Lawrence's personal characteristics of ebullience, vigor, vitality, efficiency, hard work, and humor. In

15

spite of labor distractions, Lawrence set down a strict routine for himself. He usually arrived at the mayor's office between nine-thirty and ten in the morning. He immediately turned to prepared details that needed his personal attention. Then he began a series of appointments that lasted through the day. Unless scheduled out for lunch, Lawrence ate at his desk. On many evenings he attended civic and social functions required of his office, but always tried to be home by eleven. Nearly every day after a tedious round of appointments and meetings with business and community leaders, while the staff wound up remaining correspondence and reports, Lawrence played pinochle in his office, "with people who were certainly not his intellectual or political peers." It was a relaxing time for the mayor before signing last-minute documents and departing from his office. This routine hardly ever varied when Lawrence was in Pittsburgh. He wanted to be available to constituents as much as possible. Moreover, this schedule gave the office a sense of stability.[27]

In the mayor's office, Lawrence delegated authority and generally allowed his staff to work things out themselves. Jack Robin and later Walter Giesey, executive secretaries, drafted speeches and papers, acted as managing directors of the city, coordinated development projects, and worked with community leaders. Their assistants handled all city matters that involved directors of various departments. Lawrence was available to all members of his administration, but he preferred that staff members handle their own business. John Exler, recorder of deeds and one of Commissioner Kane's protégés, verified that Lawrence "never interfered with the office in any way." Sometimes Lawrence would ask Exler to appoint a particular individual to a job, and Exler was glad to oblige.[28] At one time, some difficulty arose in the Purchasing Department. According to Pittsburgh's system of government, the department director is responsible for his particular department. A purchasing agent for the Department of Supplies was investigated and indicted. Lawrence called his former assistant secretary, Charles McCarthy, and said, "I want you to go up there. You know the business in the city; you know the law; you ought to be able to see that things operate properly." Lawrence insisted that any favors granted be done strictly within the law. A low bidder, no matter who he was, got the job.

16

"You were required to give the job under the law to the low bidder and he [Lawrence] operated that way."[29]

As mayor and head of the county Democratic organization, Lawrence controlled patronage in the city. A patronage secretary handled the details. Sometimes there would be dissatisfaction. In such cases, the ward chairman would go to the executive secretary who acted as liaison among mayor, department director, and ward chairman. Sometimes, chairmen were not willing to take the secretary's "No." Then they were free to see Lawrence personally. Walter Giesey explained, "If there was something to give away, Lawrence ought to give it away; if there was something to be turned down, I ought to turn it down."[30] Even in such a delicate matter as city patronage, Lawrence was willing to rely on others for help, a practical solution to the ever growing demands on urban administrators.

Lawrence, when inaugurated mayor, was fifty-seven years old, yet his was a "very healthy body and fertile mind." Lawrence possessed a tremendous capacity for hard work, something he demanded of his staff. When in the city, he was at his desk seven days a week. Even though City Hall was closed, he made appointments for Saturdays and Sundays. "He looked for things to do, people to talk with, calls to make, and if a fire or emergency happened he would be ready immediately. 'Come on, get your car.' " The ever present Lawrence was thus able to keep on top of everything going on. His knowledge of city matters, whether political, economic, or social, was in minute detail, most of which was stored in his mind for instant recall when necessary.[31] And there may have been more than just a personal reason for all the time Lawrence expended on his city. Lawrence's determination to keep on top of events in Pittsburgh was rooted in a nearly pathological dedication to good government. True, in his own mind he had a past to amend for, but more important than that was Lawrence's objective that his beloved Pittsburgh have the finest in government. Moreover, his success at being mayor was a great source of personal gratification. He felt the greatest job in the world was to have been Mayor of Pittsburgh. That was true when he was Governor and when he was special assistant to the President. No job that he ever had came up to the feeling of satisfaction it gave him to be Mayor of Pittsburgh.[32]

17

If indeed Lawrence's successful career as mayor was a joy for him personally as well as for his political colleagues, Pittsburgh's Republican organization suffered as a result. As will be seen, it was a Democrat, Edward Leonard, who gave Lawrence his most effective political challenge while mayor. Lawrence's success in bringing business and labor interests together for Pittsburgh's benefit prompted Frank Hawkins to write: "They [the Republicans] suffered *in extremis* one September day in 1953 when Richard King Mellon . . . figuratively draped an arm around the broad shoulders of the Mayor . . . and praised him publicly at a groundbreaking ceremony."[33] Still, the weakened Republicans did not let Lawrence forget their presence. His "Achilles' heel," municipal housekeeping, was in for some attention. Republicans, quite correctly, noted the streets were full of potholes. Moreover, garbage collection was poor and the water system worn out. "The police are controlled by district inspectors who are purely political stooges. The budget is a phoney, loaded with people who don't work but stand around on street corners and fix traffic tags. Pittsburgh is like a shiny red apple that is rotten to the core."[34] Much of the Republican criticism was political rhetoric laced with half-truths, except for the potholes. They were and still are abundant. Once, Judge Michael Musmanno, speaking at a political meeting, said, "Ah, the potholes, my friends, the potholes . . . " demeaning but not denying the charges. Most of these Republicans plaints were aired during Lawrence's second term. Giesey claims little of that appeared in the third or fourth terms.[35] Again, while people were inconvenienced by sloppy city housekeeping, they were constantly reminded of the progress being made in smoke control, redevelopment, new business and job opportunities, and recreational facilities. All these helped ease the people's frustrations with petty annoyances.

On the other hand, all was not lost for Republicans who had professional skills and were available for the use of the community. Although Lawrence sincerely believed in patronage, especially in the Police Department, which he kept within the realm of politics, where professional services were needed, he avoided political entanglements. At one time, when Pittsburgh's Health Department was completely revised, the personnel director was encouraged to hire public-health professionals solely on their credentials and qualifications, and when this caused grumblings among ward chairmen, Lawrence let it be known that the action was his and patronage was out in that area.[36]

Another phase of Lawrence's rule that was disliked and encouraged opposition, both within and without the organization, was the wage tax. On the matter of taxes, Lawrence was very careful. Lawrence felt promising no tax increases during campaigns was a foolish tactic, since a candidate never realized until in office just what fiscal demands might arise. In the matter of the wage tax, Lawrence stated that the costs for city services were inevitably rising. He knew of no other way of securing necessary funds than taxes. Lawrence argued that many people came into Pittsburgh to work but were not paying their share for city services like police, fire, mass transit, and public accommodations. Moreover, Lawrence pleaded with the "boudoir" communities not to initiate a similar tax. He knew, of course, they would not cooperate. Since Allegheny County did not come under the Sterling Act, whenever a community outside Pittsburgh added a wage tax, citizens from that community were no longer required to pay in Pittsburgh. By 1955, Lawrence's third term, all the surrounding communities had imposed the tax and it was "an established system of municipal finance." Neither Republicans nor the McClelland-Roberts Democratic factions ever opposed Lawrence because of the wage tax.[37]

When the tax became law, Lawrence consulted Mayor Hanlon of Scranton, whose city was the first to have the wage tax. Hanlon said, "Well, Dave, the way we did it, when we put it on we put a lot of money in parks and playgrounds so people could see what the money was going for." Similarly, Lawrence formed the Mayor's Management Advisory Committee, which helped the efficiency of City Hall operations. This, in addition to the ongoing building program, which was becoming more and more visible, helped demonstrate just how well tax monies were being utilized.[38] Moreover, Lawrence's reputation for honesty helped immensely in gaining acceptance for the wage tax.

One of the more popular programs growing out of the wage-tax income was Lawrence's safety campaign. Many felt his stress on

19

safety reflected the loss of his two sons in an auto accident. Lawrence never really said this, but he did demonstrate his conviction that safety contributed to a higher quality of life in urban areas, a notion that reached beyond the confines of Pittsburgh. According to Mayor James H. J. Tate, "He was the one who gave me the idea of school crossing guards in Philadelphia."[39] Toward the end of Lawrence's third term, in 1957, The National Safety Council presented certificates of achievement to Mayor Lawrence in three areas: public safety education, safety education, and maintenance of accident records.[40] Again on the national level, Mayor Lawrence was highly regarded by his fellow mayors at The United States Conference of Mayors. In 1955, the conference bestowed its Distinguished Public Service Award on Lawrence. "Mayor Lawrence was honored chiefly for being the 'crystallizing force' behind the rebuilding and redevelopment of Pittsburgh."[41] Over the years with the conference, Lawrence had been recognized as one of its outstanding leaders. When Lawrence attended yearly meetings, he always took along council members. Once, when the assembly was scheduled in New Orleans, Lawrence called the then president of the conference, Mayor Robert Wagner of New York City. "By the way, Bob, I take some of my councilmen with me and a couple of them are black. Can we get into this hotel in New Orleans?" Wagner checked it out and was told no. Wagner called Mayor Chet Morrison of New Orleans, who offered to house Pittsburgh's delegation in his home. Since the Morrison home was too small, it was decided to switch the meeting to Miami Beach. It was this type of leadership and principle that impressed Lawrence's colleagues. "Lawrence had a vision, and a quality . . . always impressed me as a hell of a fellow, good liberalism, the kind that made the Democratic Party the greatest party in the country."[42] Finally, Governor Robert Meyner of New Jersey recalled that it was Lawrence who achieved national recognition for the nation's mayors. "I think prior to this time, maybe the Mayor of New York or Chicago got some recognition, but there wasn't much attention paid to other large cities. And I think his achievements gave some impetus to the movement by which other mayors became recognized."[43] Although this was significant and, many believed, well-deserved, tribute from his colleagues, others

20

in Pittsburgh speculated that much of Lawrence's success as mayor was due to his muscling City Council. Republicans, Democrats, Independents, blacks, and whites were among those who questioned Lawrence's relationship with City Council.

In her study of Lawrence's rise as a political leader, Sally Shames tells of an unidentified Lawrence colleague who said City Council was a rubber stamp. This person claimed nothing ever originated with the council, but everything was prefabricated for presentation to the council. "It was just fortunate that Dave Lawrence did such a good job."[44] This rubber-stamp council concept was widespread during Lawrence administrations. On the contrary, according to Jack Robin, Lawrence met with the council every Monday morning behind closed doors. "Newspaper people did not like this—it was from this latter source that the notion developed that Lawrence controlled." Robin admits Lawrence was powerful but he did try to arrive at a consensus.[45]

When Lawrence took office, he was aware a strain had developed between his predecessor, Scully, and the council. Thus the reason for the Monday morning conferences was to develop a spirit of cooperation with the council. If there were problems, Lawrence wanted them out of the way before going to the council chambers. When there was too much opposition, he would withdraw proposed legislation. As a result, the council never vetoed or defeated any Lawrence proposal that came to the floor. Early in his first term, Lawrence attended every conference and public session, but later his executive secretary or a department head would sit in for him. While he was there, however, there was never anything like "now this is what we are going to do, fellows, and I want you all to vote yes." He pressed his views, but if they did not prevail, he withdrew or sought compromise. Frequently, Lawrence would bring in department heads to defend their proposals. Moreover, difficulties developed between various council members and department heads, particularly with reference to residency waivers. Since Pittsburgh had an ordinance that required all city workers to live in the city, the Department of Health and Planning was constantly seeking waivers, and this caused friction, but usually Lawrence was not in on the discussions.[46]

21

Another consideration is that many who served on the council, although all Democrats, just could not be controlled. James Knox, Lawrence protégé and Allegheny County controller for twenty years, recalled that councilmen like A. L. Wolk, Patrick Fagan, Walter Demmler, Frederick T. Weir, Craig Kuhn and Patrick Baskin "were all individuals in their own right with a very high sense of purpose and duty." Moreover, when there was a significant deviation in the council, for example, on the wage-tax issue, Lawrence admitted he had to reassess his own position on the tax and "every man in Council would have to speak for himself as a matter of conscience," since the Democratic party had originally stood against a wage-tax enactment. Councilman John Coonahan did just that. He voted against the tax, according to his conscience. Lawrence never held it against him. Moreover, Lawrence, who rarely if ever complimented anybody, constantly praised the council. When Richard King Mellon gave Lawrence credit at a public ceremony inaugurating additional development projects, Lawrence gave credit to the City Council."[47]

At the same time, Lawrence guarded the council's reputation. On one occasion, Lawrence dumped Councilman Joseph McArdle from the party. "McArdle wanted do to things that Lawrence didn't agree with as far as having black bag people around him and Lawrence couldn't buy that kind of stuff." McArdle wanted his own police inspector, but Lawrence refused. Lawrence never said why, but no councilman could appoint a police inspector.[48] At the same time, the McArdle case aside, Lawrence seemed willing to go along with sound suggestions in the council. But he hated to hear someone say, "This is no good" or "That won't work" unless the individual could answer the question "What have you got that is better?"[49] Lawrence wanted the council to function on positive rather than negative suggestions. On balance, the City Council under Lawrence, although strictly partisan, functioned efficiently and served the people well. There was give and take, and Lawrence experienced both. In addition, Lawrence was always careful about special group interests in selecting councilmen. "Although Catholics on the Council outnumber Protestants five to four, Lawrence has seen to it that Negroes, Jews, Italians, and Irish are all represented. The same policy governs judgeships and other local offices. Thus the Pittsburgh pattern is, in microcosm, that of the political parties nationally." That is how Frank Hawkins saw the Lawrence administration in 1956.[50] Still, it should be remembered, Lawrence, although he experienced significant internal opposition at times, was a powerful force, yet was rated by friend and foe alike a good mayor. Frequently, this judgment was furthered by his association with Pittsburgh's so-called Renaissance.

As European nations jousted for power in the late thirties, their increased demands on American industry were felt in Pittsburgh, the steel-making capital of the United States. Business speedup was a welcome relief for Allegheny County. Increased productivity, however, carried with it corresponding environmental inconveniences and dangers, especially increased volumes of medium and heavy smoke. Smoke and accompanying smog became a necessary facet of life in Pittsburgh. Even the City Council seemed bent on total surrender when, in 1939, it abolished the Bureau of Smoke Regulation.[51] As the tempo of war increased in Europe, greater claims were made on American industry, and Pittsburgh nearly smothered in smoke.

Late in 1940, Edward T. Leech, editor of the *Pittsburgh Press*, initiated a crusade against the ubiquitous smoke. He was joined by I. Hope Alexander, city health director, and Abraham L. Wolk, city councilman. In their campaign, they were able to push an antismoke ordinance through the council. With the U.S. entrance into World War II, however, implementation of smoke control was delayed.[52] Pittsburghers accepted the dirt and annoyance as part of their contribution to the war effort.

During the war, Richard King Mellon, Pittsburgh financier, served as Selective Service director in Harrisburg. Mellon actively recruited people to live in Pittsburgh after the war and work for Mellon enterprises. On too many occasions, Mellon was turned down because Pittsburgh "had such a reputation as a rotten place to live."[53] It was this experience that convinced Mellon and other business, civic, and political leaders that drastic action was needed to save Pittsburgh from decay and death. Unless the city could be made an acceptable place to reside, business and industry could not convince their top people to work in Pittsburgh; many businesses

23

were considering a move out of the area. There was one saving factor; these varied interests were nearly all in agreement that the first step toward making Pittsburgh habitable was the elimination or at least the control of smoke.

By the time hostilities ceased in the Pacific, the United Smoke Council had been organized in Pittsburgh, with Jay Ream as its first chairman. During the 1945 mayoralty campaign, Ream approached the candidates for support. Lawrence agreed that smoke had to be eliminated, and he developed the slogan, "Smoke must go. Let's clean up Pittsburgh." The Republican candidate refused to go along with this and did not mention smoke in his campaign.[54]

At this stage of Lawrence's official connection with Pittsburgh's Renaissance, it is difficult to say just how much support he received from Mellon interests in his first campaign for mayor. Since he won by only 14,000 votes, Republican leaders whose interests would be served by an environmentally improved Pittsburgh might well have sat on their hands, waiting to see what direction the Lawrence administration would take.

It was not long after Lawrence assumed office that it became evident he meant what he said about smoke control as well as the Allegheny Conference on Community Development, a group of civic leaders actively engaged in planning the physical, cultural, and recreational rehabilitation of the Pittsburgh area. "We fixed a date for the [smoke] ordinance to go into effect. . . . Richard K. Mellon and his associates in the Allegheny Conference gave their strong support," said Lawrence, suggesting Mellon was "a sort of a bell cow in Pittsburgh; as he moves others move with him."[55] Although Lawrence moved boldly on the issue, the norms of procedure were observed. In April 1946, the council received the recommendations for implementing the smoke-control ordinance; public hearings were held. Republicans saw this as a politically courageous step on Lawrence's part, "since many of the supporters of the Democratic Party were in the lower income group and would probably find it harder to comply with the ordinance than higher income people."[56] Nonetheless, the ordinance was revised, setting the effective date of October 1, 1946, for all users of solid fuels, except for one-and two-family dwelling units, which were to comply by October 1, 1947.

24

During the winter of 1947–48, with family units then involved, some coal retailers seemed determined to fight the law by not supplying adequate amounts of low-volatile coal for home heating and some people found it difficult to heat their homes. Pressure mounted on the Lawrence administration, and the mayor called a meeting to see what further efforts could be made to support the ordinance. Downgrading Allegheny Conference reports, one of Lawrence's principal advisors urged Lawrence to relax the ordinance. At this point, Park H. Martin told Lawrence that if he loosened the ordinance, the entire program would collapse and the Equitable Life Assurance Corporation could be lost as the prospective developer of Gateway Center, a multimillion-dollar office center in Pittsburgh's downtown Triangle. At the same time, Martin promised to call the large steel companies and get them to release some of their metallurgical low-volatile coal to retailers if the situation got worse. With that understanding, Lawrence refused to budge on the ordinance.[57] This was a significant step for Lawrence and assured Pittsburgh citizens of a better place to live even before the redevelopment and construction phase of the Renaissance began. The first year of smoke control saw a 31-percent reduction in smoke. Also, industry spent $200 million on smoke-abatement technology. An additional $15 million was spent by retailers in building new storefronts, while others spent over a million dollars to scrub their premises. By 1954, reduction in heavy smoke was 98.7 percent, moderate smoke 85.8 percent, as compared to 1945.[58] Not only did smoke control in the first eight years improve the quality of life in Pittsburgh, but its implementation sparked hundreds of jobs and increased earning power in the adjustment and cleanup process.

What became obvious in the beginning of the smoke-control program was that the city, surrounded by over 100 municipalities, needed countywide cooperation if the plan was to achieve total success. John Kane favored extending legislation to the entire county, but initial attempts at similar control in 1943 had exempted the railroads. This time, Kane wanted the rail industry included. Lawrence was delighted with Kane's position, and the two worked together writing necessary legislation for the county. In March 1947, the Allegheny County Conference sponsored a luncheon meeting

25

that included Allegheny County Republicans and Democrats. Several Republican legislators voiced concern over their role in backing smoke-control legislation for the county as well as several enabling acts for the city of Pittsburgh's improvement. Since both areas were controlled by Democrats, Republicans felt Democrats would get all the credit. Lawrence reminded them the legislation would be good for all constituencies. Moreover, if the Republicans opposed, that would be "grist for our mill." Further, Lawrence assured the Republicans the bills would be passed and the governor had already agreed to sign them. So he urged the opposition, for their own political future, for their families' welfare and for future generations, to back the proposed bills.[59] The next day, the luncheon program was featured in banner headlines on the front pages of the papers and was described as a first in Pittsburgh's political history. It was then that the pending legislation was dubbed the "Pittsburgh Package." Republicans went along, and by 1949, smoke control was extended throughout Allegheny County.[60] Moreover, the metropolitan area was now in a position to invite businesses and industries to locate in the area and plans for new buildings, parks, expressways, and educational and recreational facilities were moved forward with greater enthusiasm.

Even before having been sworn in as mayor, Lawrence activated his campaign promise to foster the Allegheny Conference program. A vacancy appeared on the City Planning Commission, and Mayor Scully suggested Lawrence make the appointment, since he would become mayor in a short time. Lawrence called Park H. Martin and asked him to take the post, which Martin gladly did. From Martin's position, he felt the appointment significant for the conference. Much of the early emphasis in the conference was on the improvement of the so-called Golden Triangle. Martin's new position enabled him "to act as the bridge" among the Planning Commission, mayor's office, City Council, and conference.[61] The arrangement proved a happy one for Pittsburgh. Speaking of the plan in 1949, Lawrence reminded his audience that "properly conducted research" was something vital the people could contribute to their community. Also, teamwork was an essential element, especially where city, county, state, and federal governments were finely orchestrated, as was the case in metroplitan Pittsburgh. Lawrence asked for and received

26

the cooperation of business, industry, finance, and organized labor and credited the Allegheny Conference for this. "The Allegheny Conference is a liaison body. It keeps us working together. It helps convert research into accomplishment. The Conference, the Economy League, the Federation of Social Agencies, and the Pittsburgh Regional Planning Association effectively accomplish their goals."[62]

One of the more significant plans pursued by the Conference was the enactment of the "Equitable Project," as it was dubbed. Pittsburgh sought a developer for land that became available on the western boundary of the Triangle after a fire destroyed the Wabash Terminal area there and the railroads decided to move. As it became evident to conference members just how significant an impact a successful project would have on the city, a groundswell developed for the enactment of city legislation creating a Public Redevelopment Authority. An enabling act was passed in November 1946. This proved an important first effort in redevelopment for the city, and since Pittsburgh would be deeply involved as a community, in this effort the conference associates felt the mayor should be chairman of the redevelopment authority. When Arthur Van Buskirk told Lawrence this, he said, "Arthur, you are putting me in a ridiculous position. I don't think there is a case in all the history of this country where any man appointed himself to a job. I just can't do that." Van Buskirk insisted, "There's nothing wrong with that. We feel that we want the prestige of the mayor's office involved in the authority." Further, Lawrence was assured that the Conference would write an open letter urging him to serve, and William B. McFall, chairman of the Pittsburgh Chamber of Commerce, wrote a similar letter. Lawrence gave in and appointed himself chairman while, at the same time, appointing three Republicans and one Democrat to the authority. Later, Lawrence joked that it was the first time he had ever appointed more Republicans than Democrats to a committee. Arthur Van Buskirk, of Mellon and Sons, was named vice-chairman; the other members were: J. Lester Perry, president of the Carnegie-Illinois Steel Corporation; Edgar J. Kaufmann, merchant and philanthropist; and William Alvah Stewart, city councilman.[63] Lawrence was thus positioned to make effective contributions to the renewal of the city, which would become a showcase in the country.

Lawrence's appointment as chairman of the redevelopment au-

27

thority certainly wedded political, business, and civic interests in postwar Pittsburgh. The immediate unknown was how Lawrence would perform. There was from the beginning no question about Lawrence's dedication to improving Pittsburgh. But in a very short time Lawrence demonstrated a keen understanding of finances associated with redevelopment and realized the necessity of attracting money. "When you need money you go the Republicans," he said when asked why there were more Republicans than Democrats on the redevelopment authority. Most jobs associated with the authority were unsalaried, and only men of means could afford the time to energetically pursue them. What actually happened in Pittsburgh was that by the end of Lawrence's second term, party lines had been dropped in city and county affairs. But Lawrence reminds us, "In national politics we both went our own ways. And I knew the Republicans would be weakened by all the successful renewal activity."[64] Clearly, Lawrence was in command, while, at the same time, he kept interested parties satisfied.

When it came to political contacts, Lawrence was in clover. His friend John Kane was well connected and opened many doors for Lawrence. Theodore Hazlett, for twenty years solicitor for the redevelopment authority, recalled he could always rely on Lawrence when problems developed in Harrisburg or Washington. "You tell me what it is you want and how I will do it, and I'll get you your votes." Once when demolition on the Lower Hill project required on-site burning, which was contrary to smoke-control regulations, Hazlett went to Lawrence. Hazlett felt the only way around the problem was to explain it to the public. "Well, whatever you feel we have to do, Ted, we'll do it."[65] It was this type of action that impressed Republicans who were involved with Lawrence in renewal. Yet, for Lawrence personally, the role of the people was paramount, and he operated in such a way as to keep the citizens well informed about projects, associated inconveniences, and expected outcomes. Lawrence once told visiting Hubert Humphrey, "If you can't organize your community in support of your efforts you are not going to get anything done even if you have under your city charter so-called powers. These powers don't mean very much until you have the support of your people."[66] Lawrence rarely hesitated

28

to lay it on the line for the community. When Pittsburgh faced a crisis, Lawrence told the people what it entailed and what he felt was needed.

Postwar Pittsburgh was indeed approaching its zero hour. The Alcoa Corporation was going to move to New York. Gulf Oil Corporation was thinking of transferring its headquarters out of Pittsburgh. The United States Steel Corporation was quietly looking for a new location. At first, Lawrence did not move in the same circles as the leaders of these corporate giants. Lawrence knew, however, that some Pittsburgh citizens did, particularly Richard King Mellon. The question was whether Mellon would use his influence. A revitalized and vibrant Pittsburgh would serve the Mellon interests well, while, at the same time, meeting Lawrence's political needs. In both cases, as long as the public interest was paramount, few saw difficulty in accepting accompanying positive outcomes for Lawrence and Mellon.[67]

Pittsburgh's financial community centered around Richard King Mellon. It was Mellon who made the first move to bring about the Mellon-Lawrence partnership that facilitated the Pittsburgh Renaissance. "One day General Mellon crossed Grant Street, walked into City Hall and offered me his family homes and ground on Fifth Avenue for a park." This was the second time Mellon offered property to the city, but the first time "So much hell" was raised in the council that Mellon dropped the offer. Lawrence told the council he wanted the land for the city's welfare. They accepted and Mellon avoided embarrassment. "That was the beginning of the honeymoon with Lawrence and Mellon."[68] Both men identified with the city of Pittsburgh as their birthplace. Lawrence recalled, "Without the joining hands of the City's Democratic administration with the Mellon economic power, the revival of Pittsburgh could not have taken place." Arthur Van Buskirk, who was Mellon's chief representative in working with the Lawrence administration said, "In the thirteen years I have worked closely with David Lawrence, I never knew him to do something that he did not feel was in the public interest." This mutual trust was sufficient for Lawrence and Mellon to exercise their "complementary powers" while taking calculated risks for the city's improvement. Moreover, some felt that a formalized relation-

29

ship might have been disastrous to their efforts. Without a systematic process, Lawrence and Mellon secured the services of "pragmatic technicians" to forge the practical outcomes of their designs. Further, labor went along. Labor was usually "quite friendly" with Lawrence and John Kane, and labor provided what they wanted once a plan was submitted.[69]

For his part, Lawrence felt that men like Arthur Van Buskirk and Wallace Richards, who were the activists for the economic and business interests, "had no built-in distrust of the government, and because they sought accomplishments not ideologies, . . . were successful negotiators between government and business." Van Buskirk and Richards proved willing to "pioneer in municipal techniques" that are now commonplace. The use of public powers to clear blight, provide parking, and construct limited-access highways was initiated under these men to bring about a better Pittsburgh.[70] Lawrence interpreted the work of these men as the sustained interest of Mellon in the entire Renaissance movement. This dual relationship then became the key to Pittsburgh's Renaissance, a fact that both Lawrence and Mellon accepted and acknowledged. Of course, there were other key individuals, like Fred Baker, Leslie Reese, David Kurtzman, Anne Alpern, and many others who developed ideas for Lawrence and Mellon. As long as Pittsburgh's welfare was served, both cooperated, and each admitted his inability in certain areas. Lawrence could talk to a Philip Murray; Mellon could not. Mellon could convince a Ben Fairless to stay in Pittsburgh; Lawrence could not get near Fairless without Mellon. "There is no doubt the leadership of the two men made this town able to turn around."[71]

Yet not everyone in Pittsburgh saw the Renaissance as progress. Mrs. Frankie Pace, a Democratic committeewoman from the Hill District, recalled Pittsburgh's blacks "had nothing" under Lawrence. "None of them was ever put on what you call a cabinet level, not a black person." Moreover, Pace did not feel that Lawrence was overly concerned about social outcomes of the Renaissance.[72] David Craig, city solicitor, felt Lawrence's work in the Renaissance was politically motivated. He felt Lawrence "saw redevelopment as extras to be added to the fundamentals of organization, patronage, and payrolls that were the liturgy of his religion." Craig's personal association

30

with Lawrence convinced him that Lawrence's goal "was perpetuation of the party in power and Mellon's goal was business revival and business health." For Craig, the Lawrence-Mellon connection was for personal advancement, although "they did not begrudge any social by-products."[73]

On the other hand, Frank Denton, Republican businessman, recalled hearing Lawrence say that the rebuilding of Pittsburgh "was the best thing that ever happened as far as he personally was concerned, because it reassured his election." But, Denton continued, Lawrence's sentiments were well known and the collaboration in Pittsburgh's renewal was such that local politics played an insignificant role. When legislation favoring Pittsburgh and Allegheny County surfaced, both sides "would land hard on legislators." Other Republicans echoed Denton. They knew what Lawrence was about, but went along for the city's well-being. Sen. John Walker talked of the Duff-Lawrence cooperation and leadership; Sen. Robert Fleming worked with Lawrence in assuring both sides they were contributing to Pittsburgh's advancement. "I was a very staunch Republican but . . . his word was his bond." Frank Magee saw Lawrence as a fine, patriotic man, "though he was not of the poltical party many of us preferred. If there had been a lesser light in his capacity, nothing would have happened around here." Alfred Tronzo, of the Housing Authority, who in his early political career was a Lawrence arch-critic, remembered, "Every time we needed help we got it from Dave. He expected nothing but excellent operation in return."[74] On balance, Jack Robin's assertion, "it could not have been done without him," is the prevailing opinion of those associated with Lawrence in the Renaissance movement.

To the very end, Lawrence exhilarated in the new Pittsburgh. At a groundbreaking ceremony for the Mellon-Stuart Headquarters on January 10, 1963, he said, "Although I am always delighted with any reason offered me to come back to this beautiful city that is my home, I am never more pleased than on these occasions when we renew our dedication to the development of Pittsburgh." He never ceased telling the Pittsburgh story of business, industry, government, civic cooperation, trust, and common cause. "When these dynamic forces for change and progress unite . . . progress will be

31

achieved." Moreover, citizen participation was a keystone to success in Pittsburgh, where a "broad cross-section of Pittsburghers . . . faced up to the problems of their city squarely and moved inventively and vigorously to find solutions which were vital to the city's future." Lawrence even dreamed a little, saying in 1966, "If only I were a big enough leader to bring our 129 municipalities in Allegheny County into a Allegheny Metro. All our million and a half people would be beneficiaries."[75] Realizing his days were numbered, Lawrence drew up a formula for the future of Pittsburgh's Renaissance consisting of "proficiency, imagination, and a certain recklessness that shocks and stirs the hardheaded men of business and politics. It is not enough to be industrious; there must be flair, a touch of genius."[76]

Most would agree that Mayor Lawrence's four terms as Pittsburgh's leader were marked with success. He acquired a nationwide reputation as a good mayor, politician, mediator, and builder. In addition, Lawrence received much of the credit for a well-organized, excellently planned, imaginative, and inventive redevelopment program whose results, even in its early stages, were noteworthy. On the surface, then, the Lawrence experience in Pittsburgh in the late forties and fifties was a happy, satisfying time for the mayor, one that saw his party, city, and people come alive. Yet this occurred in spite of opposition from Democrats and Republicans. The latter, after Lawrence's first administration, were too weak to mount any effective resistance.

It was the smoke-control policy that drew fire from within Democratic ranks. Edward J. Leonard, city councilman, local and later national leader of the Amalgamated Plasterers Union of America, and longtime Lawrence friend, led the opposition. It was a confrontation that was not unexpected by Lawrence. Shortly after taking office as mayor, Lawrence in a discussion with a friend recalled how a man named Tucker was ousted from office in Saint Louis over smoke control. Moreover, in the first months of mandatory compliance for family units, people became conscious of having to pay higher prices for a more expensive mix of coal. This was true particularly in the older sections of the city, which generally had a higher proportion of the poor and elderly. Lawrence felt the pressure, but

32

managed to maintain a firm position. Although some say Leonard's anti-smoke control position was contrived at the instigation of certain segments of labor's leadership, Leonard takes full responsibility for his crusade.[77]

Long before the advent of Pittsburgh's primary election in 1949, Leonard had voiced his opposition to the implementation of smoke control. Leonard felt large organizations like the Pennsylvania Railroad were getting away with "murder," while the little man was getting hit hard from two sides: the law enforcer and the coal dealer. "They were selling coal for twenty dollars a ton—it was smokeless. It wasn't smokeless at all." To make his point, Leonard decided to bring evidence into council chambers. He gathered ten different kinds of coal in baskets. The press was alerted. When the council opened its meeting, Leonard got the floor. He demonstrated how the coal could not possibly burn in a stove or grate. In the process, Councilmen Wolk and McArdle were covered with coal dust. McArdle and Leonard had words. Lawrence ordered Council to stop Leonard, "but he could not stop me. He taught me."[78]

Leonard carried his push for the "Little Joes" into the 1949 primary and became a candidate for mayor. From the outset, the Lawrence camp knew they were in for a fight and had to go all out to beat Leonard. "He ran an astonishingly hard campaign," Lawrence remembered, and Lawrence was forced to campaign as if it were a general election. He pulled out all the stops, but never personally vilified Leonard.[79] One of the charges that wounded Lawrence was that he was "friendly to the Mellon interests, too neutral in labor matters." Leonard denied that he ever used the phrase "Mellon interests" during the campaign. He did admit using terms like "Big Boys," "railroads," and "Consolidated Coal Company" (by innuendo including the Mellon enterprises).[80] Lawrence countered by demonstrating how he "threw politics out the window" to secure cooperation and harmony for the city's welfare. "Some men would rather be kingfish in a mudpuddle than swim freely with their fellows in a clear, bright lake." The public, according to Lawrence, despised politicians who quarreled over "who gets the credit for what" and he warned that the Democratic party would silence the "voice of the demagogue, which pretends to be liberal."[81]

33

In retrospect, Leonard suggested Lawrence actually was worried about the plight of the poor and elderly, that perhaps Leonard was correct, and that the little man really was suffering. Yet Leonard admits Lawrence had the larger problem with which to contend. Moreover, politico that he was, Lawrence correctly read the situation and knew Leonard would pull a large vote, and he did. What in effect saved Lawrence was the crazy-quilt pattern that characterized the vote in the race. Leonard recalls, "Where I lost the fight for mayor was where the poorest people were." The reason for this may have been that labor split over the two candidates, the American Federation of Labor endorsed Leonard, and the Congress of Industrial Organizations backed Lawrence. The latter came out on top with only a 20,000 plurality, having experienced the scare of his political life.

Lawrence never demonstrated any ill feeling toward Leonard or the elements of labor that supported Leonard, but became much closer to the segments of labor that had stayed with him. Some weeks after the primary, Leonard and Lawrence met at a dinner. Leonard said, "It's about time we shake hands and I offer you congratulations." "Oh," Lawrence said. "Eddie, wasn't that a good fight?" Later Lawrence told Leonard that the campaign helped pick out the weak spots in the organization. Leonard and his backers met with Lawrence the following September and gave Lawrence their full endorsement. Out of all this, Lawrence gained respect for Leonard because he put his position on the line.[82]

Leonard continued to oppose Lawrence's "closed door" policy with the council, where things were thrashed out before public meetings, but Lawrence never said anything to Leonard about his position on this. Sometimes Lawrence would wonder out loud why "Eddie won't come in and talk to me." Leonard felt since he was not invited, he had no obligation to go to the mayor's office. Despite this difference between the two men, as well as the primary fight, Lawrence never tried to dump Leonard. Immediately after the primary, a meeting was held at Democratic headquarters to pick a slate for the city. Lawrence said, "There are four Councilmen and a City Controller up. I would like to submit a name for Councilman so we get an understanding here. I would like to submit the name Edward

J. Leonard."[83] Lawrence could live with Leonard on the City Council and understood the political wisdom of openly communicating with the large following Leonard had.

Lawrence got rid of another insurgent councilman, Joseph McArdle, in the 1949 primary. Lawrence and McArdle were at odds over the dismissal of a police inspector, friendly to McArdle, who was indicted by a grand jury investigating the rackets. This was not the first time McArdle caused trouble on the council, so Lawrence decided to drop him. In his place, Patrick Fagan, a CIO leader, was slated. This was a surprise move, because Fagan had opposed Lawrence in 1938, 1940, and 1942 in his disputes with Guffey. But Lawrence, now in full control, saw Fagan's slating as a chance to strengthen labor's support of his administration, while, at the same time, getting rid of McArdle.[84] To many Lawrence-watchers, McArdle, for some unknown reason, was one of the few people whom Lawrence cut off completely. Moreover, it seemed as though Lawrence's anti-McArdle stance was personal, something uncharacteristic of Lawrence.

As party leader and mayor, Lawrence found himself in a delicate position, since the city of Pittsburgh was within the larger area of Allegheny County. He had to be careful not to step across political boundaries. The fact that Allegheny County was controlled by Democrats, under the leadership of John Kane, caused the city-county rivalry to be "within the family." Kane and Lawrence did not always see eye to eye. As early as 1937, they were on opposite sides in the mayoralty primary. In this first test, Lawrence emerged the stronger individual.[85] Yet his strength was in the party; John Kane was chairman of the County Commissioners and controlled the county government.

Still, the tension between the two prevailed. It was as if their positions required it. This was especially true once Lawrence became mayor. Kane and his followers and Lawrence and his coterie were each dedicated to taking care of their own. Thus, when the slating of candidates came up, Kane would try to get county men named and Lawrence would push for city men. However, there were those who felt the friction went beyond candidates' slating. William Block, *Pittsburgh Post Gazette* owner, suggests Kane was "a little" jealous

35

of Lawrence. Kane, "a very good public official," was not a very articulate individual, and his leadership ability paled in comparison with Lawrence's. Thus he could not function at the same level or with the same power within the party as could Lawrence, and Kane keenly felt this. Again, Kane was older than Lawrence and mildly resented the surge of prestige Lawrence gathered as his mayoralty progressed. But Kane did admire Lawrence for his accomplishments in the party and city administration. Here were two politicians who were by circumstances forced to accept each other's role in their own backyards, and when the chips were down, "they agreed when it counted most."[86]

Through all this strained relationship, Lawrence always deferred to Kane in local government. Kane would never meet with Lawrence in the mayor's office. An arrangement had to be worked out as to who spoke first on the phone. Walter Giesey remembers, "I don't know that was as much Lawrence as it was Kane who felt very sensitive." After all, Kane was chairman of the county Commissioners in 1935, Lawrence arrived in 1946, and Kane's position in the party was lessened by a "relative newcomer." Moreover, Kane wanted a party position, but seemed unable or unwilling to fulfill it. He wanted to be a member of the Executive Committee of the state Democratic party, "but he never attended any of the meetings." However, one could never throw this up to Kane. Lawrence, by contrast, was highly organized, disciplined, and very industrious. "Kane was the kind of a guy who preferred the trappings without the drudgery of political life."[87]

For city and county government to operate smoothly, Lawrence needed Kane. In a sense, politically, Kane needed Lawrence. Kane and Lawrence "used to have it out hot and heavy, but they always managed in the final analysis to get together and work out what was best for the entire community."[88] These words of Congressman William S. Moorhead constitute a fine tribute for two men who were dedicated to politics in an unselfish way. Lawrence enjoyed this kind of a political relationship. On the other hand, where opposition for opposition's sake prevailed, Lawrence bristled.

Lawrence admittedly was responsible for some of the rivalry that marked the Democratic organization. In those dark days of the

Democratic party in Western Pennsylvania, Lawrence built a coalition of independent Republicans and Democrats in order to give life and power to his foundling organization. In the process, he sought the backing of Judge Ralph Smith, then a Republican. Smith insisted that David Roberts and William McClelland had to be part of the deal. Lawrence later remarked that he regretted "some of the people they got in the bargain, but they just had to suffer them out because of the fact they got them in the package and there was not anything they could do about them." Lawrence was here speaking specifically about Roberts. Usually, Lawrence considered McClelland to be a part of the Roberts faction as it evolved, albeit a bit more intelligent, but not too much, otherwise he would not have allowed Roberts to use him the way he did.[89]

From the beginning, there was friction with the Republicans turned Democrats. Organization members who had worked faithfully for many years resented the way Smith, Roberts, and McClelland were brought into the party and, in a sense, pushed ahead of those already there.[90] What is more, with the passage of time, Roberts and McClelland set out to control Lawrence. He proved too strong for that and even recognized the possibilities of Roberts for political office. When it was suggested that Roberts be slated for prothonotory, Lawrence wryly remarked, "Well, one thing about him, he is a politician. He is a worker and he knows how to get votes." Despite the fact that Roberts became prothonotory and McClelland later was elected county commissioner, the two were never strong enough to oust Lawrence. Roberts used to lament, "There's no blood in his veins; it's ice water."[91] To their credit, Roberts and McClelland never gave up, and Lawrence learned to live with intraparty opposition.

Roberts disagreed with nearly everything Lawrence did. Moreover, if you were in the Lawrence camp, you were on Roberts's list. Andrew Fenrich recalls being put to work in Democratic headquarters by Lawrence. When he passed Roberts the next day, the latter said, "You'll never do the job; you'll mess it up; you'll foul it up!" This was a reflection on Lawrence, who had made the appointment. Roberts, however, constantly sought Lawrence's advice at meetings. Despite his devil's advocate role, Roberts relied on Law-

37

rence "because he knew Lawrence could think beyond most of us and would have the final point and would have a good one."[92]

Some saw Roberts and McClelland as harmless "mavericks." They would come with candidates that Lawrence and Kane disagreed over. There would be a lot of infighting. To Robert's and McClelland's advantage, they knew Lawrence was flexible and would rather give in than hurt the party. Moreover, for his part, "McClelland would liked to have been the boss. He would not do anything that did not put him in a leadership position."

Along with Roberts, McClelland wanted to get rid of Kane as chairman of the County Commissioners. Lawrence knew Kane to be a good administrator and did not want to see him replaced "by Roberts or McClelland or anybody else." Moreover, Lawrence understood that if Roberts and McClelland were successful in this ploy, he would be their next target, although some felt he had always held that questionable distinction. It should be understood that all this was not personal, rather "more of a jockeying for power on their part and his support of the people against whom they were posturing."[93]

In terms of political power, Roberts managed to control the Fifth Ward, which was at the time the largest black ward in the city. He was a "super ward leader," and Lawrence respected that. Roberts used this ward power as the foundation in his drive to build other bases, something Lawrence did not respect. Lawrence felt you should play on the party team, but he considered Roberts an individual "you could not trust . . . on the team." Lawrence may have been too critical here and shares the responsibility for prolonging the conflict. Through all this, Lawrence and Roberts remained cordial until the two broke over the wage-tax issue, when Roberts and McClelland united to lead the opposition. In fairness, the two major newspapers in the city also fought the tax. "They saw the newspapers attacking and so there was a chance to climb on a very popular issue and get Lawrence." Although Roberts and McClelland were unsuccessful in the wage-tax fray, they were clearly the leaders of an anti-Lawrence faction, and here Lawrence was convinced the two men did not oppose the wage tax on ideological grounds, but merely as an attempt at political regicide. For this Lawrence never

38

forgave the two men. Giesey remembers Roberts saying, "All he [Lawrence] has to do is call me . . . and I'll do anything in the world he wants me to do." Roberts knew he was cut out; he would never go beyond the prothonotary's spot, something Lawrence did not take away so as to preserve party harmony.[94]

It was not that Lawrence did not want to go after Roberts. He would often say, "If I thought I would beat him I'd go after him, but we don't want to split the party." As time passed, younger party elements urged Lawrence to confront the Roberts-McClelland faction, but Lawrence refused. In 1954, when McClelland ran for governor, everyone thought Lawrence would support McClelland. Lawrence refused and backed George Leader of York County. Roberts and McClelland were furious, but the Lawrence camp triumphed. Roberts and McClelland repaid the slight when, in 1960, they embarrassed Lawrence by their early endorsement of John Kennedy for president. For Lawrence, this action on their part had no political merit; he saw it as a cheap attempt to improve their political situation.[95] Their momentary embarrassment of Lawrence was their last hurrah. McClelland in his later years remembered Lawrence as being "mainly responsible for my political career," calling him a giant in civic life and the Democratic party. Throughout, the giant never fell to the stalking faction spawned by Roberts and McClelland. A man of lesser qualities might not have survived. These same political assets, developed in Pittsburgh, enabled Lawrence to become a force in Pennsylvania politics.

Notes

1. Sally Oleon Shames, "David L. Lawrence, Mayor of Pittsburgh: Development of a Political Leader" (unpublished Ph.D. diss., University of Pittsburgh, 1958), p. 15.

2. *Pittsburgh Post Gazette*, November 22, 1966, p. 4.

3. Joseph A. Veres, "David L. Lawrence: A Psychological Biography" (unpublished paper, Washington and Jefferson College, 1975), p. 3; Shames, p. 15.

4. *Pittsburgh Post Gazette*, July 30, 1920, p. 4.

5. H. Fuller, "Men To Watch At the Democratic Convention." *Harpers*, August 1964, p. 48.

6. *The Reminiscences of Grace Sloan*, (1975), p. 5, in the Oral History Collection of La Salle University, hereinafter Sloan.

7. Bruce M. Stave, *The New Deal and the Last Hurrah* (Pittsburgh, The University of Pittsburgh Press, 1970), p. 31.

8. Sloan, p. 5; Shames, p. 30.

9. *The Reminiscences of Joe Barr*, (1974), in the Oral History Collection of La Salle University, pp. 1, 2, hereinafter Barr.

10. Steele J. Gow, "Metro Politics in Pittsburgh" (unpublished Ph.D. diss., University of Pittsburgh, 1952), p. 230.

11. Shames, p. 111.

12. Ibid., p. 114; Stave, p. 30; *Pittsburgh Post Gazette*, October 31, 1931, p. 1.

13. *Pittsburgh Post Gazette*, March 21, 1931, p. 1.

14. *The Reminiscences of John Robin*, (1969), p. 4, in the Oral History Collection of La Salle University, hereinafter Robin.

15. Shames, p. 225.

16. *New York Times*, September 9, 1946, p. 2.

17. Ibid., September 10, 1946, p. 4.

18. Ibid., September 23, 1946, p. 17; September 24, 1946, p. 2; September 25, 1946, p. 1.

19. Ibid., November 10, 1946, p. 8.

20. *Pittsburgh Press*, November 22, 1966, p. 5.

21. *New York Times*, September 20, 1949, p. 33.

22. *The Reminiscences of William Block*, (1974), p. 3, in the Oral History Collection of La Salle University, hereinafter Block.

23. Frank Hawkins, "Lawrence of Pittsburgh: Boss of the Mellon Patch," *Harpers*, August, 1965, p. 60.

24. *Pittsburgh Post Gazette*, November 22, 1966, p. 4.

25. *The Reminiscenses of David L. Lawrence*, pp. 88–90, in the Oral History Collection of the John F. Kennedy Library, hereinafter Lawrence (JFK).

26. *The Reminiscences of Andrew Bradley*, (1975), p. 3, in the Oral History Collection of La Salle University, hereinafter Bradley.

27. *The Reminiscences of Charles McCarthy*, (1975), pp. 2-3, in the Oral History Collection of La Salle University, hereinafter McCarthy.

28. *The Reminiscences of John Exler*, (1974), p. 4, in the Oral History Collection of La Salle University, hereinafter Exler.

29. McCarthy, pp. 3, 4.

30. *The Reminiscences of Walter Giesey*, (1974), p. 22, in the Oral History Collection of La Salle University, hereinafter Giesey.

31. *The Reminiscences of Andrew Fenrich*, (1974), pp. 1-2, in the Oral History Collection of La Salle University, hereinafter Fenrich.

32. *The Reminiscences of Margaret Plesset*, (1974), p. 4, in the Oral History Collection of La Salle University, hereinafter Plesset.

33. Hawkins, "Lawrence of Pittsburgh," p. 57.

34. Ibid., p. 58.

35. Giesey, pp. 10–11.

36. Shames, p. 204.

37. Fenrich, p. 7; Giesey, p. 9

38. Giesey, p. 10.

39. Tate, p. 24.

40. Shames, p. 222.

41. *The American City*, July, 1955, p. 17.

42. *The Reminiscences of Robert Wagner*, (1975), pp. 5–6, in the Oral History Collection of La Salle University, hereinafter Wagner.

43. *The Reminiscences of Robert Meyner*, (1974), p. 4, in the Oral History Collection of La Salle University, hereinafter Meyner.

44. Shames, p. 207.

45. Robin, p. 3.

46. Giesey, pp. 2–4.

47. *The Reminiscences of James Knox*, (1974), pp. 15–16, in the Oral History Collection of La Salle University, hereinafter Knox.

48. *The Reminiscences of Frank Ambrose*, (1974) p. 13, in the Oral History Collection of La Salle University, hereinafter Ambrose.

49. McCarthy, pp. 4–5.

50. Hawkins, *Lawrence of Pittsburgh*, p. 58.

51. Stefan Lorant, *Pittsburgh: The Story of an American City* (New York: Doubleday, 1965), p. 374.

52. Ibid., pp. 377–381.

53. Block, pp. 3–4.

54. *The Reminiscences of Edward Ostker*, (1973), pp. 2–3, in the Oral History Collection of the University of Pittsburgh, hereinafter Ostker.

55. Lorant, p. 386.

56. Park H. Martin, "Narrative of the Allegheny Conference on Community Development and the Pittsburgh Renaissance, 1943–1958" (unpublished, collection of Mrs. Park H. Martin, Camp Hill, Pennsylvania), p. 20.

57. Ibid., p. 21.

58. Shames, pp. 244–45.

59. Lorant, p. 390.

60. Martin, pp. 25–26; Giesey, p. 5.

61. Martin, p. 11.

62. *American City*, 1949, p. 5; Shames, p. 260.

63. Lorant, pp. 430–31; Martin, p. 14.

64. Robin, p. 5.

65. *The Reminiscences of Theodore Hazlett*, (1974), pp. 2–3, 4, in the Oral History Collection of La Salle University, hereinafter Hazlett.

41

66. *The Reminiscences of Hubert Humphrey*, (1974), p. 1, in the Oral History Collection of La Salle University, hereinafter Humphrey.

67. Block, pp. 6–7; *The Reminiscences of Frank Hawkins* (1974), pp. 3–4, in the Oral History Collection of La Salle University, hereinafter Hawkins.

68. Hebert Kubly, "Pittsburgh," *Holiday* 25:80–81, March 1959, 86; *The Reminiscences of William McClelland*, (n.d.), in the Oral History Collection of the University of Pittsburgh.

69. Lorant, pp. 402-406; *The Reminiscences of Arthur Van Buskirk*, (1971), p. 15, in the Oral History Collection of the University of Pittsburgh; John Robin, "Lecture," pp. 5, 14.

70. Lorant, pp. 408–411.

71. Hazlett, p. 7.

72. *The Reminiscences of Frankie Pace*, (1973), pp. 22, 27, in the Oral History Collection of the University of Pittsburgh.

73. *The Reminiscences of David Craig*, (1971), n.p., in the Oral History Collection of the University of Pittsburgh.

74. *The Reminiscences of John Walker*, (n.d.), n.p.; *Robert Fleming*, n.p.; *Frank Denton*, (1972), pp. 5–6; *Frank Magee*, (1972), n.p.; *Alfred Tronzo*, (1974), p. 18, in the Oral History Collection of the University of Pittsburgh.

75. Pennsylvania State Archives, hereinafter PSA, Lawrence Collection, Press Release, January 10, 1963; Speeches, San Francisco Bay Area Council, 1965; W.H.P., Harrisburg, March 23, 1966; Adolph W. Schmidt, unpublished speech, June 18, 1975.

76. Lorant, p. 455.

77. Ambrose, p. 14; Block, p. 2; Knox, p. 8.

78. *The Reminiscences of Edward Leonard*, (1975), pp. 6–7, in the Oral History Collection of La Salle University, hereinafter Leonard.

79. McCarthy, p. 4.

80. KDKA Transcript, Edward Leonard, March 27, 1972, private collection.

81. Shames, pp. 164–165.

82. Leonard, pp. 4–5; Giesey, pp. 4–5.

83. Leonard, p. 8.

84. Shames, p. 164.

85. Ibid., pp. 130–131.

86. Exler, p. 2; Block, p. 6.

87. Giesey, pp. 7–8.

88. *The Reminiscences of William S. Moorhead*, (1974), p. 5, in the Oral History Collection of La Salle Unversity, hereinafter Moorhead.

89. Bradley, p. 5.

90. Barr, p. 6.

91. Sloan, pp. 4–5.

42

92. Fenrich, p. 3.

93. McCarthy, p. 6; Exler, p. 3; *The Reminiscences of Judge Genevieve Blatt*, (1975), pp. 8–9, in the Oral History Collection of La Salle University, hereinafter Blatt.

94. Giesey, pp. 6–7, 8–9; Ambrose, pp. 5–6.

95. Dent, pp. 7–8; Moorhead, p. 4.

David L. Lawrence, secretary of the Commonwealth, assists Gov. George H. Earle in signing legislation, as group of legislators looks on.

Pennsylvania Delegation's News Conference at 1956 Democratic National Convention. Seated from left: Mayor Lawrence, Geneiveve Blatt, Joe Barr, Richardson Dilworth, Governor George Leader, and Bill Breen Sr. Standing behind Joe Barr, Jerry Lawrence, the Mayor's son.

Mayor Lawrence huddles on the floor of the 1956 Democratic National Convention with Joe Barr, Democratic state chairman and state senator; Genevieve Blatt, democratic state secretary and secretary of internal afffairs; and Emma Guffey Miller, democratic national committeewoman and platform committee member.

Two of David Lawrence's favorites: grandchildren and sports.

January 20, 1959: Governor and Mrs. Lawrence at the Inaugural Ball in Harrisburg, Pennsylvania.

Governor Lawrence addressing a group of young people during Olympic Week, January 1963.

Governor and Mrs. Lawrence with President Kennedy.

February 1, 1963—Governor Lawrence is sworn in as chairman of the President's Committee on Equal Opportunity in Housing.

III
Keystone Politician

Burgeoning success for the Democratic party across the nation after the 1930 congressional elections was clearly reflected not only in Pittsburgh and Allegheny County, but also throughout Pennsylvania. Lawrence and Guffey accurately predicted that this would be so, and Lawrence purposefully placed himself in a position where he would benefit most upon its advent. With the Democrat's overwhelming presidential victory in 1932, Lawrence readied the arena to do battle with Western Pennsylvania's entrenched Republicans.[1]

Between 1930 and 1934, it became clear that the Democratic party in Pittsburgh had evolved into an effective and cohesive instrumentality under Lawrence leadership, whereas its Republican counterpart had became factional. Lawrence hammered away at the process of organizational development. Party policy could catch hold once the movement was an efficient machine. The Lawrence appeal was broad enough to include splinter groups of varied political persuasion so long as they functioned within the established constituency, preparing for the advent of newly established political power, and even though the new Lawrence establishment was not immediately crowned with electoral success, it possessed Lawrence and his growing charisma, which proved, over the long run, to be enough to cement his loyal and devoted followers into an effective political force in Pittsburgh, Allegheny County, and later the entire state.[2] Lawrence's organization drive at home, however, did not go unchallenged.

On May 6, 1933, J. Frank McAllister, Allegheny County Independent Democrat, wrote Cordell Hull, secretary of state, concerning Lawrence. McAllister complained that Lawrence was Democratic spokesman for Western Pennsylvania, supposedly representing the interests of President Roosevelt and his administration. Alledging that Lawrence did not even serve the interests of the "Pennsylvania district," McAllister called for Lawrence's replacement.[3] In July 1933, Anne E. Felix, president of the Jefferson Club and once defeated in a congressional race, wrote FDR charging Guffey and Lawrence with "being in league with [Governor] Pinchot." Felix wanted FDR to use his influence to have Guffey and Lawrence support John M. Henry, independent Democrat, for mayor of Pittsburgh. Felix felt this would prevent a split among Allegheny County Democrats.[4] Unaware of the Felix and McAllister letters, Governor Pinchot wrote FDR at the same time, noting he could not let the end of the Pennsylvania legislative session go by without thanking Roosevelt "for what he did for decent legislation." Pinchot further penned his appreciation for the cooperation of the Pennsylvania Democrats "and in particular that of Joe Guffey, David Lawrence, Warren Van Dyke, and, of course, the Democratic minority in the Senate."[5] Apparently, the few Democrats who were upset with the organization's cooperation with the Pinchot administration made little impression on Roosevelt. He knew Guffey and Lawrence well and trusted their political insight enough to realize that Democrats benefited just as much as Republicans from any Pennsylvania legislation they backed. Moreover, Roosevelt confirmed his trust as well as appreciation of Lawrence when, on June 8, 1933, he appointed Lawrence collector of internal revenue for the Pittsburgh District.[6] The impact of Lawrence's appointment came just at the proper time. Democrats in Pittsburgh were planning to take over City Hall.

Despite the new prestige Western Pennsylvania Democrats enjoyed following Roosevelt's election and Lawrence's selection as internal-revenue collector, Lawrence was not about to swing blindly into the 1933 mayoral race in Pittsburgh. Many colleagues urged Lawrence to run, feeling he would secure the office easily. However, Lawrence felt his religious background would hinder voter appeal and the opportunity might be lost to the Democrats. Many years later, Lawrence explained why he strongly backed perennial Democratic nominee William N. McNair's candidacy. "We needed the

49

independents. He was a Protestant, I was a Catholic; he was a single taxer and that had appeal in those days of depression."[7] Lawrence always felt religion was an issue, and perhaps it was in Pittsburgh in 1933. But Lawrence, in his continued preoccupation with organization and party growth, planned to hold, if at all possible, independents who helped send FDR to the White House in 1932. For Lawrence, independents included Republicans who voted for Roosevelt. In June 1933, Lawrence asked Pittsburgh Republicans who backed Roosevelt to support McNair. Lawrence considered these people Democrats and predicted "that if all in Pittsburgh stick to the party there will be a Democratic mayor next fall."[8]

William McNair won the Democratic nomination for mayor of Pittsburgh, and Lawrence campaigned vigorously, perhaps more so than McNair himself. However, it was a new Lawrence and a new party with a changed vision. At the windup rally of the campaign, Lawrence, speaking to party workers, predicted, "I am positive we are going to elect the next Mayor of Pittsburgh, although the Republican machine has been planning to make a super effort to steal the election."[9] Lawrence proved correct and McNair won by what modest political partisans call a landslide. When news of the victory reached Roosevelt, he was delighted and instructed a White House aide to wire Guffey and Lawrence as follows: "Congratulations to the Gold Dust twins, Colonel Joe and Captain Davey."[10] The McNair achievement quite properly belonged to Guffey and Lawrence. One Democratic observer noted that the election put Lawrence in the "political forefront. Serving as Collector of Internal Revenue, acting as joint dispenser of federal patronage with Joe Guffey, Mr. Lawrence suddenly became the chief political figure in the county. McNair was to be Mayor, but Democrats generally looked to Lawrence as the man who brought about the cataclysmic shift in the political situation."[11] No doubt Lawrence, with Guffey's leave, secured a tight grip on the Democratic county Organization, but this was probably more in the minds of the people than was actually the case, since Guffey, at the time, never conceded a partnership position to Lawrence in the matter of dispensing federal patronage. Moreover, McNair's administration did not sit well at all with the Democrats, especially Lawrence. True, the Democrats had their first Pittsburgh mayor in twenty-three years, but McNair proved an

50

eccentric in City Hall, selling apples on the street, appearing on a radio amateur hour, and, perhaps worst of all partywise, refusing to have anything to do with Lawrence. Whereas the party faithful who put McNair in office naturally expected some job opportunities, McNair shut them down completely. This put Lawrence, as well as his organization, in an awkward position, one that hindered Lawrence through 1936.[12]

Although McNair's erratic behavior bothered Lawrence and he would, in due time, handle the situation to the organization's advantage, Lawrence moved his forces ahead in the city wards, the county organization, and the General Assembly. Also, Lawrence's colleagues maintained their confidence in him and selected Lawrence as chairman of the Democratic state party on June 9, 1934. The *New York Times* reported: " . . . the organization of Joseph F. Guffey of Pittsburgh, Roosevelt leader and nominer, retained its two-year grip on the Committee." After his selection, Lawrence declared that "beneath the banners of the Roosevelt New Deal we have formed our columns for the final march upon the last trenches of Toryism and special privilege." Lawrence also praised his predecessor, Warren VanDyke, who "left a record unparalleled in the history of any political party in any State of the union!"[13] Just a little over a month later, Lawrence, preferring to retain his post as state chairman, sent his resignation as collector of internal revenue to Roosevelt. The White House did not comment on Lawrence's resignation except to acknowledge it was the first Under Secretary of Treasury Morganthau's edict that an official could not serve the treasury and a political party at the same time.[14]

Freed of his internal-revenue duties, Lawrence launched into organizing the state Democrats with the same vigor and enthusiasm utilized in Allegheny County. Congressman John Dent recalls when Lawrence first became state chairman how the Democrats built majorities in Westmoreland, Fayette, and Green counties and established a toehold in Erie County. Western Pennsylvania Democrats were able to offset Republican strongholds in the east, particularly Delaware County. At the same time, Lawrence guided the party through a difficult financial period, while keeping a close watch on pending legislation in the House and Senate. Lawrence would meet nightly with his colleagues in "an old stand-up bar" in Harrisburg,

51

treating the members to a "nickel round of beer," the while strategising pending legislation.[15] State Treasurer Grace Sloan remembers Lawrence at state committee meetings in the thirties. "He was the one that everybody talked to and looked to at the meetings. He'd put it all together when he came into the meeting. Everything sort of fell into focus when Lawrence got there."[16]

It did not take Lawrence long to serve notice that he would not tolerate what he considered unwarranted outside interference in state Democratic politics. In August 1934, Harry Hopkins asked George Earle and David Lawrence to attend a meeting during which new plans were to be worked out for relief through federal and state appropriations. Hopkins, at FDR's urging, wanted to avoid calling a special session of Congress. Lawrence and Earle wanted one, and Lawrence decided there would be no meeting, for Pennsylvanians, at least.[17] But Lawrence was not always so intransigent when White House hints were broached.

In 1934, Pennsylvania was preparing to elect its governor and a United States senator. Some White House support developed for Governor Pinchot as Pennsylvania's Democratic candidate for senator. A leader in the conservation movement, Pinchot twice beat the Republican organization in the primaries and went to the governor's mansion. Roosevelt, mindful of Pinchot's progressivism, asked Guffey to consult Warren VanDyke and Lawrence over the feasibility of Pennsylvania Democratic legislators supporting a Pinchot package. The Democrats agreed for a price; Pinchot would foster legislation outlawing primary party raiding. The legislation went through, but Pinchot refused to sign the party-raiding bill. Pinchot's possible Democratic candidacy ended.[18]

Meanwhile, the state committee, anticipating success in November, slated George H. Earle III, wealthy Pennsylvanian and minister to Austria, to run for governor and Joseph Guffey to run for the Senate seat. By the middle of October 1934, Lawrence and Guffey were able to assure Roosevelt the Democrats would sweep Pennsylvania for the first time since the Civil War. Also, in the Pennsylvania House, the Democratic majority would be increased from six to twelve Democrats, and Pinchot's suport of David Reed for United States senator would not affect the Democratic prospects. Noting that the Republicans "stole" state elections in 1932 by count-

52

ing out a Democratic majority of 150,000, Lawrence and Guffey guaranteed Roosevelt this would not happen in 1934, since the Justice Department had assigned agents in Pennsylvania to ensure an honest election.[19] A few weeks later, as the campaign moved toward its climax, the *Philadelphia Inquirer* published a story that James Farley issued orders to "knife Earle to save Guffey." Farley denied it. Lawrence commented that the Republican leadership, "panic-stricken by the imminent Democratic landslide," had given up hope of electing Reed as senator and were "desperately trying to make deals in an effort to save" Attorney General William Schnader, Republican gubernatorial candidate. Lawrence further charged, "All the old methods of the Republican gang are being resorted to. The money bags of Grundy, Mellon and Atterbury, as well as those of Philadelphia's aspring contractor boss, Jerome H. Loucheim, have been opened to debauch the electorate on Tuesday. Fearful of having their satellites driven from places of power in the state government, they are preparing to resort to intimidation and thuggery in their hopeless effort to prevent George H. Earle from being elected governor."[20]

Lawrence's withering rhetoric presaged an avalanche of Democratic votes that buried Pennsylvania's Republicans. Lawrence gleefully remarked, "The entire Democratic ticket has been elected. The victory was a sweeping endorsement of the policies and administration of Franklin Roosevelt and the New Deal. For the people of Pennsylvania, [this is] . . . a red letter day, marking the emancipation of millions from the yoke of Mellon-Grundy industrial and financial autocracy."[21]

A new era had dawned for Pennsylvania Democrats, an age that saw Lawrence's toughest political competition, Joseph Guffey, move to Washington, while Lawrence assumed greater direction in the Earle administration, along with significant political power and prestige in Democratic circles.

Just a few days after his election as governor, Earle appointed Lawrence secretary of the commonwealth. This was generally conceded to be a logical choice for Earle, since it gave Lawrence an occasion to engineer the consolidation of Democratic advances in heretofore Republican bastions.[22] At the time, neither Lawrence nor Earle realized just how significant a move Lawrence's appointment would prove. As the Earle administration unfolded, it became evident that Governor Earle lacked certain persevering qualities needed as the state's chief executive. Earle's reputation as a playboy governor is generally accepted even among Democrats, but at the same time, the Earle administration was able to pursue a rather steady course. It was indeed helmsman Lawrence who kept the ship of state afloat much of the time between 1935 and 1939. However, Lawrence's unassuming demeanor in grasping the helm was such that Captain Earle's braid remained untarnished. Lawrence could have secured the bridge with great eclat, but his personal instincts favored preservation of party unity and tranquillity, thus preventing his becoming a source of embarrassment to Earle and the other Democrats. Ready or not, in 1935, Lawrence was thrust into a position requiring courage, leadership, statesmanship, and an abiding understanding of the common good. Lawrence, according to Robert L. Meyers, Jr., deputy attorney general in 1935 and later secretary to Governor Earle and secretary of banking in the Leader and Lawrence administrations, was not found wanting. A capable public official, Lawrence was an ardent partisan politician who knew how to balance public service and party politics. "In his capacity as head of the Democratic Party, he was a dynamic and aggressive person. Consequently, the Republicans always thought of David Lawrence as a consummate partisan Democrat and were perhaps never willing to give him credit for the statesmanship he displayed in so many areas."[23] Whatever the merits of the Earle administration proved to be for the Commonwealth of Pennsylvania, Lawrence deserves recognition for having front-run the Earle government while keeping his political organization in good order.

When Lawrence was secretary of the commonwealth, the Metropolitan Plan, calling for one unit of government to serve both Pittsburgh and Allegheny County, surfaced again. Lawrence continued to favor the idea, although the urgency of the twenties had faded in his view, since Democrats now controlled both city and county government. Lawrence went along with those seeking metropolitan status, even to the point of accepting Mellon money so that Democrats could at least make a show of supporting the drive.[24] And if, in the final analysis, the plan did not come to fruition, at least the Democrats, with Mellon money, had trumpeted their in-

54

terests. Whatever transpired, metropolitan government or not, Lawrence did not plan to sit back and allow McNair's defiance of Pittsburgh's Democratic organization to continue.

Early on in the 1935 legislative session of the General Assembly of the Commonwealth, the so-called "Ripper Bill" was introduced, which would have, if passed, removed McNair from office. At the same time, Lawrence watched the Civic Club of Allegheny County file suit against McNair charging fiscal mismanagement. Pittsburgh's city charter permitted twenty freeholders to start impeachment charges against city officials where mismanagement was evident. The *Pittsburgh Post Gazette* editorialized: "From every angle the purely 'ripper' moves carries the label of politics." Moreover, McNair asked, "Is it right? Dave Lawrence cracks the whip in Harrisburg and McNair walks out in Pittsburgh. It is the [public's] right to say who should be Mayor—not Davey Lawrence's." McNair threatened to appoint a deputy before the bill passed. Meanwhile, Lawrence insisted that Democratic members of the House pass the "ripper." Lawrence said he felt responsible for McNair's election. "I put him in and I'll take him out."[25]

Even though the bill, after much bitter partisan wrangling, was defeated, Republicans felt they had an opportunity to embarrass Lawrence. Republican assemblymen initiated an investigation that attempted to demonstrate that deals had been offered both Republican and Democratic state senators in return for support of the Ripper Bill. Lawrence fumed, calling the inquest an "S.O.S. broadcast by the rapidly sinking Allegheny County Republican Machine." The investigators were labeled "three representatives of privilege who led the slaughter of social, labor and humane legislation in the last session of the legislature." Lawrence's rhetoric, and that is all it was, did not stop the inquiry, which was at a point where Lawrence was about to be called to testify. Lawrence then issued a formal statement. "I wish to tell them at no time did I ever solicit the vote or influence any Democratic or Republican member of the House or Senate for the so-called Ripper Bill or any other bill in return for patronage or any other consideration." Perhaps so, but it was clear from other testimony that Lawrence made no bones about wanting McNair out. However, the investigation stopped suddenly when Republicans discovered Coyne-McNair deals over the Ripper

Bill.[26] Finally McNair resigned on October 4, 1936, due to difficulties with an intransigent Democratic City Council, which, in this case, danced while Lawrence fiddled.

Despite the heavy-handed methods Lawrence used in the McNair incident, his loyal following in Democratic ranks seemed not at all shaken. After his 1936 reelection as state chairman, Lawrence told the state committee that not a single Pennsylvania county would be Republican after the 1936 election: "Never in the history of our party have the prospects been better in Pennsylvania than they are today. Our forces are powerful and united. Our opposition is disorganized and discredited." Lawrence explained further that Western Pennsylvania was almost solidly Democratic, Central Pennsylvania and the anthracite region were moving steadily into the Democratic columns, and the only uncertain battleground would be Southeastern Pennsylvania, although here Lawrence predicted victory. Lawrence felt great hope for Philadelphia, since he had just avoided a revolt there through negotiations that saw Matthew McCloskey step aside in favor of George Earle as Democratic national committeeman.[27]

As the 1938 gubernatorial election approached, Pennsylvania's Democratic leadership split—not only over specific candidates, but also over the roles Lawrence and Guffey were to play in the Democratic party. Since George Earle could not, constitutionally, succeed himself, finding a candidate for governor was paramount. Given Lawrence's role in the Earle administration, many Democrats felt he should run. Lawrence was interested in the post, and he knew Guffey would be in a very difficult position should the senator openly oppose Lawrence's candidacy. Moreover, there was a significant groundswell for Lawrence. One Frank Zak wrote Roosevelt that he chaired a committee of 100 people representing over fifty organizations and nine nationalities in Pennsylvania that were unanimously in favor of David Lawrence for governor. Also, Zak warned it would be difficult for any other candidate to win the election.[28] Actually, it was Lawrence who took himself out of the primary race. Judge Genevieve Blatt explains that Lawrence, having had a survey taken, was convinced in 1939 that a Catholic could not be elected governor.[29]

56

With Lawrence definitely out, it was unfortunate for the Democrats that there was no one individual the Lawrence and Guffey factions could agree on. Warren VanDyke may have been acceptable to all parties, but he died unexpectedly.[30] Accordingly, Democrats were in for a tough primary.

The Guffey forces backed Earle's Lieutenant Governor, Thomas Kennedy. Kennedy had important United Mine Workers support. Moreover, Attorney General Charles J. Margiotti pressured Lawrence to back his candidacy. Margiotti, onetime Republican leader in Western Pennsylvania, swung over to the Democrats at Lawrence's urging in the 1934 campaign. He was rewarded with the post of attorney general in Earle's Cabinet and claimed in 1938 that Lawrence, in 1934, had promised to support him for governor. Lawrence refused and Margiotti, in a series of speeches, charged graft and corruption in the so-called "Little New Deal." He said Lawrence "bought" legislation, took graft in buying gravel for the state, and was responsible for payroll kickbacks.[31] Despite these charges, Lawrence remained unflappable and sought the man who in his opinion was the best suited for the post of governor, Charles Alvin Jones.

Before finally endorsing Jones, however, Lawrence wanted Roosevelt's advice. Governor Earle, Lawrence, J. David Stern, and Guffey all met with FDR. Roosevelt would not agree to running Jones and suggested Ambassador William C. Bullitt as a compromise. Guffey offered himself as a compromise candidate, but Roosevelt claimed he wanted him in the Senate. Bullitt was vetoed by the Lawrence forces. Following this meeting, the Democratic state committee, at the urging of Lawrence, John B. Kelly, and Matthew McCloskey, endorsed Jones for governor and Earle for the Senate.[32] It turned out to be a strange primary for Democrats in Pennsylvania, who saw their two leaders, Lawrence and Guffey, backing different slates. When the polls closed on primary day, Lawrence wired Roosevelt proclaiming another victory for "Roosevelt Democracy." FDR wired back with seemingly little enthusiasm: "Thank you for your telegram. The registered voters have been duly recorded in primary election. I wish every success to my friends George Earle and Charles Jones."[33] Roosevelt realized that now two important

Democratic forces in Pennsylvania were disgruntled—the UMW and Guffey's followers. What Roosevelt did not know was how serious the consequences of the 1938 Pennsylvania race would be. Guffey's message to party faithful "that only the grave will part us," referring to him and Lawrence, convinced no one, and for Democrats, including Lawrence and Guffey, things would never be the same in Western Pennsylvania.

Pennsylvania Republicans had not been idle while Democrats fell apart in 1938. They planned well and used every opportunity to invite the disenchanted into their ranks. As a result, in a complete aboutface, a record vote was cast in the election and Pennsylvania Democrats lost every state office, the United States Senate seat, and many other congressional races. Arthur H. James was elected governor. Republicans asserted the rout was an indictment of the New Deal as well as reaction to graft and corruption charges against Earle's administration.[34] This was a stinging blow for Lawrence, shattered the Lawrence-Guffey friendship, and splintered Pennsylvania Democrats. Not satisfied with party shambles, Democrats continued to gouge each other, in this case in a series of devastating indictments brought against David Lawrence and a political war to the death between Guffey and Lawrence.

Lawrence, according to his time-honored custom, spent the 1938 holidays at home in Pittsburgh. Family festivities were a bracing tonic for a disappointed Lawrence. Following the Christmas and New Year recess, Lawrence returned to Harrisburg to close out the Earle administration. With the formalities of changing administrations completed, Lawrence returned to Pittsburgh in late January 1939 and began the painful process of preparing his Democratic followers for reorganization. It was a gigantic task, since the splintered forces seemed unwilling to move toward unity against the Republicans. Lawrence was, of course, stripped of his power base as long as the Democratic party in Western Pennsylvania was in shambles. There were those within the party who were bent on taking revenge against Lawrence, no matter what the cost to party unity was, especially Charles J. Margiotti.

Joe Barr remembers Margiotti as a "darned good lawyer." But "he was one of those who did not want to wait his turn. He wanted to be the candidate for governor in 1938; it wasn't in the wood."[35]

58

Margiotti was deeply upset by this. Along with Guffey, Margiotti felt the only way to destroy Lawrence was to put him in jail. So earlier accusations by Margiotti against Lawrence were pushed to formal proceedings.

Lawrence was indicted by a special grand jury on charges of violating the election law, statutory blackmail, and conspiracy on January 7, 1939. On February 27, 1939, Lawrence was brought under grand-jury investigation on charges of payroll padding and other fraudulent waste of state highway funds totaling more than $600,000 in Luzerne County; conspiracy to misuse the power of state office to compel the awarding of surety bond business to a favored agency; and conspiracy to extort money from state employees for political purposes.[36] The grand-jury investigation carried through to the fall of 1939. On October 14, 1939, Lawrence was indicted for statutory blackmail, violation of election laws, and conspiracy to cheat and defraud the state.[37]

Margiotti's plan was working well. Already Lawrence had suffered public humiliation and disgrace, and once the indictments were handed down, there was no turning back for either side. Those were bitter days for State Democratic Chairman Lawrence. An election defeat was one thing, but being brought to trial was a much more severe test. He was particularly embittered by the way in which his family was dragged into the limelight through his political activities, especially in view of the fact that, according to Lawrence, there was not one shred of truth in the accusations. Lawrence's one consolation lay in the loyalty displayed by his friends and a sizeable majority of the rank-and-file Democrats.

In late November 1939, Lawrence was tried on the charge of conspiracy to cheat and defraud the state. A jury consisting of nine Republicans, two Democrats, and one Independent was selected, while a Republican judge presided. The indictment charged Lawrence conspired with John J. Verona, a former Pittsburgh ward leader, and others to allow the state to purchase substandard gravel, drew fraudulent bids in concert with the Pioneer Materials Company, of Kittanning, Pennsylvania, and influenced state officials for these purposes. Moreover, the state further tried to demonstrate that Lawrence extorted $5,000 from Spurgeon Bowser, president of Pioneer Materials, as a political contribution, which Lawrence al-

59

legedly failed to hand over to the Democratic state committee. In the midst of the trial, while news of the Bowser extortion was being aired, Lawrence noted for the press that he had never received any money from Bowser. Further, he realized that Bowser and Margiotti were friends and that the former attorney general was "very bitter towards me because I had blocked his ambition to be governor and would wreak his vengence on me."[38] Joe Barr recalled the Harrisburg trial as a "ridiculous thing. I remember the judge, a Republican judge, who later sat on the Supreme Court, in his charge to the jury said that he thought that it should not even have gone that far." When asked if the judge actually said that, Barr replied, "Well, there were times during the trial when he thought it should have been thrown out."[39] The *New York Times* reported that the judge in his charge to the jury said the testimony that had been offered "raised a reasonable doubt as to the accuracy and credibility" of witnesses for the prosecution. Moreover, the conspiracy charge had been built on "circumstantial evidence."[40]

After a three-week trial, with the jury deliberating five and one-half hours, Lawrence, on December 8, 1939, was acquitted of blackmail, conspiracy, and violation of election laws. However, Roy Brownmiller, the first to go on trial, was found guilty of padding payrolls for political purposes. Lawrence's close friend and city treasurer of Pittsburgh James Kirk, along with his associate James P. Skoh, were convicted of conspiring to create a monopoly of the state's insurance and banking business.[41] These latter convictions were a severe personal setback for Lawrence, since he felt these men were being made scapegoats in a vendetta toward him. Still, for the public, Lawrence took a positive stance. "Of course, I am delighted with the verdict. At all times I have had an absolutely clear conscience, since I had done no wrong, and somehow I felt I would be vindicated."[42] Below the surface, however, Lawrence realized that all was not well. Some of his friends were deserting him. Lawrence the politician understood their position, but Lawrence the person was stung to the quick. The White House, so much in debt to Lawrence, was silent. Shortly after the first trial, Roosevelt wrote himself a memo captioned, "Letter to Dave Lawrence by me asked by Joe Guffey." The memo continued to the effect that since

Lawrence was going to be tried again, FDR was going to "forget" the request.[43] Aside from the cheering crowd that met his train upon his return from Harrisburg after the trial, Lawrence had little to buoy his spirits over the holidays as he awaited his second trial on charges of conspiring to tap the public payroll.

During his second trial, which began in late March 1940 and lasted seventeen days, Lawrence, along with seven other Democrats, drew an all-Republican jury. In effect, Lawrence's Democratic state committee had been accused of sponsoring "three to five percent clubs." State payrolls were allegedly padded and then employees "kicked back." This resulted in a fund of well over $1 million according to the prosecution, which was said to have been spent illegally by Democratic state officers in the political campaigns of 1936 and 1938.[44] When the case was completed, the jury deliberated four hours before reaching its decision. Lawrence and his seven colleagues were acquitted of "macing," as it was known in Pennsylvania. The not-guilty verdict saw Lawrence launch a vicious attack on Guffey and Margiotti, accusing them of having instigated the charges that led to the trials. "For the second time a judge and jury have definitely given answer to the calumny and lies against the Earle Administration in the 1938 primary by the Margiotti's and Guffey's and their slimey speech writers and press agents, all of which wrecked our chances of electing a great Democrat, Charles Alvin Jones, as Governor, and George H. Earle to the United States Senate." Happy with his vindication, Lawrence deeply regretted the "heartaches of my wife and daughters."[45] Lawrence's bittersweet reaction to his second acquittal gives but scant indication of the resentment Lawrence harbored over the trials. His personal belief that this was done purposefully in order to destroy him made Lawrence more bitter toward Margiotti. But the realization that his political mentor, Guffey, had turned on him and his family in such a seemingly shameful and reprehensible fashion puzzled rather than angered Lawrence. At the same time, Lawrence's experience gained for him an empathy for colleagues who had to face accusation and trial, whether in the courts or another public forum.

For all practical purposes, Lawrence left no personal record of his indictments and trials save the brief remarks noted above. Generally, his friends and colleagues remember his treating the episode with silence. Robert L. Meyers said he never saw Lawrence worry. He was always self-confident and aggressive and gave "the appearance of being complete master of himself and the situation. Convinced the indictments were politically inspired, Dave was not despondent or didn't give evidence of having lost his courage or confidence."[46] A Lawrence protégé, Judge Charles McCarthy, remembered Lawrence in 1940 during the trial. "He didn't like to say anything about it, except that he didn't want to have anything to do with Margiotti. My impression was that he just did not trust Margiotti at all."[47] McCarthy stated further that the history of the Lawrence indictments demonstrated there was no basis whatsoever for the charges. Andrew Bradley, a longtime political crony of Lawrence's, also alludes to the distrust of Margiotti: "He [Lawrence] felt in a sense that he [Margiotti] was intellectually dishonest. . . . Many who knew Margiotti well would say they had occasionally walked up on Margiotti when he would be standing behind doors listening to conversations and that sort of thing." Moreover, after the trial, Lawrence shared his thoughts on the matter with Bradley. Admittedly, the affair was a harrowing experience, but Lawrence felt that since only Roy Brownmiller was found guilty, and that based on a technicality of having signed papers sent to his office that were audited by someone else, the Earle administration was vindicated.[48]

Frank Ambrose claimed to be a bit more involved. He recalled his experiences relating to the grand-jury investigation. When Ambrose was questioned by the grand jury, they tried to make a case against Ambrose as a bagman. "The man wouldn't condone anything like that." When Ambrose told Lawrence about the questioning, he laughed.[49]

In his care and concern for the Democratic organization in Western Pennsylvania that he had nurtured, Lawrence had put great emphasis on youth. One of his favorite young protégés was Genevieve Blatt. Judge Blatt remembers her reaction to the indictments as a young Lawrence follower. Blatt felt shocked and hurt at the implications, because "I just couldn't imagine that he'd have anything to do with it, the whole sleazy business." Feeling he had been dealt a "very hard blow" in the indictment, Blatt was "gratified and relieved" when Lawrence was acquitted.[50] It was the young people in his party like Blatt that Lawrence worried more about than any other group, save his family, during those beleaguered years. Lawrence realized many young people had put their faith in his leadership and had been, at a young age, put to a serious test of confidence. In Lawrence's view, some would fall by the wayside and he could not hold it against them. Lawrence accusers were to blame, and this helped deepen his resentment.

Grace Sloan recalls a very sad event during the trials. Lawrence attended a local meeting of state committeemen one night outside Pittsburgh. When he rose to speak, someone in the audience threw plastic bags filled with gravel onto the platform. When Lawrence's son Gerald was asked about the incident, he had never heard of it. Moreover, Jerry was in college before he realized the trials had taken place. He explains, "The first time that I realized that the trials had gone on was seeing some flyers that were put out at La Salle College when we had candidates day there. . . . At the Republican rally . . . there were some flyers that had the headlines 'Lawrence Indicted, Cronies Convicted.' " This occurred when Lawrence ran for governor in 1958. After that, Jerry began to ask questions. He gives his impressions of the indictment phase in his father's life as follows. His dad never forgave Margiotti and when others would be indicted or on trial, Lawrence would recall the horror of the experience for himself and his family and how the children were abused by other children in school. Moreover, Alyce Lawrence was pregnant with Jerry at the time of the trials and had to go to Harrisburg to testify. This infuriated Lawrence. In later years when Margiotti would try to strike up a conversation with Jerry while at the races, his father would say, "Stay over here." In his dying days, Margiotti sent word he wanted to be forgiven. Lawrence replied, "As a Catholic I may have to forgive you, but I don't think I could ever forget." Lawrence felt the abuse of police or political power was a most heinous crime. "The thing they don't realize is the suffering they put people through and these people should know what it is like to be under indictment."[51] Walter Giesey confirms Lawrence's lifelong intransigence toward Margiotti. " . . . he [Lawrence] refused to indicate anything of forgiveness for Margiotti. Frankly, that whole period had such a tremendous effect on his life and the lives of his family that he carried it with him all his life. . . . . He treated him [Margiotti] with absolute disdain. He considered him the most untrustworthy person he had ever met."[52]

In his own way, then, Lawrence dealt with Margiotti, and although Margiotti had a sizable following, some of which were influential in Western Pennsylvania, he was no longer a political threat to Lawrence. Any public acclaim or political power once possessed by Lawrence was no longer available to Margiotti. In imperturbable silence, Lawrence moved in Allegheny County circles, rarely publicly acknowledging Margiotti's existence.

Guffey was another problem entirely. Distasteful as it was personally for Lawrence to admit Guffey's entanglement with Margiotti over the indictments, Lawrence accepted the reality of Guffey's political appeal in Western Pennsylvania, as well as his access to the White House. In handling his relations with Guffey, Lawrence realized full well in 1940 he could not just ignore Guffey, as much as he hated dealing with him. Moreover, the evolution of the Guffey-Lawrence set was rooted in friendship, admiration, and gratitude, much like that of a successful student for an excellent teacher. Here, however, it was a case of the student overtaking the teacher. It was a natural process—one, no doubt, Guffey expected to happen—and as Lawrence began to move forward, it became clear to Guffey that Lawrence might soon replace him in power, prestige, and influence. Hence a friction developed between these two loyal, dyed-in-the-wool Democrats, the worst result of which was Guffey's role in the indictments. The contention first appeared when Pennsylvania Democrats enjoyed full-blown political success in the middle thirties. Here Lawrence was forced to steer a very careful course. One mistake and he was on the rocks of political double-cross, the graveyard of many aspiring statesmen.

In his autobiography, Guffey philosophized about those in politics with whom he disagreed. "In my lifetime I have always considered opponents as the people on the other team and never as personal enemies."[53] It is difficult to say whether or not Guffey considered Lawrence his "enemy." That there was a rift in the Guffey-Lawrence relationship in the thirties is well documented. Yet there is little agreement over just what caused these two men to part, a separation that damaged the Democratic party in Pennsylvania for some years. Just when Pennsylvania's Democrats wrested control from the Republicans, Lawrence and Guffey, in the hurlyburly of newfound success, drifted apart. Lawrence's success should have been the crowning achievement of Guffey's career, yet it did not happen that way, and neither said what drove them apart. Fellow party workers and the rank and file worked under this cloud. In a conversation with William Block, owner of the *Pittsburgh Post Gazette*, Lawrence recalled his early days with Guffey at the latter's home at 5050 Ward Terrace. Shortly after World War I, Guffey had phoned Lawrence and asked him to come to his home. Guffey, standing in his nightshift when Lawrence arrived, said, "You see before you, Dave, an economic, physical and political wreck." Lawrence had commiserated with Guffey and then chatted a long time that night about Guffey's troubles.[54] This was not, for Lawrence and Guffey, an unusual occurence thereafter. Just what significance Guffey attached to these sessions he does not say.

By early 1935, workers in Allegheny County's Democratic headquarters knew there was serious friction. Still, Guffey would appear at headquarters on a regular basis. He and Lawrence were politically cordial, but there was an undercurrent of disagreement. Some felt Lawrence wanted to be chairman of Pennsylvania's 1936 delegation to the Democratic National Convention. Guffey vetoed this and Lawrence was piqued.[55] Guffey, a United States senator, felt he should be national spokesman for Pennsylvania's Democrats. Politically, Lawrence accepted this, but personally he found it hard to take, more so because of his misgivings about Guffey's leadership ability. Still, Lawrence played along and kept Allegheny Democrats united with other Pennsylvania Democrats.

For his Democratic constituency in 1937, however, Lawrence's guidance took a strange turn. The Railroad Brotherhood Unions, whose numerical strength was impressive in Pennsylvania, pushed for railroad full-crew legislation. Lawrence and the Earle administration backed the unions, and a bill was introduced into the Pennsylvania Assembly. Guffey, since he was not consulted in the matter,

65

was irked by the proposed legislation and wired state senators to vote against it.[56] For the first time, Lawrence publicly opposed Guffey and won. Guffey then realized that in his absence Lawrence was becoming an opposing force in Pennsylvania political circles. Moreover, Governor Earle's term was due to expire the following year, and it seemed likely to Guffey that Lawrence might seek the governor's chair. This would give Lawrence more patronage and might further chip away at Guffey's power base. However, Guffey noted that he remained on "terms of close intimacy" with Earle and Lawrence while he was in Washington. "In order to free myself for my duties in Congress, I had turned all matters of patronage, State and Federal, over to the State Committee, of which David Lawrence was Chairman."[57] It was evident to Guffey that he no longer held a key position among Pennsylvania Democrats. That he really placed federal patronage in Lawrence and Earle's control was questionable, and whatever intimacy Guffey had at one time shared with Lawrence and Earle, seemed, to most observers, lost in the 1938 primary campaign and the so-called scandals that ensued. Father Woody Jones recalled: "Guffey and Lawrence fell out on this [the 1938 primary]. They never quite made up. When the let's-all-make-up meeting occurred at the Penn Harris, Guffey said, 'The Guffeys and Lawrences will part only at the grave.' I said to Clair Ross, 'He means the political grave.' "[58] Jones, a lifelong friend of Lawrence, felt Lawrence was wrong in this matter. On the other hand, a Lawrence man all the way, Joe Barr saw the primary dispute as the beginning of the Lawrence-Guffey feud that culminated when Guffey backed Tom Kennedy, vice-president of the United Mine Workers of America. Barr felt Kennedy was reluctant to run, but Guffey kept pushing him. "After it was over we had to get all the shreds and put it back together. That was the beginning, you might say, of the cooling between Guffey and Lawrence."[59] Andrew Bradley, another Lawrence devotee, suggests Lawrence took himself out of consideration because the Catholic issue could hurt the party. He submerged his feelings and backed Jones. "I am sure that he felt the Guffey activity was not of that same motivation, that it was more selfishly motivated."[60] Robert Meyers, Jr., saw the fight as one between two men who really, for the most part, agreed with each other. Still, Guffey had wanted to be governor for a long time. When it became

66

obvious Guffey would not be the party choice, Guffey joined forces with, Margiotti. Meyers said, "I just don't know what Margiotti's ambitions were." But clearly Guffey wanted to take state control away from Lawrence. Guffey wanted to be the "Power behind the throne."[61] Finally, John Dent, Democratic congressman from Jeanette, Pennsylvania, traces the effects of the falling out on the Democratic party as follows. After the primary, "Joe's boys" wouldn't unite and the Lawrence versus Guffey undercurrent lingered through 1946, when Guffey lost his bid for reelection. With Lawrence and Bill Green, of Philadelphia, together, Guffey was finished.[62]

Another consideration is, however, that professionals both within and without the Lawrence-Guffey organizations saw the dispute more along the lines of personalities rather than political infighting. James Farley experienced grave concern over the Pennsylvania rift and suggested, "Joe Guffey was a pretty tough fellow. . . . There were few fellows who were closer to Roosevelt than Joe was, but I think Joe was a pretty selfish fellow. . . . Guffey wouldn't want anyone else around to grow up and take his influence or power, and Dave probably found that out himself when he got into position . . . jealousy enters into that you know, everybody has that kind of situation, particularly in politics."[63] Farley, at the time, wanted to believe jealousy motivated the fight, since, given the proper national leadership, Pennsylvania could be saved for the 1940 national election. As it turned out, Farley was, for the most part, correct.

In Pennsylvania, Grace Sloan saw the feud as one between two strong men thrown together in politics. "I think each wanted what they wanted . . . basically I don't think they ever in their hearts fell out."[64] Art Rooney, a Republican and close personal friend of Lawrence, felt Lawrence and Guffey fell apart because their ideas were different. Rooney suggests further that Lawrence was a much stronger man than Guffey and, given their roles in the Democratic party, one could readily understand how the two could come to loggerheads. Rooney also observed that many things Guffey did upset Lawrence because he construed Guffey's actions as not always being in the best interest of the party.[65] This links with Farley's characterization of Guffey's selfishness, while, at the same time, many people agree that Lawrence was generous to a fault when it came to party well-being.

At the same time, some felt Lawrence shared responsibility with Guffey for the primary fracas as well as the November trouncing in 1938. Also, Margiotti's role here was important. But Lawrence, rightly or wrongly, saw Guffey as a supporter of Margiotti's crusade, a posture Guffey never admitted or denied. Guffey revealed that Margiotti knew he could not make his general claims of graft and corruption in the Earle administration stick, but enjoyed playing the martyr role for the cause of righteousness. Moreover, Margiotti goaded Governor Earle into firing him as attorney general by refusing to back off on accusations that Lawrence, McCloskey, and Ralph Bashore had purchased legislation in 1935. When Earle asked for proof that Margiotti claimed he had, the attorney general refused to show Earle the evidence. Earle then fired Margiotti. Thus Margiotti, using his undisputed legal skills in concert with the Republican district attorney of Dauphin County, provoked a full-blown grand-jury investigation of Earle's administration. Earle, in attempting to counteract the move, called the legislature into general session to mount its own investigation to supplant the grand jury. However, the state supreme court said the legislators could not legally do this.[66] In the meantime, the elections took place and the Earle administration was defeated.

While under indictment, Lawrence cut back on public political activities, while, at the same time, planning to strike back at Guffey. Early in January 1940, a group of Western Pennsylvania Democratic leaders asked John B. Kelly, chairman of the Philadelphia Democratic Committee, to lead a movement to oppose Guffey's renomination in the primary. Although Lawrence did not allow his name to be used publicly in the matter, it was understood Lawrence and Kelly had already agreed that in order to avoid a fight similar to that of 1938, Guffey should be forced into retirement.[67] A move toward this goal followed Lawrence's acquittal. At the same time, Lawrence announced he would campaign vigorously for Walter A. Jones to replace Guffey as the party nominee for United States senator. Guffey replied that he hoped Lawrence's statement was the result of "momentary hysteria." Guffey's position was that of surprise at the Lawrence outburst, saying he held no ill feeling and had even contributed $1,000 to Lawrence's defense fund and appeared as a character witness. Lawrence retorted, "Joe Guffey did not contribute one cent to any defense fund for me. Apparently, the hysteria is in the Guffey camp. He was not a character witness for me. He was called like a number of others to testify about a fictitious meeting in Philadelphia at the last Democratic National Convention."[68] Interestingly, this was Lawrence's last major salvo against Guffey. Lawrence carried on his promised energetic campaign against Guffey's renomination for the Senate.

Despite signals received from the White House indicating Roosevelt would not be a party to Guffey's removal,[69] when Pennsylvania's State Democratic Committee met in February, they were still determined to block Guffey's nomination. After an all-night, vigorous, bitter meeting with the committee, Guffey declared he would enter the Pennsylvania primary whether or not he was approved by the committee. Further, he let all federal officeholders know that he still controlled the patronage and power in national politics. In view of Guffey's gauntlet, the committee ordered a "free and open" primary race for United States Senate seat.[70]

By early March, the notion of a "free and open" primary had begun to wear on some Democratic leaders. Many felt the open race was ruining the Democratic party. Accordingly, word was passed along to Walter A. Jones, chairman of the Pennsylvania Turnpike Commission, suggesting that Jones step aside in favor of Guffey and party harmony. Since Guffey was already a United States senator, had White House favor, and was not under indictment, as was Lawrence, it seemed only natural the Democrats could easily pull together under Guffey's banner. Moreover, the Guffey camp asked, "Why drag the fight on? Obviously, Guffey is going to win." Jones refused to back away. "If my opponents are so confident of victory, why are they so anxious to have me withdraw? If their confidence is real, why are they interested?" Jones's stonewalling caused concern that reached Washington.[71]

In the meantime, John B. Kelly declared he would remain neutral. He was allegedly told to do so by President Roosevelt. The president, upset at the situation in Pennsylvania, indicated that if

69

the "right" candidate was not chosen in the Keystone State, then Kelly and Roosevelt would sit down in the middle of the summer "and see that the best available candidate is on the ticket."[72] Roosevelt's stance did not augur well for Jones and the latter's political power base. Lawrence, then under a cloud of indictment, was really in no position to negotiate or challenge the president in the matter. Moreover, the Lawrence-Jones forces continued to press the accusation, once Lawrence was exonerated, that Guffey was responsible for originating the graft and corruption charges against the Earle administration. Interestingly enough, John Kane agreed with Lawrence that "vested interests" had shattered party unity. "The big interests knew they couldn't attack us on our record so they started a campaign of intrigue and they got the Margiottis and the like to bore from within." Whether or not the charge was correct, the White House did not want to hear it. This was a national election year. Guffey, apparently acting on White House orders, disregarded Lawrence's barbs and denunciations while, at the same time, offering the olive branch. Guffey recalled his twenty-five–year political friendship with Lawrence, declaring he felt Lawrence personally honest both in and out of office. Further, Guffey pleaded, Lawrence was an innocent victim of despicable Republican conspiracy to blacken the Earle administration.[73]

Just how far Guffey's protestations went toward preserving party unity during the primary is difficult to say. Moreover, in the waning days of the primary campaign and just one week after Lawrence was found not guilty, Sen. Alben Barkely, commenting on the political situation in Pennsylvnaia, said President Roosevelt "devoutly hopes" Guffey will be reelected. "When Guffey enlisted under the banner of Woodrow Wilson, one of his fellow soldiers in the cause was FDR."[74] Thus Roosevelt's long friendship with Guffey served the latter well in the 1940 primary. The president did not reject Lawrence outright, but made it clear that Guffey's friendship was very important to him. Further, Jones had at one time opposed a third term for Roosevelt, although he changed his position at the urging of the Pennsylvania State Democratic Committee. All this was too much for the Jones-Lawrence forces, and Guffey defeated Jones handily by 100,000 votes, a resounding defeat for Lawrence. The man Lawrence once called "party wrecker" was in control of the Democratic party in Pennsylvania.[75] As a result, Lawrence resigned as state chairman, a post he had held since 1934. At the same time, Lawrence, ever concerned for the welfare of the party, announced he would support the party's candidate, Guffey, in his Senate bid. Guffey noted that "our friendship continued."[76]

Guffey, with some slight help from Lawrence, was reelected to the Senate in 1940, and Pennsylvania, much to the relief of Roosevelt's crowd, was saved for the Democrats. Moreover, despite Roosevelt's friendship with Lawrence, Guffey continued to command clout in federal circles. In May 1941, Lawrence protested the removal of William Driscoll as collector of internal revenue for the Western District of Pennsylvania. He was to be replaced by William Miller, who had been selected by Guffey. After a series of memoranda passed among the White House, Guffey's office, and Lawrence's office, the Guffey appointee was picked by FDR.[77] Lawrence accepted the decision as "part of the game" and continued to serve Pennsylvania Democrats. Although others noticed a coolness between Guffey and Lawrence in the early forties, the two Pennsylvania leaders did speak and work together on party matters.

As the 1942 primary date in Pennsylvania neared, many Democrats felt Guffey would run for governor, and Guffey gave every evidence that he was certainly considering such a move. Guffey realized, however, that the Democrats in his state were, to a degree, split. It would be difficult to overcome that division, especially in a state where Republicans already controlled the governor's mansion. When decision time arrived, Guffey opted out of the governor's race and decided to back Judge Ralph H. Smith. John Kane and William D. McClelland were also in the Smith camp. Lawrence was backing Pennsylvania auditor general F. Clair Ross. At the same time, Luther Harr ran with the backing of David Stern and Albert M. Greenfield, two political heavyweights from Philadelphia.[78] Again Lawrence and Guffey were apart at primary time, much to the disgust of several Philadelphia leaders. Still, the split in the '42 primary lacked the open acerbity of those of 1938 and 1940. Lawrence backed Ross because he thought Ross was the "best candidate." Moreover, there was much private jocularity over the diminutive stature of the two

71

major candidates, Smith and Ross. Lawrence remarked one day, "What do you think? This looks like the battle of the midgets." Further, many members of the state committee assembled in Harrisburg saw Lawrence and Guffey together in public in an apparently friendly and jovial exchange. As the deliberations of the state committee progressed, there was some obvious cooperation on the part of both Guffey and Lawrence, but the two men remained separated until after the primary. F. Clair Ross won the nomination, and Lawrence, in effect, again became state Democratic chairman.

As the 1942 campaign progressed, the Democrats seemed unable to pull things together. The two Western Pennsylvania factions remained at odds. Lawrence's victory in the primary was a hollow accomplishment without accompanying success at the November polls. At first, Guffey sat on his hands. However, the state Democratic leadership, under Lawrence's guidance, appointed Ramsey Black, a Guffey protégé, state campaign chairman. John Kane responded to the gesture by directing his colleagues in the labor area to form a Central Labor Union movement and mount an endorsement of all Democratic candidates.[79] However, these efforts proved futile in stemming the Republican tide. Lawrence was concerned over the election outcomes to such an extent that he felt something had to be done to arouse labor, liberals, and other New Dealers. He suggested a fireside chat by Roosevelt might do the trick. Also, Lawrence wanted Roosevelt to meet with Philip Murray.[80] Unfortunately for Lawrence, the Democratic cause was too far gone. Gen. Edward Martin was elected governor and the entire Republican slate won in the other races. Democrat Ross carried Allegheny County and Pittsburgh, but lost by substantial margins in a majority of the remaining counties. "In Philadelphia it was a bad year for getting out the vote; it was a war year, you see, and not too many people were interested in voting," said James Tate. Lawrence, despite a statewide defeat, saw a bright future for Democrats in Western Pennsylvania. The returns proved just how effective his organization had grown to be in the face of overwhelming odds.

During World War II, only a few minor events marked the political scene in Pennsylvania. Lawrence continued to build his organization, and it worked effectively in contributing to the election

72

of the Roosevelt-Truman ticket in 1944. At the same time, Pennsylvania Democrats elected Francis Myers to the United States Senate. The evolution of the Myers candidacy marked a new era in Pennsylvania's Democratic politics. According to James Tate, then state representative from Philadelphia, Myers was nominated because Lawrence and Guffey got together in opposing James McGrannery, of Philadelphia, for the nomination. Lawrence, who had an obsession about Catholic candidates, felt McGrannery's name was too Irish and too obviously Catholic. Moreover, McGrannery was a difficult individual to handle. Since Guffey and Lawrence opposed McGrannery, Philadelphia leaders picked Michael Bradley. Again, Lawrence objected because of the Irish-Catholic name and Bradley's negative record in Congress on draft and lend-lease legislation. Lawrence and Guffey asked about Myers, because with his name he could be Jewish, German, or Irish. Jim Clark, chairman of the Philadelphia Democratic City Committee, said Myers was all right but unknown. Lawrence replied, "Anybody but McGrannery or Bradley."

Tate, as Clark's lieutenant, was sent to poll the Philadelphia delegation on Myers. With the understanding that if they accepted Myers, Philadelphia would get the Senate nomination, the group agreed to accept Myers. When word went back to Clark, Guffey, Lawrence, and other state leaders, after a short consultation, Guffey announced he would take Ramsey Black for state treasurer, G. Harold Wagner for auditor general, and Myers for United States senator. The general reaction was, who is this fellow Myers? Some said he was the head of the Holy Name Society in Philadelphia, and he was! Myers, satisfied to stay in the background, said, "I came to Harrisburg to nominate Mike Bradley. In fact, he and I slept in the same bed together." When things settled down, Lawrence pledged to go from county to county and plead with the people to get together and resolve their differences. This helped bring Philadelphia into the Democratic column in 1944, according to Tate, but Myers barely won, by about 16,000 votes. The Democrats took Pittsburgh and Allegheny County, but Myers did not do as well as Roosevelt. "Roosevelt won by a big majority, and history shows Roosevelt was in pretty bad shape at that time, 1944."[81]

The Lawrence and Guffey forces now presented a public image

of working together, and Allegheny County's Democratic organization was again a major force in state politics. In this newfound unity, that Lawrence did not cut Guffey off completely as he did Margiotti was, according to some, due to Lawrence's friendship with Emma Guffey Miller, Joe Guffey's sister and Pennsylvania Democratic national committeewoman. So, despite the grief that Lawrence had experienced over the party split, scandals, indictments, and trials between 1938 and 1940, there did seem to be a healing between himself and Guffey in the early forties, and during the 1946 senatorial campaign, when Guffey was accused of swindling several corporations and individuals, including Lawrence, in a stock transaction in the early twenties, Lawrence came to Guffey's defense. He explained that it was Guffey's partner, Gillespie, who had engineered the swindle. Lawrence, referring to press reports, said, "Why, it's a damned outrage to talk about Senator Guffey that way."[82] Lawrence, in 1946, could afford to be publicly magnanimous in Guffey's regard. Guffey, by then in his midseventies, could not win reelection, in Lawrence's estimation. Roosevelt died in April 1945, and with his passing Guffey's power ebbed. Lawrence, in November 1945, had led the Democrats to victory in Pittsburgh, occupied the mayor's chair and was in full control of the Pittsburgh Democratic organization, despite Guffey's persistent faction, and with Truman in the White House, Lawrence now controlled Pennsylvania's federal patronage. The damage of the bitter years with Guffey had passed, and Lawrence had no wish to stain the Democratic organization further with personal revenge. The Guffey-Lawrence conflict was over, their friendship to a degree restored.

Toward the end of 1944, both the Lawrence and Guffey factions were surprised when Pittsburgh's mayor, Cornelius D. Scully, approaching the end of his first full term, informed Democratic leaders he would not try to retain his office in 1945. Scully's surprise move forced the Democrats to seek out a possible nominee, a process that in the past had proved detrimental to party harmony. Whoever the nominee proved to be, he would need the active support of Commissioner John Kane's followers, as well as Lawrence's. When news of the Scully decision filtered through the ranks, many felt Lawrence would be a good candidate, one that John Kane could, without too much difficulty, support. But Lawrence at first proved reluctant. Frank Ambrose recalled asking Lawrence to run for mayor. "I am not interested in being mayor" was the reply. Lawrence further related he had been thinking of running Eddie Fry, for many years Pittsburgh's controller. Ambrose objected that Fry, once in office, would turn on Lawrence. "Oh, come on, Frank" was Lawrence's reaction. Lawrence then proceeded to call in all thirty-two ward leaders, one at a time. Only one, Frank Good, favored Fry for mayor. Good lived in Fry's ward and had been made a police inspector through Fry's support. Ambrose again urged Lawrence to run. "I don't want to run; I don't want to run for political office," Lawrence said.[83]

Lawrence continued to maintain his unwillingness to be designated mayoral nominee until a very late date. When the Democrats finally convinced Lawrence to accept, they were close to a point where a bitter primary battle loomed as a distinct possibility. John Kane could accept Lawrence, but could not back candidates Lawrence had in mind, and the reverse was true. Later, Lawrence liked to tell the story about the time when city and county Democrats had been in conference three days discussing mayoral candidates. One day, Terrence O'Toole, onetime Democratic city councilman, met Lawrence and said, "How are you coming?" Lawrence replied, "We're not getting anywhere." O'Toole said, "Why the hell don't you take me?" Lawrence, said, "Well, we could go further and do worse." A few days after Lawrence had been selected candidate, he met O'Toole, who said, "How is it coming along?" "Well," Lawrence said, "they picked me and I have to take it." "Well, by God, Davey, you did it." "What do you mean?" O'Toole said, "You went further and done worse."[84]

So in 1945 the die was cast, and Lawrence found himself in a situation he said he really never wanted. Lawrence's disenchantment over his personal involvement in seeking public office in no way affected the stamina and fight he brought to his mayoral campaign.

First, intraparty strain had to be relaxed. Lawrence wisely asked John Kane to be his campaign manager. Thus the very strong pockets of Kane followers situated within the city limits of Pittsburgh looked favorably on the Lawrence candidacy. At the same time, Lawrence evolved a seven-point program for Pittsburgh that was, in effect, the Lawrence platform. In setting up his goals, Lawrence was reminded by Kane that his campaign structure had to reach beyond politics into civic matters. Lawrence was well known politically, but in civic circles he needed updating and exposure. As a result, George E. Kelly, who was handling publicity for the Democratic party in the city and county, was directed by Kane to meet with Park H. Martin, chairman of the Allegheny Conference. Kane pushed for the conference program, which he felt Lawrence should endorse as part of his campaign strategy. This then became the keystone in Lawrence's seven-point agenda.[85] Allegheny Conference endorsement had broad appeal, although at first some members, unaware of Lawrence's capacity for follow-through, saw it as campaign rhetoric.

During the campaign, bitterness surfaced between Lawrence's followers and those of Robert N. Waddell, his opponent, an insurance executive, and onetime football coach at Carnegie Tech. Naturally, the Waddell forces had significant ammunition merely in past events involving Lawrence, all of which were a matter of record. Moreover, the boss issue surfaced almost immediately. But Lawrence reminded the public he made no apologies for seeking the mayor's office. "I helped to take the party from an abject minority to a place where it is solid in the county." In Lawrence's mind, since he did not actively seek the nomination, once it was offered and accepted, he had every right to it. Lawrence further reminded the people of his "solid backing of the labor movement," a factor that would better enable him as mayor to bring business and labor together for Pittsburgh's benefit. Finally, the charge that he as boss gave himself the nomination was dismissed outright. "I am not a candidate of my own choosing. I had my work cut out for me in larger fields. But when they decided I was the man to make the fight, I was willing."[86] In effect, Lawrence had sacrified his interests in state and national politics to run for mayor, and he would fight as only he knew how, as the man who had struggled within the minority party for years. Still, despite muckraking opposition, his deep love for his native city made his race for mayor a joy.

Lawrence stuck to the issues and avoided personalities. He

stressed the city's need for leadership and the desirability of stamping out bickering and glory hunting among politicians. Some years later, Lawrence recalled that industries were pulling out of the city in great numbers. Smoke was killing the city. Lawrence thus decided to call upon the people to put "P for Pride" back in Pittsburgh, a slogan that became characteristic of the Lawrence campaign.[87] As the contest drew to a close, Lawrence appealed to the people of Pittsburgh's civic pride. He pointed out his race was not based on the "tried and tested political standbys." Lawrence sensed a "new spirit" in Pittsburgh that matched his proposed community program. "When I am Mayor, we will work together and we will make that program come true. And we will let history worry about who gets the credit."[88]

Lawrence's message hit home and despite deprecating personal attacks on his character, Lawrence outpolled Waddell by over 14,000 votes. Lawrence interpreted the election outcome as both a vote of confidence in him personally and a clear directive for initiating his seven-point platform. He vowed to make every effort to meet his elected responsibility. "I have not been elected Mayor of a political party . . . but of a great city and all its varied people."[89]

Despite success at home, Lawrence, along with other Pennsylvania Democratic leaders, struggled to keep the Keystone State in Democratic ranks in state and national elections, but 1952 proved a low point for Pennsylvania Democrats because of the great voter appeal Dwight Eisenhower had in Pennsylvania. At the same time, according to Lawrence, the Democrats were not united even at the top. There had never been a close connection between Truman and Stevenson "that was so desirable in a situation of that sort." Stevenson had "inflicted" Steve Mitchell on the national committee. This was a bad move, since it upset Truman's friends, and the latter sat on their hands during the Stevenson campaign.[90] As a result, Eisenhower swept Pennsylvania and the country, but Lawrence still controlled Democratic politics in the state.

Whatever disappointment Eisenhower's victory held for Lawrence vanished in 1953, when Lawrence was returned to the mayor's office for a third straight time in a smashing victory. Lawrence then trained party sights on the governor's mansion for 1954. He wanted

77

Richardson Dilworth to make another bid for governor in 1954. Dilworth, however, had been elected Philadelphia's district attorney and would have had to resign to run for governor, so he opted out. In the meantime, Allegheny County Coroner William McClelland threw his hat in the ring, supported by Commissioner Kane, Prothonotory Roberts, and the John Exler factions. Kane's cronies expected Lawrence to go for McClelland since he was a local, but Lawrence sat on the fence till the last minute. On the day the state policy committee met to pick a gubernatorial nominee, Lawrence told George Leader, a York County poultryman, that he would be tapped. Leader met Lawrence that morning (the committee was scheduled for two in the afternoon) and went over the policy-committee list with Lawrence indicating what support he had. Lawrence finally said, "Yes, you'll be the person." No doubt Lawrence wanted to see what Leader had accomplished on his own before endorsing him. Naturally, the Kane, Roberts, McClelland, and Exler crowd was furious with Lawrence for selecting Leader, but Lawrence felt Leader was the only man who could win over the entire state. McClelland campaigned in the primary without committee endorsement as an independent Democrat. His chief issue was the wage tax that Lawrence backed and initiated in Pittsburgh in 1953. McClelland swept Western Pennsylvania and this was a great victory for Kane. But as John Exler explained, "We did all right till we got to the other side of the mountains, and that's where the state organization came through." Leader won the primary, and when Lawrence was questioned about the outcomes in his backyard, he said, "I have no statement to make. What is there to say? Leader was nominated and that was what we were trying to do."[91]

McClelland was embittered over the election, and Lawrence realized Leader needed all the support he could muster in Western Pennsylvania. As a result, Leader met with McClelland, who, Leader remembers, "supported me moderately well, I suppose." Leader did not feel McClelland's support was a big factor, because after a vigorous campaign, engineered by Lawrence, Leader did well throughout the remainder of the state.[92]

In the early stages of the campaign, Lawrence warned Leader to be very careful about taxes. He suggested Leader tell the people

78

the only thing "you know about finances is what you read in the papers," and Lawrence advised, "Once you are elected you will then determine what is best for the people of Pennsylvania." At the same time, Lawrence asked Jim Finnegan and Matthew McCloseky to help with the financing. Moreover, Leader recalls Lawrence was a "great organizer." In contrast, Joe Clark said at the time, "It's too bad. He's [Leader's] a nice fellow, I hate to see him be the sacrificial lamb." Lawrence never had a "sacrificial lamb" philosophy about any campaign, Leader recalled, and although Lawrence was very much in demand as a speaker during the campaign, he never took the limelight off Leader. Leader remembers, "He did all the things an effective leader should do."[93] As a result, Pennsylvania Democrats, for the first time since 1934, elected a governor, symbolic of the evolving power base Lawrence was building in Pennsylvania.

That Lawrence had become one of the top men in the national Democratic party became evident at the 1956 Democratic National Convention. From the outset, Lawrence worked with Stevenson in the primaries. Lawrence believed Stevenson to be "the best qualified man in either party to be president." Lawrence felt many people underestimated the intelligence of the American voter when arguing that Stevenson talked over their heads. Lawrence remembered critics said the same of Woodrow Wilson "because he was president of Princeton University." Further, Lawrence was convinced that many who voted for Eisenhower as a military hero would not vote for him in '56 as a great president.[94] The Democrats at least believed Lawrence, and Stevenson secured the presidential nomination with little effort at the convention.

Prior to the convention, however, both Estes Kefauver and Stevenson experienced fiscal difficulties that led to a deal for the vice-presidential nomination. Lawrence explained both sides were fiscally weak, and so he suggested to Howard McGrath, Kefauver's campaign manager, that Pennsylvania would support Kefauver for the vice-president if the primary fights could be ended. It was agreed.[95]

This all worked out well, except for the fact that when Lawrence arrived in Chicago for the convention, "John F. Kennedy was a candidate for Vice-President and David Lawrence had pledged his

79

word to be with Kefauver. So you can see the position I [Lawrence] was in with the Pennsylvania delegation. It was pretty much the Pennsylvania delegation that deprived him [Kennedy] of the nomination." Many people could not understand why Lawrence was against Kennedy, but according to Lawrence, "I had to keep my word."[96]

Once nominated, however, Stevenson found some fairly strong opposition to the Kefauver nomination. Lyndon Johnson and Sam Rayburn wanted Stevenson to name Kennedy as his running mate. A meeting was held at Chicago's Stock Yard Inn with Johnson, Rayburn, Finnegan, and Stevenson present. With Johnson and Rayburn pushing for Kennedy and Stevenson and Finnegan wanting Kefauver, the meeting stalled. Stevenson then suggested an open convention. Meanwhile, Finnegan, near panic, sought out Lawrence and said, "Oh, I need you. I need you. I don't think I can handle those fellows," meaning Johnson and Rayburn. Lawrence went into the meeting and took the open-convention position, explaining that anyone running against Eisenhower had an almost insurmountable job. Maybe it was time to do something new; it would be dramatic to have the convention pick the man. Rayburn was disgusted with Lawrence over this and said, "I never saw a convention where anything like this ever happened."[97] Nonetheless, the convention went open, and Lawrence was free to back Kefauver as promised.

Back in the Pennsylvania delegation, Lawrence received extended support for his Kefauver push. Both Richardson Dilworth and Bill Green of Philadelphia, surprisingly enough, agreed that Kennedy should not be "thrown away" in the '56 vice-presidential race, which seemed quite precarious at the time, and Bill Green had to take some heat over his decision to go with Lawrence for Kefauver. Charles Buckley angrily shouted at Green, "What the hell kind of Irishman are you? Christ Almighty, here's a chance for a fellow like Kennedy and you're for that goddamn guy!" Moreover, Kefauver's Senate investigating committee had "raised a lot of hell with a lot of Democrats," according to Lawrence, and that is what bothered the Buckleys. Another embarrassing thing for Lawrence was that Kennedy had nominated Stevenson.[98] Still, the Pennsylvania delegation backed Lawrence in this, and Kefauver went on to

80

defeat Kennedy, with Pennsylvania the deciding factor. When all was over, Lawrence observed, "This is the most democratic convention I have ever seen and I've been coming to them since 1912. Sure, we could have put Kefauver over that way, but Mr. Stevenson wanted an open convention and I certainly wouldn't cross Jim Finnegan."[99]

John Kennedy, although disappointed, seemed to take Lawrence's role goodnaturedly. Some few months later when Kennedy spoke in Pittsburgh, Lawrence, in his introduction, spoke about Kennedy's grandfather Honey Fitzgerald and finished by saying, "Ladies and gentlemen, I give you the junior senator of Massachusetts, John Fitzgerald," and immediately sat down. Kennedy got up and said, "Gee, Mr. Mayor, I wish you'd said that out in Chicago!"[100] The crowd roared and applauded for several minutes. Some years later, the question of Lawrence's position at the open convention surfaced again. As a result, Lawrence wrote Robert Kennedy saying, "The fact is I was not against your brother. I was for Senator Estes Kefauver. I promised Senator Kefauver I would support him, as did the then Governor of Pennsylvania, George M. Leader, several months before the convention."[101] As the '56 campaign opened, Stevenson wrote Lawrence with gratitude, promising to mount a great campaign.[102] Lawrence reciprocated in bringing every power at his command to secure the election of the Stevenson-Kefauver ticket. It was a futile struggle in Pennsylvania. Judge Blatt felt "not three Stevensons rolled into one" could have beaten Eisenhower in Pennsylvania. Joe Clark remembered, "We were all slugging for a straight ticket, and I went all out for Stevenson at the end of the campaign, which many Democratic leaders did not, but Lawrence did." Stevenson lost Pennsylvania by 615,000 votes, although Joe Clark won his senate seat by 17,500 ballots.[103] The Lawrence organization, despite losing the presidential vote, looked good, and it augured well for the future.

The following November, Lawrence was elected mayor of Pittsburgh for the fourth time. With very little effort and only slight opposition in the campaign, Lawrence outlined a plan to reform county government, while reminding Pittsburghers of all the improvements in the city. According to Walter Giesey, "Lawrence had

81

it made in Pittsburgh," and there was no political post that interested Lawrence or would have provided more prestige for the mayor. However, Pennsylvania Democrats would ask Lawrence to leave his favored and happy Pittsburgh role to bring unity to the party in 1958.

Lawrence surely hoped the Democrats could replace Governor Leader, who could not lawfully succeed himself, with another Democrat, but the question of who would be the candidate became a vexing problem. True to form, Lawrence never publicly backed Richardson Dilworth in the early considerations, but when Dilworth suggested Red China be admitted to the United Nations, it became clear the resultant furor would weaken Dilworth's possible candidacy. One evening Giesey, Robin, and Lawrence met for dinner to discuss the candidacy, since Dilworth was out. Robin wrote a list of five characteristics the prospect needed. Lawrence said, "That's a very good question; that's what we have been trying to find out." Robin said, "But it's you Dave, you're the one who can do it." Lawrence replied, "Oh, no, I'm too old for that. I really don't want it."[104] Lawrence continued this stance even though the state policy committee was foundering.

The committee met three times, getting nowhere. Finally, Andrew Bradley, while acknowledging the religious issue, indicated Lawrence was the only one who could unify the party. Jim Clark, Dilworth, and Green, "who were at each other's throats" over the candidacy, all agreed. Lawrence smiled and said, "Well, the last thing in the world I thought of when I left Pittsburgh this morning was ever walking out of this room as the candidate for governor. . . . If this is the decision of the group, I suppose I'll have to do it." Many committee members saw no other way out, because they could not support a candidate that Green opposed.[105] At the same time, it was agreed the candidate for lieutenant governor should be from Philadelphia. Leader wanted Philadelphia City Councilman Victor Moor, and Joe Clark blocked that move by calling Moor no good, a turncoat Catholic who had left the church, and questioned the wisdom of having two Catholics on the ticket. John Morgan Davis was selected even though Dilworth claimed he did not remember him. Joe Clark quipped, "Well, he's just the type you wouldn't remember."[106]

82

Earlier in the proceedings, Leader vowed he would run for the Senate only with Dilworth. But after Lawrence was selected, Leader backed off and became the candidate for United States Senate. Leader recalled, "I thought I had an agreement with Dick that he would run with me and he thought he had an agreement with me. He thinks I deserted him and I am confident he deserted me. Dick and I would have been unbeatable according to the polls."[107]

With the ticket set, Lawrence planned a broad-based appeal for his campaign. He voiced his concern over Pennsylvania's ability to compete with states like New Jersey, Delaware, Maryland, New York, and Ohio. He was convinced all Pennsylvanians had a role to play in making the Keystone State a better place in which to work and live. "Unless we are able to develop a type of climate and atmosphere that will encourage new industries to come into the State, and the industries we have to expand their facilities, we will slide behind the other states," Lawrence said.[108] This was the campaign theme. Moreover, Lawrence's proven ability to work closely with business attracted nominal Republicans. At one Lawrence speech, E. L. Nixon, a chain-store marketing official and uncle of then vice-president Nixon, said, "I don't want to do anything to hurt Dick, but this man Lawrence's program appeals to me."[109] In Philadelphia, with Dilworth's help, bankers and industrialists gave Lawrence a big day. Of course, they heard the opponent, but McGonigle's day was different. "It was rigged," admits Saxe. In addition, Dilworth got the people at the prestigious Mid-City Club to support Lawrence, arguing Lawrence got on very well with the Mellons. Much of Lawrence's campaign travel was done alone on commercial flights. In Pittsburgh, the only one to meet him was his city chauffeur in an eight-year-old city car. Someone referred to the car, and Lawrence fired back, "That car is in good condition." When Lawrence appeared before youngsters, his manner mellowed. He answered sometimes impertinent questions with candor. According to Giesey, "The kids could ask him things no one else would dare."[110]

The campaign went well aside from the religious issue. Very early in Lawrence's candidacy, one individual wrote, "What is your position relative to the principle of separation of Church and State? Would you endorse the establishing of diplomatic relations with the Vatican?" Lawrence answered he would fight the union of church

83

and state and diplomatic relations with the Vatican were certainly out of his jurisdiction. Leslie Conrad, executive secretary of the Luther League of America, asked Lawrence to comment on a report that the Catholic lawyers in Pittsburgh had to clear with the chancery before taking divorce cases of Catholics, Protestants, and Jews. Lawrence replied, "As Mayor, I have absolutely nothing to say about Catholic Church rulings, or as a matter of fact, about the rulings of any religious group. I am sure the Mayor of Philadelphia has never been asked to approve or reject the policies of your religious organization, nor would you ask him to do so."[111] In a more sensational vein, Lawrence received large numbers of anti-Catholic letters. Despite his previous concerns about the religious issue in a race of that kind, Lawrence was shocked at both the volume and contents of the hate mail. Some letters were so bad he turned them over to the FBI.[112] Summing up Lawrence's gubernatorial campaign, James R. Doran, editor of the *Harrisburg Evening News*, stated that it was because of Lawrence's skills, talents, and honesty that his newspaper supported his candidacy. "For that I was branded a dirty Democrat, a Catholic-lover and a part-time Communist."[113]

Just how much impact the religious issue had is difficult to say. Lawrence won, but came nowhere near his predicted margin of 250,000 votes. Moreover, Leader lost the Senate race. At three o'clock the morning after the election, a none-too-jubilant Lawrence snapped at a photographer, "Come back in four years. Then we'll see how many victory pictures you'll be taking."[114] Lawrence was obviously upset over Leader's defeat and his own poor showing in many counties. Typical of the postelection mail was Columbia County Democratic chairman Rollin Brewer's letter. "Ten days before the election a splendid Democratic victory locally seemed assured. Religion was injected into the fight and a vile whispering campaign was waged. That not only spelled defeat locally for our candidates of the Catholic faith, but materially weakened our entire ticket."[115] Lawrence urged Brewer, a Protestant, and other Democrats in Columbia County to forget what happened. "I think our job is to give the people a good administration and make those who injected the issue ashamed of themselves for what they did."[116]

As for Leader's defeat, a dejected Lawrence wrote, "He developed very strong newspaper opposition, and we could not overcome it."[117] Leader, however, did not accept this. He felt he was "cut" by Democrats in some western counties. "They wanted to get Dave Lawrence elected governor. . . . Hugh Scott was the 'darling' of the Mellons, and Dave was the darling of the Mellons; so it was a natural thing for them to work with candidates that were popular with the Mellons."[118] Leader went to Lawrence three times over the issue. The third time, Lawrence became furious and said, "I don't want to hear any more about it. There is nothing to it." Leader had no way of knowing if Lawrence knew what was being done or had anything to do with it. Giesey said that Lawrence absolutely did not cut Leader, that it was the press and not the Democratic party.[119] Although Lawrence and Leader remained friends, Leader continued to believe he was cut in Western Pennsylvania, while the majority of Lawrence's colleagues said this was not so. If the Leader polls were correct, Lawrence may have made some compromises to save the governor's chair for the Democrats. What is more, when Lawrence went to Harrisburg he had only a two-vote majority in the House and a Republican-controlled Senate. Lawrence's tenure as governor would indeed be a challenge, but his role as party leader was still intact despite Leader's defeat.

Democratic headquarters in Pittsburgh became the hub for the Democratic state organization. Lawrence, who wanted top-notch personnel at the headquarters, asked Huck Fenrich two or three times to take over headquarters management, but Fenrich stalled. Late one evening, while signing an ordinance and without looking up from his writing, Lawrence said, "Huck, Monday morning you're going down to headquarters." And that was it; Fenrich took over, no arguments. And Lawrence always kept a close watch on headquarters operations. He used to tell Fenrich, "Be careful down here; there are flaws; there are pitfalls." Every day while Lawrence was mayor, he and Fenrich would go over headquarters business for that day. It was a very closely controlled situation.[120]

Lawrence's personal concerns went beyond the confines of headquarters, however. In 1955, when Leader's tax bill came up in the House, thirty Democrats were opposed to the measure. By the time the final vote came, 108 Democrats out of 112 had voted for

85

the bill. As soon as the vote was taken, "Lawrence mounted the speaker's rostrum in the House to urge delay in submitting the Bill to the Senate." Lawrence wanted time to get support before the Republican-controlled Senate could put their "quick-kill" plan into action. Commenting on Lawrence's action, one reporter wrote: "It dramatized as well as emphasized again, for the edification of the doubting and wayward Democrats, that the Mr. Big of the Party in Pennsylvania, when the chips are down, is still Mayor Lawrence."[121]

Perhaps Mayor Jakomas of McKeesport did not see it that way. In 1956, Jakomas resented Lawrence's selection of Elmer Holland as nominee for United States representative. Jakomas said he was launching a drive to "break King David's hold on the suburbs." "It's bad enough that Mr. Lawrence has Pittsburgh in the palm of his hand, but when he can pick who shall represent us outside the City of Pittsburgh, that's going too far." A few weeks later, Jakomas, after meeting with Lawrence, denied the "King David" remark.[122] Jakomas accepted the Holland nomination and worked along with the party while, at the same time, he was not cut off by Lawrence. The persuader was at work, and Lawrence kept control.

Even outside Western Pennsylvania, in the two largest Democratic strongholds, Philadelphia and Lackawanna counties, Lawrence seemed in the driver's seat. In the early fifties, Philadelphia leaders Myers, Finnegan, Jim Clark, McCloskey, and Jack Kelly, Sr. never were in doubt as to who the real leader of the party was. None of them felt he was. Later, Frank Smith and Tate never claimed Lawrence's role. When Bill Green replaced Finnegan as chairman in Philadelphia, there was an uneasy alliance between Lawrence and Green. Lawrence respected Green as a powerful leader and knew Green could deliver Philadelphia with a large majority. For the first time, Lawrence saw Green as a potential rival, and some felt Green wanted to replace Lawrence as Democratic national committeeman.[123] Green's untimely death ended any possible rivalry. Joe Clark, who often needled Lawrence, saw the mayor as a politician of great experience and common sense, with a "keen understanding of partisan politics." Clark felt Lawrence was as close to being the boss as anyone could be without being a boss. "If you saw how he operated, you would have great difficulty in distinguishing between

86

what he did and being a boss."[124] Yet the respect Lawrence commanded among Philadelphia leaders was sufficient to smother most flare-ups that could have been interpreted as threats to Lawrence's leadership.

In Lackawanna County, Lawrence made it his business to know a lot of people in the small towns and boroughs. He had an amazing knowledge of the area and was well liked there. Moreover, his Lackwanna County counterpart, Michael Lawler, was very influential in the county, particularly through the *Scranton Times*. Judge Richard Conaboy remembers both Lawrence and Lawler had the same political style: "You don't hurt anybody as you go along in politics, be friendly with everyone, and government is something apart from politics."[125] On the other hand, some were none too complimentary about the Lawler Lackawanna machine. Joe Clark called it "as corrupt a Democratic political organization as I have run into, although nicely papered over." Lawler ran a tight ship, "and you did what Mike Lawler did or else." Clark felt Lawrence paid too much attention to the three big counties: Allegheny, Philadelphia, and Lackawanna. And he raised the issue with Lawrence, reminding him "there are sixty-five [sic] other counties." He said those constituencies did not care for Lawler, "but you seem to think his word is the word of God." Lawrence did not like Clark's remarks, but continued to follow Mike Lawler's advice. Further, Clark contends Lawrence did not pay any heed to Democrats in Luzerne County, which is adjacent to Lackawanna County. Lawrence, according to Clark, did not like Daniel Flood, who controlled Luzerne.[126] Apparently, the feeling was mutual. But aside from these minor squabbles, it is clear that Lawrence remained in control. Moreover, his record as governor helped to reaffirm his strong position in Pennsylvania.

As unusually heavy snowfall in January 1959 forced the inauguration ceremony of David Leo Lawrence as governor of Pennsylvania indoors. Despite treacherous travel conditions, over 10,000 people looked on in the Harrisburg Farm Show Arena as Chief Justice Alvin Jones administered the oath of office. Heavy snow was not the only unusual occurrence that January 20. Lawrence, at sixty-nine, was the oldest governor in Pennsylvania's history when entering office;

he was the first Roman Catholic governor and the first Democrat to succeed a Democrat as governor of Pennsylvania. Lawrence's short inaugural address called for bipartisan cooperation to solve Pennsylvania's fiscal problems, pointing out that programs requiring $400,000 in new taxes might be needed. At the same time, Lawrence announced the appointment of the Kennedy Tax Committee, broadly bipartisan and representing management, labor, and public service, to study the most feasible format for future taxes. With the formal swearing in completed, the traditional inaugural parade was cancelled, but two inaugural balls, held at the Zembo Mosque and the adjoining Scottish Rites Cathedral, saw Governor and Mrs. Lawrence lead the grand marches.[127]

With the inaugural hoopla out of the way, Lawrence set to work determining goals for his administration. His first priority was to provide Pennsylvania's citizens with the services necessary "to lead lives of maximum usefulness in their own communities." Second, Lawrence saw these services requiring funds through "taxation which distributes the tax load fairly among all levels of our society." Finally, Lawrence set down as a major objective the wise use of tax monies "so that the services we must provide are made available at the lowest possible cost."[128] With his broad-based philosophy, Lawrence sought to appeal to legislators on both sides of the aisle, as well as big business, management, labor officials, and the working class. For Lawrence, the commonwealth was paramount, although he realized, as an experienced public administrator, that all could not be perfect. In his inimitable style, however, Lawrence tried to have a near-flawless administration.

From a practical point of view, Lawrence ran the governor's office much as he operated the mayor's office in Pittsburgh. In Harrisburg, he usually spent eight hours a day at his desk when in the office. At irregular hours, a snack would be bought from the capitol cafeteria. Thus Lawrence could get in about thirty-five appointments a day. "He claps his hands together three times . . . very much like a football coach's 'hurry up—let's go' routine—and the appointment is on its way." In addition, Lawrence averaged about six speeches a week, while setting aside one hour weekly for photographs with organizations, charities, school groups, and individuals.[129]

88

Despite a heavy schedule, Lawrence managed to keep tensions at a minimum. Once, when Mayor Richardson Dilworth of Philadelphia visited Lawrence with a large package of needs, Lawrence threw his head back and laughed, saying, "I just want to know how you are going to act when you are in this chair and Jim Tate comes up here as Mayor of Philadelphia."[130]

Since, as governor, Lawrence's jurisdiction was broader than it had been as mayor, he would be out of the office much more than he was in Pittsburgh. He liked to see things as they happened in order to better understand what was going on. While he was out of town, the government continued to run smoothly, since Lawrence delegated responsibility. He never kept strings on his people once he gave them a job to do, but he would tear into anyone who failed to perform assignments. Moreover, he always watched what was going on. Once, when a member of Lawrence's staff equipped a communications room with very expensive material, Lawrence went to see it, and this caused a stir among the press. When asked why he made the visit, Lawrence replied, "I am a dumb cluck. I don't understand these things unless I see them."[131] In this instance, having had the benefit of the new equipment explained, Lawrence was satisfied the expenditures were justified, and nothing further was said.

In his cabinet relationships, Lawrence always opened himself to explanation and suggestion. He relied particularly on his cabinet for ideas. Cabinet members were invited to help in the decision-making process, while, at the same time, Lawrence bounced his ideas off the cabinet for reaction. In many instances, he already had his mind made up, but wanted to be sure. In other circumstances, he wanted his cabinet members to run their departments with the highest integrity. At every cabinet meeting over four years, Lawrence asked to be informed immediately of any wrongdoing or corruption. Obviously, this was a throwback to the experiences of the Earle administration, something he was determined to avoid in his tenure.[132] Still Lawrence acknowledged that he was not well versed in every area and relied heavily on his department heads. When Lawrence took over as governor, he retained Robert Meyers as secretary of banking. The Philadelphia Democratic organization wanted Lawrence to restrain Meyer's operations in the Banking

89

Department, particularly where Philadelphia interests were concerned. Lawrence told Meyers, "Bob, be fair to both Democrats and Republicans. . . . Don't lean over backwards to help a Republican where under the same circumstances you wouldn't help a Democrat."[133] In addition, Meyers admittedly did not always see eye to eye with Lawrence on banking problems and there was give and take on both sides to the extent that Lawrence would say, "Well this is your area of responsibility, I defer to your judgment in the matter." Finally, Lawrence demanded members of his cabinet be punctual. At this very first meeting with the cabinet, when some members showed up late, Lawrence snapped, "If I call a meeting for nine o'clock, I expect you to be here at nine o'clock, not five minutes after."[134] At the same time, Lawrence pushed to make himself readily available to cabinet members when the need arose.

One of the chief criticisms concerning Lawrence's operations in the governor's office was that he was too concerned with what was going on in Pittsburgh; he appeared to be trying to run Pittsburgh and the state at the same time. Lawrence's successor as Pittsburgh's mayor denies the allegation that Lawrence interfered. Joe Barr admitted he tried to do things Lawrence had programmed. As a result, "a lot of people thought that perhaps Dave was telling me what to do. But he was never that type."[135] What may have reinforced the notion Lawrence was interfering was the fact that Lawrence returned to Pittsburgh nearly every weekend. Moreover, while there, Lawrence was very visible, particularly when, as was his custom, he went into various neighborhoods for wakes and funerals. Lawrence always kept a close watch on the obituaries and had friends call if someone in the organization died. Whenever possible, Lawrence would appear, and naturally, as he was governor, his presence would be noted. Once, while Lawrence was attending services for Viola Turner, a committeewoman, the preacher noticed him and called upon him to speak. Lawrence spoke in glowing terms of Viola for twenty minutes, "and he meant every word of it."[136] Even outside Pittsburgh, Lawrence would visit friends, particularly party workers. When passing through Centralia one day, he called at the local Catholic parish. Lawrence told Msgr. William Burke he just wanted to see "where Woody Jones worked for a living."[137] All this was part of the Lawrence style, a method of keeping contact with the people within the party who worked at the all-important local level. With their backing, confidence, and enthusiasm, Lawrence felt he could do for Pennsylvania what he knew had to be accomplished, although in some cases, all concerned would have to make sacrifices.

As governor, one of Lawrence's major efforts was directed toward bringing about fiscal stability in the state while continuing to provide and expand needed services. One of his first official acts was to cancel an order of a $10,000 limousine ordered for the governor by the previous administration. He used a car that had traveled 90,000 miles.[138] With this example, Lawrence hoped his advisors and the people would participate in bringing fiscal stability to Pennsylvania. Once the Kennedy Tax Committee proposals were filed, Lawrence had his staff work up the necessary legislation to secure funding. The sales tax, long anathema to Democrats, was retained, although some labor members of the Kennedy committee grumbled. Lawrence said, "The sales tax is here to stay." In addition, the gasoline tax was raised two cents, while, at the same time, Lawrence signed a bill permitting pari-mutuel betting on harness racing for the first time in Pennsylvania. Moreover, Lawrence signed a bill exempting churches from real-estate taxes. All these innovations allowed the Lawrence administration to overcome the $177 million state deficit, while providing new and expanded people-oriented programs. In addition, Lawrence sought more funds for school buildings, hospital care for the indigent, workmen's compensation and occupational disease benefits, and anti-skid row legislation limiting the concentration of taprooms. As Giesey recalled, "In terms of increased taxes, there was nothing like it in Pennsylvania history. Those were not easy things to do, certainly not with a split assembly." In all this, Lawrence's leadership and political expertise shone, and once he led Pennsylania out of fiscal distress, Lawrence, ever the financial watchdog, kept the state in the black. In a radio and television reply to Governor Scranton in March 1963, Lawrence stated, "When I left office on January 15th of this year, there was a surplus of over ten million in the General Fund. The Highway Fund was solvent despite the greatest highway construction program in the state's history."[139]

91

Another area that became a matter of personal interest and pride for Lawrence was his highway-safety program. Somewhere in his life, Lawrence turned completely around on highway safety. As a younger man, Lawrence had a heavy foot on the gas pedal when driving. Mrs. Lawrence recalled how Lawrence was stopped for speeding one time in Florida. Lawrence told the trooper his wife had a toothache and asked for the location of a dentist. The trooper said, "Follow me." Lawrence thought he had wiggled out of the ticket, but they were taken to the Squire's office. When Lawrence posted his fine, the trooper took him outside and said, "Now across the street and up the steps you'll find a dentist." Conversely, when Lawrence was governor and attending a Bonds for Israel rally in Ohio, a friend from Erie complained of having been stopped by Pennsylvania troopers and given a ticket. Lawrence said, "How fast were you going?" "Seventy," came the reply. Lawrence said, "You shouldn't have been going that fast."[140] This seemed to have been Lawrence's entire approach to highway safety, which was such an obvious concern to him once he was in a position to push for it as governor. He never missed a chance to spread the gospel of highway safety. He called radar, physical examinations, and chemical tests "effective tools in the battle for highway safety." And although some Lawrence highway-safety legislation failed to become law, his administration saw several significant advances. The point system came into effect; radar, physical examinations, the no-fix ticket, and painting outer edges of highways became part of Pennsylvania's system. Moreover, Lawrence laid the groundwork for the Keystone Shortway, a convenient highway across the northern-tier counties that incorporated the most advanced technological innovations in highway construction.[141]

In providing the best safety program for Pennsylvania, Lawrence encouraged its citizens to enjoy the natural beauties and recreational opportunities the state possessed. Once Lawrence assured himself he had provided adequate highway safety, he turned to environmental considerations.

Midway through his term as governor, Lawrence initiated "Project 70," which called for a $70 million bond issue for the acquisition of open space around Pennsylvania's urban areas, particularly

Philadelphia, Pittsburgh, and the Wyoming Valley. The plan was similar to New Jersey's "Green Acres" project. Another $20 million was earmarked for the Bureau of Community Affairs to buy parkland within the cities. The title Project 70 referred to the year 1970, which was the target date to achieve four major goals. First, Lawrence hoped to develop three federal recreation areas at Allegheny Portage, Fort Necessity, and Hopewell Village. Next, he wanted "to ring our population centers with a green belt of regional parks and reservoirs." Third, Lawrence wanted to develop "a new American vacationland along the new interstate highway system in Pennsylvania." Finally, vital fish and wildlife areas were to be preserved for the future. In all this, Lawrence encouraged Maurice Goddard, secretary of forests and streams, to bring his expertise and knowledge into action so that the plan would become a reality. Lawrence supported Goddard to the hilt, and a major portion of the project became a reality before 1970.[142] Project 70 proved one of the most beneficial, ongoing facets of the Lawrence administration for the welfare of Pennsylvania's citizens, as well as for visitors and tourists.

Lawrence energetically pursued other aspects of citizen welfare and interest, even though not all segments or needs required legislation. As governor, Lawrence worked toward bettering conditions for the handicapped. Pearl S. Buck wrote: "I wish I could put into words, and I can only try, what it has meant to me to be working with you and under your guidance for the handicapped citizens of Pennsylvania."[143] At the same time, Lawrence singled out deaf people for his particular attention, explaining, "For over twenty years I have taken a deep interest in the problems of the deaf, who in most parts of the country are pretty much forgotten because apparently they do not have the special appeal that goes with the effort toward helping the blind and are sort of shunted aside."[144]

Along broader lines, Governor Lawrence succeeded in having a fair-housing bill passed in Pennsylvania in 1961. This was the first such legislation in any state, the fulfillment of a campaign pledge. In addition, Lawrence pushed the community-college concept and the state-related university programs. In 1961, as a humanitarian gesture in the midst of a highly emotionally charged atmosphere,

Lawrence suspended executions in Pennsylvania until the legislature acted on capital punishment legislation.[145]

In the area of social welfare, Lawrence looked to women for a brighter future and greater contributions. He wrote "I have always believed that our Democratic women were in large part responsible for the advance in social welfare made possible during the late thirties. We are now privileged to greet a new generation strengthened by the leadership of those who have done the work in the past."[146] At the same time, Lawrence strained against Pennsylvania's constitution toward greater reform in social welfare. In Lawrence's view, the constitution was overregulative. "A constitution reflects the issues and the needs of the time when it is written. It is not an ironclad, final document. It is a human document set down by human beings—and it is subject to human error."[147] The very constitution Lawrence wanted changed forced him out of office before the constitutional convention process could be inaugurated. Still, it was Lawrence's push toward reform that eventually realized a revised constitution for the commonwealth.

As governor, Lawrence's influence was felt outside Pennsylvania. At the annual governor's conferences, "he was sound. He would always come up with the right answers in a calm, cool, deliberate way," according to Governor Pat Brown of California. Soapy Williams described Lawrence "as part of the middle, which is generally a strong position to be in." Lawrence's experience both as mayor and governor was impressive at these meetings. "You had to listen to him as having sound and reasonable ideas you wouldn't disagree with."[148]

Internationally, Lawrence's visits to Ireland, Israel, and Italy were noted by the American press, particularly Israel, for which Lawrence worked diligently in fund-raising affairs. But the highlight of Lawrence's international experience was his speech on national television when Chairman Khrushchev visited Pittsburgh. He reminded Khrushchev "politics stops at the waters' edge" and "President Eisenhower speaks for a united country."[149] Later Lawrence remembered the event with great satisfaction. "I felt my responsibility very keenly, due to the fact that I was probably the highest ranking Democrat who was to have the opportunity to tell Mr.

Khrushchev the position of the Democratic Party."[150] These plain and simple words demonstrate Lawrence's sense of service to nation and party. Khrushchev knew where the opposition party stood on international relations, and this may have had some effect on his approach to Eisenhower the next day. And Western and Eastern Europeans were impressed by the courage and forthright declaration Lawrence made before the leader of the Soviet Union. Many Europeans had heard of Lawrence; relatives and friends who emigrated to the United States now lived within his industrial state and spoke well of the courageous politician, mayor, and governor, the voice of the workingman, labor's friend.

From his earliest days as a clerk-stenographer with William Brennan, Lawrence was exposed to the workingman's struggle in the early twentieth century. As he matured in politics, Lawrence became a leading voice for labor in Pennsylvania and later the nation. Responsible for the Little New Deal package in 1937, Lawrence backed the State Labor Relations Act, the Unemployment Compensation Act, the Anti-Injunction Act, and similar labor-oriented programs.[151] Throughout his career, "trade union members and their leaders found Lawrence to be their unswerving friend and co-worker in supporting the long struggle to make life better for working men and women and their families," according to an AFL-CIO publication. Labor legislation in Pennsylvania over thirty years stands as a testimonial to Lawrence's efforts. "He was a man of the people who never lost the common touch amid nationwide recognition that came to him as leader of his party and intimate colleague of three presidents."[152]

Nicholas Unkovic, Pittsburgh mediator, describes Lawrence in action during labor disputes. "He would go from one side to the other and be with us throughout various meetings. He was an individual who knew how to get along with people. And he deserves a great deal of credit for improving Pittsburgh's labor-management atmosphere. He always looked at the constructive side."[153] There was a fairness in the Lawrence approach to trade-union problems, and he never hesitated to remind labor of its responsibility. "The union cannot limit its obligations to obtaining higher wages and better conditions." He emphasized that unions had the additional

95

responsibility to attract new industries, to retrain the "economically dispossessed," and to provide an adequate labor future for younger generations.[154] Most reasonable labor proponents could accept Lawrence's position. Moreover, Lawrence clearly understood the necessity of solid, professional, honest, fair relationships between management and labor if American society was to prosper.

Again, Lawrence was not above going right to the top to spread oil on labor's troubled waters. In 1964, Lawrence wrote President Johnson over his concern that the power struggle among steelworkers would initiate increased demands upon the steel companies for higher wages and more benefits. Lawrence feared this would bring about either a strike or higher prices, both of which he saw as having a damaging effect on the national economy. "My advisors in Union circles lead me to believe that [David] McDonald is up against very stiff opposition; and I have also been urged by many in the Pittsburgh area to ask that you use your influence to effect a compromise on their differences."[155] As the Democrat's "elder statesman," a term Lawrence detested, his direct line to the White House saved labor and the country from a dispute that could have had severe consequences. The party and country were indebted to Lawrence, whose unfailing interest in labor as politician, mayor, and governor was responsible for enlightened labor-management relations, especially in the mining and steel industries.

Before Lawrence left the governor's office, he was asked which accomplishments he was happy about. Surprisingly, Lawrence did not mention labor. Highway safety was, for Lawrence, the greatest achievement on the "human side." He also noted public welfare, particularly concerning the mentally ill and mentally retarded children; the library program; balancing the state budget; road building, where the incoming governor still had funds to carry on; and education, where more had been done than ever before, as being the high points of his gubernatorial tenure.[156] Generally, Lawrence's administration as governor was rated highly. Emma Guffey Miller wrote to him. "Without question you are the best governor the state has ever had and we are all proud of you. Please don't give up politics but go back to Pittsburgh and reorganize our Party there for certainly the McClelland and Roberts outfit cut Dilworth outrageously in the hope of taking control of the organization."[157] In a less political vein, Edward H. Litchfield, chancellor of the University of Pittsburgh, stated: "I feel that we are all indebted to you for what you have done. It has been a most successful chapter in the long story of your contributions to your city, your Commonwealth, and your Nation."[158] Despite some postelection barbs by Governor-elect Scranton, the Lawrence record stands as one of the best in the history of the Keystone State. His stature and reputation in the late fifties and the early sixties were well deserved among Pennsylvania's Democrats. How bright would the Lawrence star shine in the rough and tumble of national politics?

Notes

1. Stave, p. 45.
2. William Burns and Dennis Mulvehill, "The Damned Fool." (Unpublished senior paper, Princeton University, 1969), p. 37.
3. J. Frank McAllister to Cordell Hull, May 6, 1933, Franklin D. Roosevelt Library, Personal File, hereinafter FDR Library under "Governor Lawrence."
4. Ibid., Anne Felix to FDR, July 13, 1933.
5. Ibid., Governor Pinchot to FDR, May 15, 1933.
6. *Pittsburgh Press*, June 9, 1933, p. 1.
7. Stave, p. 44.
8. *Pittsburgh Press*, June 5, 1933, p. 1.
9. Stave, p. 77.
10. Ibid., p. 78.
11. Shames, p. 118.
12. *Pittsburgh Post Gazette*, November 22, 1966, p. 4.
13. *New York Times*, June 10, 1934, sec. 2, p. 1.
14. *Pittsburgh Post Gazette*, June 22, 1934, p. 1; *New York Times*, August 24, 1934, p. 17.
15. *The Reminiscences of John Dent*, (1974), passim, in the Oral History Collection of La Salle University, hereinafter Dent.
16. Sloan, p. 2.
17. *New York Times*, August 31, 1934, p. 2.
18. Shames, p. 20.
19. *New York Times*, August 31, 1934, p. 2.

20. Ibid., November 5, 1934, p. 12.

21. Shames, p. 122.

22. *New York Times*, November 11, 1934, p. 25.

23. *The Reminiscences of Robert L. Meyers, Jr.*, (1974), pp. 3–4, in the Oral History Collection of La Salle University, hereinafter Meyers.

24. Gow, p. 277.

25. Stave, pp. 95, 101–102.

26. Shames, pp. 123, 125.

27. *New York Times*, May 23, 1936, p. 2.

28. Frank Zak to FDR, Feb. 2, 1938, FDR Library, Personal File, under "Governor Lawrence."

29. Blatt, p. 5.

30. Shames, p. 23.

31. *Pittsburgh Post Gazette*, November 22, 1966, p. 4.

32. Shames, p. 26.

33. Telegram, Lawrence to FDR, May 18, 1938; telegram, FDR to Lawrence, May 18, 1938, FDR Library, Personal File, under "Governor Lawrence."

34. Shames, p. 30.

35. Barr, p. 5.

36. *New York Times*, February 28, 1939, p. 2; Shames, p. 32.

37. *Pittsburgh Post Gazette*, October 15, 1939, p. 1.

38. Hawkins, p. 39; Shames, p. 33; *Pittsburgh Post Gazette*, December 5, 1939, p. 1.

39. Barr, p. 5.

40. *New York Times*, December 9, 1939, p. 7.

41. Ibid.

42. *Pittsburgh Post Gazette*, December 9, 1939, p. 1.

43. Personal Memorandum, FDR Library, Personal File, under "Governor Lawrence."

44. Shames, p. 35.

45. *New York Times*, April 13, 1940, p. 18; *Pittsburgh Post Gazette*, April 13, 1940, p. 1.

46. Meyers, p. 3.

47. McCarthy, pp. 1–2.

48. Bradley, p. 4.

49. Ambrose, p. 4.

50. Blatt, pp. 3–4.

51. Gerald Lawrence, II, pp. 12–13.

52. Giesey, pp. 5–6.

53. Joseph F. Guffey, *Seventy Years on the Red Fire Wagon* (privately published, 1952), p. 51.

54. Block, pp. 2–3.

55. Ambrose, p. 5.

56. *Pittsburgh Post Gazette*, November 22, 1966. p. 4.

57. Guffey, p. 100.

58. *The Reminiscences of Father Woody Jones*, (1974), p. 2, in the Oral History Collection of La Salle University, hereinafter Jones.

59. Barr, p. 7.

60. Bradley, pp. 1–2.

61. Meyers, p. 2.

62. Dent, pp. 3–4.

63. Farley, pp. 3–4.

64. Sloan, p. 1.

65. *The Reminiscences of Arthur Rooney*, (1974), p. 5., in the Oral History Collection of La Salle University, hereinafter Rooney.

66. Guffey, pp. 110–111; Charles Harris, *Tiger at the Bar: The Life of Charles J. Margiotti* (New York: Vantage Press, Inc.), pp. 374–77.

67. *New York Times*, January 7, 1940, p. 31.

68. Ibid., April 14, 1940, p. 4.

69. Ibid., January 19, 1940, p. 26.

70. Ibid., February 4, 1940, p. 1.

71. Ibid., March 10, 1940, p. 3.

72. Ibid., March 19, 1940, p. 14.

73. Shames, pp. 37–38.

74. *New York Times*, April 21, 1940, p. 2.

75. Ibid., April 28, 1940, sec. 4, p. 6.

76. *Pittsburgh Post Gazette*, May 1, 1940, p. 1; Guffey, p. 117.

77. Memorandum, May 26, 1941, FDR Library, Personal File, under "Governor Lawrence."

78. Shames, pp. 142–43; Tate, p. 6; Jones, p. 2; Barr, p. 7.

79. Shames, pp. 144–45.

80. Memo, Lawrence to FDR, November 4, 1942, FDR Library, Personal File, under "Governor Lawrence."

81. Tate, pp. 9–11.

82. Shames, p. 159.

83. Ambrose, pp. 2–3.

84. Dent, p. 3.

85. Park H. Martin, p. 10.

86. Shames, pp. 150–51.

87. Ibid, E. Selby and A. Selby, "Democrats Tough Old Pro," *Saturday Evening Post*, March 14, 1959, p. 80.

88. Shames, pp. 154–55.

89. Ibid., p. 157.

90. *The Reminiscences of David Leo Lawrence*, (1966), p. 34, in the Oral History Collection of the Harry S. Truman Library, hereinafter Lawrence (HST); *The Reminiscences of George Leader*, (1975), p. 1, in the Oral History Collection of La Salle University, hereinafter Leader.

91. *The Reminiscences of Natalie Saxe*, (1974), pp. 3–4, in the Oral History Collection of La Salle University, hereinafter Saxe; Leader, p. 3; Exler, p. 5; Shames, pp. 57, 58.

92. Leader, p. 5.

93. McCloskey, p. 9; Leader, p. 4, 6.

94. Shames, p. 84.

95. Fuller, p. 51.

96. Lawrence (JFK), pp. 5–6.

97. Selby and Selby, p. 78; Lawrence (JFK), pp. 78–79.

98. Saxe, p. 6; Lawrence (JFK), pp. 77–78.

99. *Pittsburgh Post Gazette*, August 18, 1956, p. 2.

100. Gerald Lawrence, I, pp. 6–7.

101. Lawrence to Robert Kennedy, November 19, 1959, PSA, Lawrence Papers, General File (24).

102. Stevenson to Lawrence, August 23, 1956, private collection.

103. Blatt, p. 7, Clark, pp. 2–3.

104. Giesey, p. 25.

105. Bradley, p. 12; Clark, pp. 3–4.

106. Giesey, pp. 28–29.

107. Leader, p. 8.

108. Lawrence to E. W. Dressler, n.d., private collection.

109. *Newsweek*, October 20, 1958, p. 41.

110. *Pittsburgh Post Gazette*, November 22, 1966, p. 4; Saxe, p. 8.

111. Lawrence to Leslie Conrad, June 28, 1958, private collection.

112. *The Reminiscences of Thomas McCloskey*, (1974), p. 3, in the Oral History Collection of La Salle University, hereinafter Thomas McCloskey.

113. Speech, James R. Doran, January 20, 1971, private collection.

114. *Pittsburgh Post Gazette*, November 22, 1966, p. 4.

115. Rollin B. Brewer to Lawrence, November 5, 1958, private collection.

116. Lawrence to Robert K. Brewington, December 10, 1958, private collection.

117. Lawrence to Adlai Stevenson, November 10, 1958, private collection.

118. Leader, p. 11.

119. Ibid.; Giesey, pp. 29–30.

120. Fenrich, p. 2.

121. Shames, p. 67.

122. Ibid., p. 190.

123. Saxe, pp. 2, 4–5.

124. Clark, pp. 1, 10.

125. Conaboy, p. 5.

126. Clark, pp. 10–11.
127. *New York Times,* January 21, 1959, p. 23.
128. PSA, Lawrence Papers, press release, December 14, 1959.
129. Ibid., July 5, 1959.
130. Saxe, p. 8.
131. Giesey, pp. 32–33; *The Reminiscences of Maurice Goddard,* (1974), p. 1, in the Oral History Collection of La Salle University, hereinafter Goddard.
132. Giesey, pp. 30–31; Sloan, p. 4.
133. Meyers, p. 5.
134. Bradley, p. 8.
135. Barr, p. 5.
136. Ambrose, pp. 7–8.
137. Jones, p. 3.
138. Geisey, p. 30; PSA, Lawrence Papers, speeches, November 1963.
139. Ibid.
140. The Reminiscences of Robert Aiken, (1974), p. 3, in the Oral History Collection of La Salle University, hereinafter, Aiken.
141. PSA, Lawrence Papers, press releases, December 4, 1961; Aiken, p. 6; Fenrich, p. 8; Hooper, p. 2; Tate, pp. 22–23.
142. Lawrence to Emma G. Miller, November 17, 1961, PSA Lawrence Papers, General File 65; press releases, March 12, 1962; Goddard, p. 4.
143. Pearl S. Buck to Lawrence, November 30, 1962. PSA, Lawrence Papers, Subject File, "Handicapped."
144. Ibid., (25), Lawrence to Michael DiSalle, October 8, 1962.
145. *New York Times,* March 28, 1961; Giesey, p. 33.
146. Lawrence to Mrs. Katie Loucheim, April 29, 1959, PSA, Lawrence Papers, General Subject (24).
147. Ibid., press releases, March 1962.
148. Brown, p. 1; Williams, p. 2.
149. PSA, Lawrence Papers, press releases, September 1959.
150. Ibid., Subject File 24, Lawrence to Arthur B. VanBuskirk, October 13, 1959.
151. Shames, p. 22.
152. "AFL-CIO Tribute," 1966, private collection.
153. *The Reminiscences of Nicholas Unkovic,* (1973), p. 8, in the Oral History Collection of the University of Pittsburgh.
154. PSA, Lawrence Papers, Central Catholic High School, May 13, 1963.
155. Memo; Lawrence to Johnson, December 9, 1964, LBJ Library, General File, under "Governors."

156. PSA, Lawrence Papers, press releases, December 30, 1962.

157. Ibid., Subject File, Emma G. Miller to Lawrence, January 9, 1963.

158. Ibid., Edward H. Litchfield to Lawrence, December 26, 1962.

IV
Statesman

Long before David Lawrence became involved in the Allegheny County commissioner race in 1931, he had been working with Pennsylvania Democrats to push their national interests. Lawrence had learned the bitter lesson of politics that without a strong, influential, and patronage-doling national organization, local political gains were difficult to achieve. Congressional elections in 1930 gave Democrats in Western Pennsylvania some hope. As a result, their efforts at bringing about the candidacy of a Democrat who could take the White House in 1932 increased.

It was clear from the outset that Lawrence and Guffey were supporting Franklin D. Roosevelt. Lawrence admits that when Al Smith lost the presidency in 1928, while Roosevelt won the governorship of New York, "I first figured Roosevelt was our man for '32." As luck would have it for the Lawrence-Guffey faction shortly after Roosevelt became governor, a close friend of his, Vance McCormick, attacked one of Roosevelt's policies in an acrid editorial. Lawrence stated, "A political colleague of mine clipped the editorial and sent it to Guffey. The next morning Guffey phoned me in great excitement. Over lunch he read me McCormick's editorial. 'You should write Roosevelt and send this to him,' I told Guffey. That afternoon he mailed the editorial to Roosevelt. Roosevelt replied immediately, saying how wrong McCormick was. 'Joe, the first time you are up Albany way, pop in and see me,' the letter ended."

Lawrence and Guffey lost no time in going to Albany, and "Guffey came back convinced he had no cause to worry about any other politician in the state taking over the Roosevelt movement. Or about Roosevelt remembering who his friends were."[1] From

Lawrence's account, it appears that it was his idea to send the editorial, which, in turn, cemented the Guffey-Lawrence image in Roosevelt's mind. Clearly, Lawrence and Guffey were in with Roosevelt, and if Roosevelt won the White House, Lawrence, Guffey, and Allegheny County Democrats would be remembered. Still, the goal was distant, and, under Guffey's acknowledged leadership, much work had to be done.

It was most important for Lawrence and Guffey to deliver Pennsylvania for Roosevelt at the 1932 convention. So 1931 and 1932 were busy preparation years, as Guffey explained. "I spent practically all my time canvassing the State and lining up Roosevelt support. I was ably assisted by Warren VanDyke of Harrisburg, David L. Lawrence, John O'Donnell of the former Philadelphia City Committee, J. David Stern of the *Philadelphia Record* and a number of others."[2]

In March 1932, Governor Roosevelt was in direct communication with David Lawrence concerning John A. McSparran, Pinchot's secretary of agriculture. The McSparran issue is not significant for the whole preconvention preparation, but Lawrence's response to Roosevelt demonstrates his understanding of Western Pennsylvania politics. Lawrence thought McSparran an individual of narrow views. He was against Al Smith in 1928 and bolted Pennsylvania Democrats in 1930 over the "wet" issue. Lawrence told Roosevelt that if McSparran backed him, "it could be of no benefit. In rural districts where he has a number of friends, you are going to get the delegates anyway."[3] Some years later, Lawrence said, "When we came to the convention, Pennsylvania had the largest number of votes for Roosevelt of any state—more than New York. We were very proud of that fact and exploited it fully after Roosevelt was in the White House."[4] Still, the Pennsylvania delegation was not unanimous for Roosevelt. That Pennsylvania held more Roosevelt votes than FDR's home state was a circumstance pleasing to Roosevelt and gave Lawrence and Guffey every reason to work harder. But the Pennsylvania delegation was a hard nut to crack.

John M. Hemphill of West Chester, Pennsylvania, had made a very strong showing in the 1930 gubernatorial race. Because a group of Republican industrialists who called themselves the Liberty

Party threw their support to Hemphill, since they were disenchanted with Republican Pinchot, Hemphill commanded a significant power base. Former state chairman John Collins and national committeeman Sedgewick Kissler, along with their many supporters, went for Al Smith. One notable exception was Al Zimmerman, secretary of the Democratic state committee. Zimmerman went with the so-called Guffey-Earle combo of which Lawrence was a part.[5] Despite this split in the Pennsylvania delegation, the Guffey-Earle-Lawrence faction remained in the Roosevelt camp. A victory in the 1932 convention for FDR, followed by a November win, would leave Lawrence and Guffey in the driver's seat in Pennsylvania. But the convention was not yet won.

Someone or something had to project Roosevelt into the nation's eye so that he would captivate the country and the Democrats would be almost forced to nominate him. Jim Farley, Lawerence, and others searched for an electrifying issue, and they were rewarded when Roosevelt said, "If I am elected, I will repeal the Prohibition law." There was no stopping him from then on, according to Congressman John Dent.[6] Whether Lawrence played a role in this maneuver is difficult to say. At the convention, the issue was discussed at great length by the Resolutions Committee and their thrust toward the repeal of the Volstead Act met with some major opposition. Lawrence was not on the committee, which was handpicked by James Farley. Moreover, whatever politicking Lawrence accomplished at the convention was carried out in consultation with Guffey, the key Pennsylvanian at the convention.

Many years later, Lawrence confirmed his novice role at the '32 convention by explaining his first impressions of Huey Long. A discussion evolved at the meeting over the two-thirds rule for selection of the presidential nominee. Lawrence said, "I was seated in the front of the room. Suddenly, I heard a stentorian voice yell out from the rear. I looked back and there was a reddish-haired, wild-eyed individual demanding that we abolish the two-thirds rule. It was defeating the will of the people. Majority rule prevailed elsewhere in America. It should prevail here and we were cowardly if we did not go into the convention and change that rule." However, FDR took the wind out of Long's sails when he informed Democratic

105

leaders that if the rule was changed, he would not accept the nomination. If a change was to be made, it would have to come after 1932.[7]

Thus, as the Roosevelt forces expected, FDR received only a majority of votes on the first ballot. According to Lawrence, "On the second, we threw in some additional strength, including some Pennsylvania Smith votes we were able to change, and we pulled up the total, but not enough."[8]

Roosevelt was nominated on the third ballot, only after deals were made for the vice-presidency. Farley feared Catholics would resent Garner on the ticket with Roosevelt, since Garner and Texas went against Al Smith in 1928. Lawrence and Guffey agreed that Garner should be offered the second spot, because Garner ran second only to Roosevelt in delegate strength. An arrangement was transacted through Sam Rayburn, Garner's manager. Lawrence remembers, "Pat [Harrison, of Mississippi] briefly outlined our proposition to Rayburn over the telephone. He hung up the receiver and said, 'That gentleman is very receptive'—meaning that Sam was going to work with us."[9]

Lawrence and Guffey left the convention convinced they could win Pennsylvania for Roosevelt. Both moved right into the campaign. At home, Lawrence seemed to take a more active role. His was the responsibility for making major decisions about the conduct of the campaign in Allegheny County. In October, Lawrence wrote Roosevelt asking him to speak in Pittsburgh, because Lawrence felt that for the first time since 1856, Pennsylvania could possibly go Democratic.[10] Roosevelt agreed to appear in Pittsburgh, and instead of renting a hall, Lawrence went out on a limb and hired Forbes Field, which had nearly 37,000 permanent seats and additional temporary seating. Given the condition of the Democratic party in Allegheny County, some Lawrence colleagues viewed the Forbes Field caper as political suicide—with it a sure bet that candidate Roosevelt would be embarassed by the small turnout. Lawrence's hunch proved correct; over 50,000 people jammed the site for Roosevelt's speech. Lawrence recalled, "It was a depression year. The people wanted to feel hope. And I knew they would come to hear Roosevelt speak of a New Deal with security for all."[11]

Despite Hoover's victory in Pennsylvania overall, election results in the Lawrence-Guffey bailiwick matched the Forbes Field success. The Democrats, at long last, were a viable party in Pittsburgh, Allegheny County, and Western Pennsylvania. Lawrence recalled that he was not completely surprised at the election outcomes, since the Democrats had been victorious in 1930 congressional elections. "Anyway, the economic conditions of the country, especially Pittsburgh, shook the people. The people were looking for relief. FDR's coattails and the economic conditions were the main impetus to building the organization."[12] As much as Lawrence wanted to take advantage of his burgeoning success at home, demands on the national level continued apace. Moreover, the growth of the Pittsburgh-Allegheny County Democratic organization worked hand in glove with the FDR charisma sweeping the nation. So it is not surprising that we find Lawrence very active, more independently so, in the 1936 presidential campaign.

Before the 1936 Democratic National Convention, Lawrence had been elected chairman of the Pennsylvania Democratic party. This gave him an important role at the convention. In 1936, it was clear that the Keystone State delegation was for Roosevelt. Lawrence, when questioned about Roosevelt's chances in Pennsylvania, answered that in Pittsburgh "Democratic registration exceeds Republican registration for the first time since the Civil War." Calling Philadelphia "the very citadel of Republicanism," he noted that the Democratic vote in 1935 was the "largest in history." Lawrence further explained that Pennsylvania's Republicans were in the embarrassing position of having bitterly fought every liberal, social, and labor measure pledged by the Republicans in 1934, as well as the Republican national platform of 1936.[13]

Despite this positive picture painted by Lawrence, he made every effort to bring Pennsylvania in for Roosevelt. At the last minute, he prevented the Union Party, whose candidate was William Lemke, from appearing on Pennsylvania's ballot by preempting the Union Party name. Lemke had to run under a different moniker.[14] That William Lemke was any threat to Pennsylvania Democrats in the 1936 presidential elections is certainly open to challenge.

107

Nonetheless, Lawrence wanted no slipups in his state.

When the Democrats met in Philadelphia in 1936, it was a foregone conclusion that Roosevelt would be the party nominee. Some talk of Al Smith's opposing Roosevelt was heard, but no one took it seriously, except perhaps the Republicans. During one of the initial general sessions, some Al Smith banners were displayed and fisticuffs broke out in the balcony. As host state chairman, Lawrence mounted the podium to apologize for the incident and said, "We have investigated and learned that the young men who caused the disturbance were merely hoodlums from the Second Ward in South Philadelphia. Their leader has been identified as a Republican worker in that precinct. I want to take this opportunity to serve notice upon the Republican machine of this city and state that the day of such tactics as well as ballot-box stuffing and other election skullduggery is over in the State of Pennsylvania."[15]

As the 1936 campaign blossomed under newspaper predictions of a sweep by Alf Landon, Lawrence, exercising his leadership as state chairman, wrote James Farley, again Roosevelt's campaign manager, suggesting a threefold campaign strategy. Feeling the press was anti-FDR, Lawrence suggested a radio committee to work to get Roosevelt's message across in spite of the press. Next, given Landon's poor record on education, Lawrence wanted to organize "schoolteachers of the country for Roosevelt." Finally, he suggested using as many independent Republican speakers as possible, men like Senators Morris, Hiram Johnson, and LaFollette.[16] Farley's reply to Lawrence was properly polite and grateful. Yet Farley's tone seemed to say, "Slow down, young man." Even so, the suggestion about using Republican speakers was sent to the White House, indicating David Lawrence was the source. It was almost as if Farley was afraid Roosevelt would have an adverse reaction. Lawrence then, in his own way, carried the fight to Pennsylvania's Republicans.

Allegheny County, the center of the United States steel industry, was deeply shaken by Roosevelt's 1932 sweep. Steel interests were determined to rid the White House of the Hudson River baron-radical. Lawrence charged the steel companies with forcing their employees to register Republican. Jim Farley was not too concerned. But Lawrence, in a campaign speech, declared, "In several of the industrial towns around Pittsburgh, where the registration is normally Republican two to one, we are now getting three Democrats registered for every Republican. We are going to carry Pennsylvania by 250,000." Guffey nodded agreement, "Yes, 250,000 is the figure for the Roosevelt plurality in Pennsylvania."[17] Just how accurate Lawrence's registration statistics were in August 1936 is open to question. It was his way of letting steel workers know that many of their colleagues were defying company orders on Republican registration and suggesting that the fence-sitters and the fainthearted should join the winning side.

Lawrence's call for Democrat registration paid off. In early October he wired Roosevelt: "The box score the day after the night before. Enrollment Friday two thousand five hundred fifty-four. Republican enrollment nine hundred thirty-five." Roosevelt wrote Lawrence the next day: "My hearty congratulations on the final enrollments. Keep up the good work."[18] Roosevelt hardly need use the "good work" platitude with Lawrence. Like a human dynamo, Lawrence joined the Roosevelt caravans, one of Farley's ideas, as they visited every corner of Western Pennsylvania. Fr. Woody Jones recalls the caravans covered all the towns in which people usually wouldn't go to political rallies. Using a man, woman, and youth speaker, they would stop at factories, mine entrances, or general stores.[19]

When the election results were posted, Lawrence, in his first presidential campaign as state chairman, made a powerful showing. The Democrats carried Pittsburgh by 190,000 votes, while sweeping Philadelphia with a 210,000 plurality, with a state margin of more than 244,000. This achievement tended to focus ample national attention on Lawrence. Some Democrat colleagues tagged him "one of Big Jim Farley's fair-haired boys." Twenty years later, Lawrence seethed with resentment when reminded of the moniker.[20] It was a cruel epithet from Lawrence's own camp, since he was well aware of the long, bitter struggle he personally endured to build the Democratic organization in Pennsylvania into a powerful political force. FDR's charisma aside, the 1936 Pennsylvania Democratic landslide served notice to national and state Democratic organizations that David Lawrence was now a power to be considered. There were

109

indeed some Pennsylvania Democrats who saw Lawrence's meteoric rise in Pennsylvania politics in the thirties and asked themselves, "What hath Guffey wrought?"

When the Pennsylvania Democratic State Committee met at Harrisburg on February 3, 1940, Chairman Lawrence was still under indictment and awaiting trial. This fact did not seem to negate his influence. It was then that the committee, at Lawrence's behind-the-scenes urging, refused to back Senator Guffey's bid for renomination and declared an open primary in the senatorial race. The question of a presidential candidate was another matter.

Lawrence issued a strong appeal to the delegates to endorse FDR for an unprecedented third term. "Fellow Democrats, there is only one man in this nation fit to carry on the work begun by Franklin D. Roosevelt. That man is FDR, and I call upon this convention to lead the way. Insist that President Roosevelt become a candidate for re-election. His work is not yet done and he alone can do it."[21] The convention rose in unison and roared its approval. If Roosevelt decided to run, he had Pennsylvania's seventy-two delegates, courtesy of Dave Lawrence.

Two months later, cleared of all charges by the courts, Lawrence swung back into national politics with great vigor. He continued to push the Roosevelt candidacy and accomplished much in Pennsylvania to bring about that reality.

Likewise, Lawrence proved very active in the 1940 Democratic National Convention. With FDR a sure candidate, the major issue was Roosevelt's running mate. Here Lawrence was at odds with FDR, since Lawrence backed Paul McNutt, governor of Indiana. Lawrence and McNutt had met in an American Legion Hall, and Lawrence was impressed with McNutt's political fight in Indiana. Roosevelt would not buy McNutt. Henry Wallace of Iowa was his choice, and Roosevelt told Lawrence that as presidential nominee, he should have much to say about his running mate. McNutt withdrew, and Lawrence, although disappointed, was satisfied, since FDR explained that Wallace's being on the ticket would help Democrats in the farm states.

In the fall of 1940, when Wallace campaigned in Pennsylvania, Senator Guffey asked Lawrence, at Roosevelt's request, to accompany Wallace so as to dispel the impression that Lawrence was unfriendly to Wallace. Lawrence agreed, and while riding with Wallace between stops he said to Wallace, "Well, Henry, I guess we'll do all right in Iowa." Wallace answered, "Oh, no, we'll lose Iowa. In fact, we'll lose nearly all those states," meaning Nebraska, the Dakotas, and so on. Wallace said those states were basically Republican and anti-Democratic and had been heavily against Smith in '28. Also, they felt Democrats were the whiskey party, according to Wallace. "They're just not going to vote for the ticket this year." In view of his conversations with Roosevelt about Wallace and the farm states, Wallace's answer chagrined Lawrence. He later threw it up to Roosevelt, who just laughed and said, "Well, that's just one of those things."[22]

Despite Lawrence's misgivings about Henry Wallace, he continued to campaign vigorously for the entire Democratic ticket. In mid-October, Lawrence informed the White House that Willkie's swing through Western Pennsylvania did not compare in size and enthusiasm with Roosevelt's. Also, Lawrence heard it rumored that John L. Lewis contemplated coming out against the president, but Lawrence felt this insignificant in view of the fact that Philip Murray, leader of the United Steel Workers of America, had come out strongly for FDR, despite Lewis's attitude. Lawrence felt confident Roosevelt would carry not only the western portion, but the entire Keystone State.[23] He was correct. Roosevelt won big in Pennsylvania and the rest of the nation, and the White House was pleased with Lawrence's work in Pennsylvania. And when the Roosevelt organization was ready to move out again in 1944 they looked to Lawrence.

With the U.S. entrance into World War II, politics on the national level shifted. In 1944, it was no longer a question for the Democrats of a precedent-setting third term; Roosevelt was the man to lead the nation all the way through the emergency. It would be politically foolish, from the Democratic standpoint, to change presidential candidates at such a critical time. However, the question of the vice-presidential nominee was another matter, particularly in view of Roosevelt's rapidly deteriorating health. James Farley, who claimed to be an innocent bystander at the 1944 Democratic National Convention, remembered talking with a number of Democratic lead-

111

ers who told Farley they could not possibly back Wallace because, in their view, the president was not going to live long. Farley was glad at the time that Wallace was turned down, since, in 1940, he had tried to prevent Roosevelt from naming Wallace as his running mate. Farley told Roosevelt Wallace was a mystic, and Roosevelt later mentioned this to Wallace. Wallace approached Farley at the time and said, "I thought you were a friend of mine; why did you say that?" Farley answered, "Well, sure I am a friend of yours. I said the truth. I wouldn't like to see you president of the United States, Henry, and you might be if you are elected vice-president. I have a lot of good friends that I like more than you that I wouldn't want to see Vice-President."[24] Farley's remarks reflected the feeling among many Democrats in 1944.

Prior to the convention, Lawrence was in contact with many leaders over the Wallace issue. His political colleague Allegheny County commissioner chairman John Kane had seen Harry Truman in action on the Truman Senate Committee to Investigate National Defense Programs and been quite impressed. Truman was doing a "great job" in getting war contractors to live up to their obligations. Bob Hannegan, chairman of the Democratic National Committee, and Edward Kelly, Chicago's mayor, also saw Truman as an attractive possibility. But Lawrence and Guffey parted company on the Truman candidacy. On this, Lawrence found himself in the middle, since his labor friends, Philip Murray and Sidney Hillman, were leading a movement for Wallace at the convention. "It was a little bit hard to be on the opposite side from Mr. Murray and I think he was a little provoked at me." Guffey was a part of this action, although Lawrence went out of his way in later years to explain Guffey's position. Guffey had talked with Senator Truman about the vice-presidency, and Truman dismissed the idea. Guffey then felt free to support Wallace. Truman confirmed the incident to Lawrence. "A lot of people misjudged and misconstrued this action on Guffey's part, but it was perfectly honorable. President Truman has on a number of occasions since said that he really was to blame for that himself."

In April, a few months before the convention, Senator Truman spoke at a Pittsburgh Motor Association banquet. Lawrence and

112

Kane were invited and spent the better part of the evening with Truman. The following day, Lawrence drove Truman to York, Pennsylvania, where both were scheduled to address the Young Democrats. They had about a five-hour chat during the trip, and Lawrence came away very impressed with Truman. Lawrence was particularly moved by Truman's loyalty toward Tom Pendergast, Truman's mentor, who was then in jail. That Truman did not deny his friendship for Pendergast when the latter hit hard times meant much to Lawrence, who sorely remembered his lonely indictment months.[25]

Lawrence's April rendezvous with Truman, as well as John Kane's good impressions, still did not put Lawrence on Truman's bandwagon. As was his custom, Lawrence used all the time at hand to investigate every possibility for a successful 1944 ticket. Moreover, even when he was absolutely sure Roosevelt was going to cut Wallace from the ticket, Lawrence continued seeking advice.

A short time before the convention assembled in July 1944, Lawrence and Andrew Bradley discussed James Byrnes as a possible nominee. Bradley and Lawrence were in Washington at the time, and the latter had just come from the White House. "Andy, in your estimation which of these men would be the best insofar as colored voters would be concerned, which one of these would be the safest candidate for vice-president?" Lawrence named Truman, Bankhead, Byrnes, and two others whom he could not recall later. Bradley said he assumed Wallace was out and Lawrence confirmed it. "Wallace has been very popular among colored voters, but if he is not going to be in it, then the safest among the five is Harry Truman, and the worst . . . Byrnes." Bradley explained that Byrnes was a "left footer," a fallen-away Catholic. But, most of all, Byrnes "took unholy delight in snipping at appropriations for Howard University or anything having to do with colored people" when he was in Congress. This matter would, according to Bradley, be dredged up during the campaign. Further, he warned that Truman might have some rough going because he was from Missouri, but "in the final analysis, the issue will be the reelection of Roosevelt, so on balance it would be better to go with Truman."[26] Interestingly enough, Lawrence, in his own recollections and those of his colleagues, did not apparently raise the issue of the black vote again. Bradley's information may have moved Lawrence closer to backing Truman, but Lawrence never did say.

With the Roosevelt nomination a foregone conclusion, the vice-presidential nominee was a hot and confusing issue, especially for the Pennsylvania delegation. James Tate, then a state legislator, in recalling the convention noted the confusion. When the Philadelphia delegates headed for Chicago, they were under the impression Lawrence was going along with Guffey and supporting Wallace. This seemed acceptable to Jim Clark, Philadelphia Democratic chairman, Bill Teefy, Philadelphia finance chairman, Matthew McCloskey, congressional candidate Herbert McGlinchey, Joe Donahue, and other Philadelphia leaders. However, Clark got word from Bob Hannegan that Truman was to be the vice-presidential candidate. "Lawrence was flabbergasted." Hannegan confirmed this to Lawrence, and Guffey was very upset. Of course, he knew Lawrence would go with Hannegan. Also, Jim Clark passed the word to his delegation through Tate that Truman was it. All but one, Charles Weinstein, switched to Truman. When Clark relayed this to Lawrence, he said, "The heck you say." This put Lawrence in the middle, especially with labor, and effectively split the Pennsylvania delegation. Lawrence called around the various Pennsylvania delegates, and eventually the Pennsylvania delegation went for Truman.[27]

Contrasting Tate's story, Lawrence explained the ebb and flow of his position at the convention and how, in his view, the decision came about. "I sat in on the strategy with Bob Hannegan, Mayor Kelly, Frank Hague, and Frank Walker." The main meeting took place under the stage after the convention was adjourned. The adjournment was by prearrangement. "Senator Jackson, the presiding officer, was to recognize me, and I made the motion that we recess until the following day and that carried." The leaders, Lawrence explained, felt it was necessary to halt the huge demonstrations being engineered by the CIO and others from stampeding the convention in Wallace's favor. "Wallace was very close to the nomination, and we felt that if it had gone into another ballot, some of the weaker-kneed delegates might run away from some of the other candidates and go to Wallace." That night, plans were laid to check

114

all delegations and have them hold the next day. Hannegan, according to Lawrence, worked among the members of the national committee that night to hold for Truman. Also, Lawrence stressed, it was Hannegan who had selected Jackson as convention chairman and when Hannegan asked Jackson to recognize Lawrence that tumultuous night, "that was a *very vital* and important moment in the convention." Lawrence stated later that the leaders were provoked at Roosevelt because of the confusing letter he wrote Hannegan in which he fence-sat over the Wallace-Truman choice. Also, FDR was quoted in the press as saying that if he were a delegate, he would vote for Wallace. The leaders then were pressed to secure the famous Truman-Douglas letter wherein Roosevelt admitted he was friendly toward Truman "or would take Douglas." With that letter in hand, Lawrence and the others were able to convince a number of delegates they were not working against FDR's wishes.[28]

One interesting sidelight that took place during the balloting for vice-president, something Lawrence failed to mention, found Lawrence and Truman in an office under the convention floor. Truman quipped, "What are you chewing your nails for? I'm going to make it."[29] The nail-chewing was typical for Lawrence, whose great anxiety at the time was the need to put together a ticket that would attract all elements of the party and keep them in the fold come November.

Both the Tate and Lawrence reminiscences clearly attest to Lawrence's full involvement in Truman's nomination. Lawrence told Andrew Bradley, "Andy, it was not a matter of being affirmatively for Harry Truman. When I got to Chicago Jimmy Byrnes had it sewed up. I, Ed Flynn from New York, and Cooke from Chicago went to Bob Hannegan and protested that we could not accept Byrnes as a candidate for vice-president. Hannegan told us, 'Well, how about Harry Truman?' We were delighted to take anybody but Byrnes, so we said sure that would be fine." Further, Bradley relates that his friend Bill Dawson, of Chicago, was asked by Ed Cooke to go over to the Blackstone Hotel to a particular room and meet with a mystery person. When Dawson arrived, he found Jimmy Byrnes in the room. Byrnes spent an hour with Dawson indicating why he would be safe for vice-president. Dawson said, "I heard him out

115

courteously, and then I went back to Cooke and said, 'Well, I couldn't possibly sell him.' " It was on that basis that Cooke joined Lawrence and Flynn in protesting the choice of Byrnes to Hannegan.[30] Still, it is difficult to understand why Lawrence failed to mention the Byrnes affair. On the other hand, Lawrence may well have emphasized the Byrnes account with Bradley, since Lawrence sought Bradley's advice in the matter regarding the black vote. That Lawrence did a lot of switching and fence-sitting at the 1944 convention is evident. Most seem to agree that his motive was basically the party's well-being. Nonetheless, Harry Truman, rightly or wrongly, always credited Lawrence with a major share of the responsibility for his 1944 nomination. A few weeks after the dedication of the Truman Library on July 6, 1957, Truman played host to Lawrence and other Democratic leaders. Truman toured the library with his guests and, at one point, looked at Lawrence and said, "You got me in all this trouble. You made me the vice-president and then president."[31]

After the 1944 convention, Lawrence returned to Pennsylvania a stronger man politically. As the campaign progressed, Lawrence became concerned about Roosevelt's health. In the middle of October, Lawrence called on the president to discuss details of his visit to Philadelphia. "I was really shocked when I saw him. Of course, he was at a disadvantage. He hadn't had a haircut for some time and he looked rather shaggy and had thinned out a lot." About a week later, Lawrence rode with Roosevelt in a Philadelphia campaign appearance. "He was spruced up and he looked much better than he did before. I was really shaken that morning I went in."[32] Aside from Lawrence's surprise over FDR's health on that one occasion, he did not feel that the president's health was a serious issue in 1944. Moreover, the ever-confident Lawrence on the eve of the election predicted victory for the Democrats in Pennsylvania despite a Republican registration of 2,681,707 to the Democrats' 1,886,393. "Party enrollment figures have meant nothing in Pennsylvania for years. With registrations overwhelmingly against us we carried the state in 1934, 1936, and 1940, and we will carry it in 1944."[33] Lawrence proved correct, and Pennsylvania helped Roosevelt back in the White House for a fourth term, which lasted a little less than

116

three months. Lawrence remembered how poorly the president looked at his 1944 inauguration. Although Democratic leaders were not surprised, the world was shocked by Roosevelt's death on April 12, 1945. When Truman succeeded Roosevelt, Lawrence's contact with the White House proved firmer.

Depending on one's politics, Truman's initial White House performance ranged from fair to good. In any case, it was such that Lawrence felt justified in having stuck his neck out for Truman in the '44 convention, and it was no coincidence that Lawrence and Pennsylvania's senator Francis J. Myers were appointed cochairmen of the 1948 Democratic National Convention Committee.[34] Truman wanted the 1948 nod from the party, and he felt Lawrence and Myers would set up the convention in his favor. Moreover, there was no question of where Lawrence stood on the '48 national ticket. He was, long before the convention convened, squarely behind Truman.

With most of the opposition out of the way prior to the convention, the Democrats in 1948 were destined for a repeat performance; a national convention whose major purpose was the selection of a vice-presidential nominee, building a party platform, and roasting the Republicans.

In his welcoming address to the delegates, Lawrence lashed the Republicans in his inimitable fashion. He accused Senator Grundy of having brought about Thomas Dewey's nomination as Republican presidential nominee in the same manner as Boise Penrose had dominated another Republican convention, which nominated Warren G. Harding. The local color was not lost on the crowd. Lawrence proclaimed, "Joseph Grundy watched the snarling pack of candidates with amused and cynical eyes and selected the nominee from among them. The deal doesn't sit well on Pennsylvania stomachs. With us, who know Joe Grundy the best, it should defeat Grundy two to one." Lawrence then turned on Hugh Scott, Jr., newly appointed chairman of the Republican National Committee, arguing Scott was selected "by the grace of Grundy and the shameful acquiesence of the Republican nominee for president." Lawrence predicted, "Scott sits in that chairmanship as a trustee for the Grundy interests in the Dewey deal. He will protect the high tariff, special

117

privilege, duck-the-taxes, beat-down-labor, forget-the-world Republicans, the dominant element in the Republican Party."[35] The convention literally rocked as the Democrats wildly applauded Lawrence's rhetoric, and they were off to a vigorous start. Some say that his welcoming speech was the cause for a small movement that developed later in the convention to have Lawrence become a "favorite son" candidate for the vice-presidency. Lawrence crushed the movement in its infancy, calling the idea "utterly silly."[36]

Meanwhile, in the early stages of the convention, vestiges of a dump-Truman movement were circulating. Some Democrats were "flirting" with Eisenhower. It was felt that if Lawrence would give Eisenhower a nod or would join any rump meeting of Eisenhower's followers, Truman would lose the nomination.[37] Even though many state leaders felt Truman was not strong enough to carry the party in 1948, Lawrence would not budge. It was Lawrence's firm conviction that Truman was the best candidate. "And so, therefore, I think if we would have admitted by not nominating Truman that we felt he wasn't a good president, I don't think that anyone else would have done near as good." Admittedly, according to Lawrence, there was a strong movement among Democrats in favor of Eisenhower, including the Americans for Democratic Action, but "they didn't know where Eisenhower was—whether he was a Democrat or a Republican." This seemed to deflate the Eisenhower balloon, and his backers faded.

In the meantime, Truman's nomination was in some difficulty over the civil-rights issue, which eventually caused the South to walk out of the convention. Lawrence recalled, "Truman stood up like a major on the whole civil rights program, and, of course, the famous Humphrey resolution that was in there—the minority report on the platform. That was the big item in Philadelphia in the '48 convention." Moreover, Lawrence was convinced the walkout was due solely to the civil-rights plank in the platform and that it had nothing to do with Truman's being a weak candidate. "Back in those days the people weren't anywhere near as liberal on civil rights as they are today, and so you can see that this hit some of those southern delegates very severely and they just got up and walked out."[38] Nonetheless, Truman's nomination was saved and the convention looked for a running mate.

Alben W. Barkley electrified the delegates with his keynote address. According to Lawrence, the speech thrust Barkley into the vice-presidential race. "He made a terrific speech. That won him the nomination without any question—without any question." Of course, Lawrence made no bones over the fact he backed Barkley from the outset and, as convention cochairman, he handpicked Barkley as keynoter. When asked in 1966 about Truman's having requested Supreme Court Justice William Douglas to run with him as vice-presidential nominee, Lawrence snapped, "I know nothing about that. I was, of course, for Barkley and centered on that from the start."[39] Thus the Truman-Barkley ticket was approved in Philadelphia and moved out into the hustings under a cloud of near-universal press predictions of certain defeat.

Even Lawrence had misgivings. This was an unusual frame of mind for him, and in retrospect he recalled how buoyant Truman was. A week before the election, Mrs. Lawrence was saying good-bye to Truman and said something along the line of, "Let's hope everything will be all right Tuesday." Lawrence recalls: "And I remember how quick he snapped back, 'We're going to win Tuesday. There's no question about it.' "[40] Moreover, Lawrence admitted he was so sure the Republicans would be victorious that during the 1948 Republican convention, he prayed Senator Taft would be the Republican nominee, even though Taft and Lawrence were poles apart politically. Lawrence knew Taft to be able, competent, and honest. He did not feel the same way about Dewey.[41]

Here, of course, Truman proved correct; Lawrence and many other Democratic and Republican leaders guessed wrong. Truman was elected president, and Lawrence's political star rose in the nation. Still, Lawrence had been known in national Democratic circles for some time, especially through the Democratic National Committee.

Shortly after Pennsylvania Democrats, in a stunning upset, siezed the governor's mansion and state legislature in 1934, David Lawrence, with Joseph Guffey's encouragement, helped secure the speakership of the United States House of Representatives for Rep. Joseph W. Byrns of Tennessee. Guffey gleefully predicted this would make Pennsylvania a power in the Congress of the United States.[42] But, by 1938, the Guffey-Lawrence organization had split apart over

119

the gravel scandals and the ensuing trials. Guffey's victory in the 1940 primaries convinced Lawrence he should save himself additional humiliations at Guffey's hands. Hence Lawrence resigned his position as Democratic state chairman before Guffey had a chance to force him to step down. What Lawrence did not seem to realize when he offered his resignation was that his followers still held him in great esteem. Some felt the Democratic party in Pennsylvania would suffer a severe loss if Lawrence was allowed to fade away. As a result, the day Lawrence submitted his resignation, Lawrence forces nominated and elected Lawrence the Democratic national committeeman from Pennsylvania. Guffey's candidate, Meredith Myers, lost out in the display of loyalty for Lawrence. At the same time, Guffey's sister, Emma Miller, was reelected as Democratic national committeewoman.[43] The Lawrence selection proved a stinging rebuke to Guffey, whose candidates in the Pennsylvania primary a few days before had thrashed Lawrence-backed nominees. Also, his election served to lift Lawrence's spirits and saved Lawrence for the Democratic party. Moreover, Guffey was convinced he had better mend his rift with Lawrence, since it was becoming clear Lawrence was the man of the future, not only in the state, but also in the councils of a national party that controlled the White House.

Shortly after having become national committeeman, Lawrence had written FDR: "Due to the shortness of my visit yesterday, I may not have emphasized enough my desire that you invite M. H. McCloskey, Jr., to come to see you." Lawrence explained that McCloskey had done an outstanding job for Democrats in '34 and '36, but in '38 was made a target "by some of our misguided friends in the Democratic Party" and retired from politics. Realizing the Democrats were going to have trouble raising funds, Lawrence put McCloskey on the delegate-at-large slate to try to get McCloskey interested again. Although McCloskey admired FDR, he resented the treatment given him by "Guffey, Stern et al." in '38. Lawrence was sure that if Roosevelt invited McCloskey to the White House, "it would further enthuse him, and he would be very helpful to me in trying to raise funds for the National Committee" and general campaign. Roosevelt accepted Lawrence's request, asking General Watson to arrange for a ten-minute visit in the White House "absolutely off the record."[44] This was typical of the way Lawrence pursued his national committee work. He would try to get all the facts in a situation, ask colleagues in Pittsburgh and around the country for opinions, sometimes three or four times, and then get on the phone to the national chairman, with his argument for or against an issue well in hand.[45]

At first, although Lawrence had a direct line to FDR, few on the national committee were aware of his ability, and this, in part, explains why Lawrence was never elected national chairman. In the early forties, when Lawrence was available, he was not too well known. After 1945, once elected mayor, he would not accept the position "because he had a home base that was a source of strength and gave him a voice at all levels."[46] Nonetheless, Lawrence, in the minds of his colleagues, was never hurt personally by this, nor did the party suffer by his not accepting the chairmanship.

Postmaster General James Farley, onetime chairman of the Democratic National Committee, recalled Lawrence as a great leader. "He was the kind of man who would attract, and one of the reasons was that he would tell the truth. [We] had confidence in Dave. A political party is built on confidence."[47] Mayor Tate suggests that Lawrence was well recognized over the country. Naturally, a position on the national committee "was a big role for anybody," but if you were from a large state like Pennsylvania this position proved even more significant. However, Lawrence's personal qualities were a more important factor. Lawrence was recognized as having the necessary stature to provide big state leadership on the committee, while, at the same time, his liberalism was projected in such a fashion that Lawrence was able "to have the utmost respect of all the Southern senators" in a period when there was quite a strained feeling between North and South.[48] In addition, within the national committee, Lawrence's prominence grew to such an extent that he became spokesman for the committee members from the large eastern states, as well as some midwestern areas. According to Carmine DeSapio, Lawrence assumed the prolocutor role "by virtue of our faith and confidence in his experience." DeSapio notes further Lawrence did not come on strong; "he was very, very discreet, very analytical, very considerate of other political persons' posture or point of view as to the type constituency they may be representing." Lawrence went out of his way to understand other sections of the country, especially the regions west of Ohio. If he was going to make any contribution to the party, Lawrence felt this understanding on a political and social basis had to be exercised in favor of committee members from the far western and southwestern states. "This is the reason why a number of the members of the National Committee looked up to Dave for some guidance by virtue of his experience in the area of politics."[49]

Throughout his tenure with the national committee, Lawrence tried to establish a pattern and framework for the structure of the committee in the selection of presidential candidates. Through a process of education and political assessments, Lawrence wanted to list presidential hopefuls who reflected a broad base of opinion and nationwide support. Lawrence was in large measure responsible for the development of formulas, information, voting patterns, and vitae of acceptable presidential candidates. In this, he was somewhat hampered by what the more radical wing of the party considered Lawrence's philosophy. Although held by a certain segment to be outmoded in his thinking, Lawrence still managed to provide the national committee with proper candidates, while, at the same time, assisting the committee in addressing important issues.[50]

As Lawrence's influence on the national committee grew, it was not long before White House aspirants, as well as so-called lesser political-office seekers, found themselves checking with Lawrence. Moreover, in presidential campaign times, "all the leaders throughout the United States, at one time or anther, would be in touch with Dave to see where Dave was going," states Matthew McCloskey.[51] McCloskey's "all" is overstated. Still, Lawrence's leadership was paramount in a quiet way. Governor Hughes, of New Jersey, was impressed with Lawrence. "He was a settler; he was the judge. People would come to him and they would trust him and he could bring factions together."[52] Mennan Williams, who admittedly did not agree with Lawrence on many issues, saw him as one of the "top few" that made the Democratic party a significant factor in the thirties and forties. "I think he was a very constructive voice in the Party. I think we were fortunate to have him as a leader in the

Party."[53] Finally, Chicago's Jacob Arvey, who went on the Democratic National Committee in 1950, attests that Lawrence had more influence on the committee than any other man. "And I was happy to follow him. Dave was easily the dominant, not domineering leader on the National Committee. In some respects I think he had more influence than the Chairman."[54] Even though Lawrence and Arvey were friends, Arvey's comment about being more influential than the chairman might have had some truth to it, a factor that caused some choppy times for Lawrence within the committee.

Shortly after Paul Butler was appointed Democratic National Committee chairman in December, 1954, he decided to move Matthew McCloskey out as party finance chairman. Lawrence was upset. One day Butler met Lawrence and Arvey while the latter two were lunching at the Mayflower Hotel in Washington. Lawrence said to Butler, "Paul, you have just undertaken the fight of your life. You don't like him [McCloskey] personally because he won't yes you like these other stooges. You try it. You try to oust him and you are going to oust yourself."[55] Butler backed off and McCloskey remained. After the hotel confrontation, tension between Lawrence and Butler heightened.

As the 1960 Democratic convention approached, a growing disenchantment with Butler surfaced among other leaders. Much of the dissatisfaction was channeled to Lawrence in hopes he would take action against Butler. President Truman wrote Lawrence in July 1959; "The thing I am most interested in, Dave, is the Democratic Party and the Democratic Convention in 1960. We seem to have a chairman who thinks it's his business to break up the party before the convention meets." Truman felt Bulter was not supporting Democratic-party policy that had been set at the '56 convention. Also, Butler, in Truman's view, was establishing party policy without the convention's approval. Truman disliked this and wanted Lawrence to do something about it.[56] The following month, George F. Rock, Democratic national committeeman from Colorado, wrote to Tracy S. McCracken, Democratic national committeeman from Wyoming: "If Dave Lawrence or some of his associates would lead a move to oust Butler it could be accomplished easily. It is going to take someone of the Governor's stature, however, to lead the

123

movement rather than someone from the South or West."[57]

In the meantime, Lawrence received a variety of oral communications that convinced him there was a significant groundswell both in and out of the national committee against Butler's holding the chair. In September 1959, Lawrence wrote: "I thnk most people are thoroughly convinced that Butler's usefulness to the National organization is at an end. His squabble with Senator Johnson and Speaker Rayburn, and his hassle relative to Ed Pauley, and the many people who are upset with him, certainly hampers the Party."[58]

Butler knew there was a growing movement to oust him, and he knew Lawrence to be the prime mover. Thus Butler decided to attack Lawrence prior to the national committee's meeting in New Orleans in September 1959. He accused Lawrence of having allied himself with southern segregationists. Few people believed that. Even the contentious Sen. Joseph Clark exclaimed, "Governor Lawrence's record on civil rights speaks for itself. Any attempt to suggest that he allied with Southern segregationists against civil rights is nonsense."[59] Lawrence recalled some years later, "I think he [Butler] was trying to needle me, you know, because I had a big Negro following in Pittsburgh and Pennsylvania. Of course, they didn't like him for one reason; I didn't like him for another."[60]

Lawrence never did like Butler's leadership qualities, having opposed him for chairman in 1954. After that "it was sort of a running fight between the two of us." Lawrence remembered there was much dissatisfaction with Butler because "Butler was a bitter sort of fellow. He brought personalities into all this stuff. . . . He sort of had it in for Arvey and myself." Along with his move to dump Butler in 1959, Lawrence backed Philadelphia's Jim Finnegan for the post. "Finnegan took sick on me and could not get down there, so we were badly beaten."[61] Some five months later, things had not improved between Lawrence and Butler when the former wrote a constituent; " . . . I am not on friendly terms with the Chairman of the National Committee. Therefore I hesitate to ask him for anything."[62] Butler bowed out of the chairmanship in July 1960.

Sen. Joseph Clark was likewise a problem for national committeeman Lawrence. Lawrence and Clark had, for the most part, agreed to disagree in Pennsylvania politics. However, once Clark

124

went to Washington, he seemed to resent Lawrence insofar as the latter's stature in national politics overshadowed Clark's. Lawrence never really had to get anything in Washington through Clark's office, since he had long since gained entry to more prestigious party and nonparty forces in the capital. Natalie Saxe, Richardson Dilworth's executive secretary, suggested, "Joe went out of his way to create problems for the Democratic national committeeman while he was United States senator that could easily have been negotiated. He made life very miserable for the man."[63] If such was the case, Lawrence never complained publicly and Clark was always welcome in Lawrence's political circles. Moreover, in 1963, Clark went hat in hand to Lawrence asking for support in securing a position on the platform committee, indicating he had been turned down "four years ago." Clark's purpose was to assure "an adequate plank on Congressional reorganization."[64] Lawrence backed Clark on this, and their differences seemed ended.

Lawrence remained on the national committee until his death in November 1966, and immediately afterward, the Lawrence forces, still an effective group at the time, urged President Johnson to appoint Joseph Barr in Lawrence's place. Francis Smith, of Philadelphia, had announced in the papers that he was interested in the position. The Lawrence group felt a Smith appointment would create internal quarrelling with Joseph Clark and Barr would be the more effective committeeman in the '68 campaign.[65] The Lawrence forces prevailed, and Johnson threw his support to Barr. It was Johnson's conviction that Lawrence, as Democratic national committeeman, during his twenty-six–year tenure, had been an effective, sagacious leader. Johnson wanted whatever carryover from Lawrence that could be had in the person of Barr on the national committee.

Aside from Lawrence's role as Democratic national committeeman, a series of events in the fifties seemed to determine his future. In a span of ten years, Lawrence was twice reelected mayor of Pittsburgh, twice engineered the presidential candidacy of Adlai Stevenson, and was elected governor of Pennsylvania. By the end of the decade, Lawrence was a recognized force in the Democratic party, yet the events of 1950 seemed an inauspicious beginning.

Early in 1950, we find Lawrence working behind the scene in

125

party affairs with President Truman. The latter was plotting to wrest control of the party from southerners, giving northern "liberal" Democrats more power. Lawrence, fully aware of the Truman plan, used the opportunity to urge Truman to achieve his goal partly by campaigning vigorously in Pennsylvania for the not yet chosen gubernatorial candidate. Surprisingly, Truman agreed.[66]

Shortly thereafter, the Pennsylvania Democratic State Committee, with Lawrence's blessing, chose Richardson Dilworth, the mayor of Philadelphia, as their candidate for governor. From the outset, Lawrence worked hard for Dilworth. He briefed Natalie Saxe on every individual who should be seen in each county, but cautioned her that she should, first, pay a call on John Kane, chairman of Allegheny County Commissioners and, second, call on Mrs. Kane, "partly because I [Natalie Saxe] was a female, and partly because Lawrence felt she had some influence on Commissioner Kane." Lawrence further gave Saxe his unlisted phone number, urging her to call any time help was needed.[67]

Despite the Lawrence plan and President Truman's help, the Republicans carried the state and held the governor's mansion for another term. Lawrence was none too happy with the returns. One ward leader who went to Democratic headquarters with returns smelled of alcohol. Lawrence exploded, "This is an election and this is no way to walk into this office. If that's the way you do in the field, no wonder we don't win elections."[68] Dilworth lost by a margin of only 80,000 votes. This was a "drop in the bucket" for a statewide election, and Lawrence was much encouraged by the tally. The following day, Lawrence called Dilworth and suggested that since he had come so close, he ought to run again in 1954. At the same time, he suggested Dilworth send his executive assistant to all the legislative sessions to maintain good communications.[69] Although the outcomes of the 1950 election were somewhat disappointing, Lawrence looked ahead eagerly to the 1952 presidential race.

What Lawrence did not realize then was that President Truman would remove himself from the race. Lawrence remembered, "There was no thought of it, at least in my mind at the time, and it was just a shocker."[70] The entire Democratic leadership scrambled for a nominee after Truman's surprise announcement. Lawrence had heard Adlai Stevenson speak the same night Truman withdrew and was impressed with Stevenson's intelligence, although Lawrence was friendly with Harriman, Symington, and Barkley, he sensed much enthusiasm in the country for Stevenson. While Lawrence was not in the original draft-Stevenson movement, Lawrence admits, "I was one of the early advocates for Stevenson." At the time, Lawrence did not make his feelings on the matter known.

In the spring of 1952, Stevenson was resisting suggestions that he run for the presidency. Even Truman urged Stevenson to accept. But Stevenson remained adamant. It was then Lawrence was quoted as saying, "Why support a man who doesn't want the job?" And between the spring primaries and the July convention, Lawrence was reportedly backing Barkley. Lawrence denied this, citing Barkley's age. Shortly before the convention, after consulting Truman, Lawrence stated, "We are a Truman organization. We'll keep an open mind in Chicago and see."[71]

In the meantime, Joe Clark, then mayor of Philadelphia, met Stevenson in the Chicago airport. "Adlai, what's all this talk about your being a candidate for the presidency? I would like very much to support you," said Clark. Stevenson replied, "For God's sake, don't, Joe. The last thing I would want is to be candidate for president." With that in mind, Clark and Dilworth, (the latter did not like Stevenson) decided to go for Kefauver, and since Lawrence was keeping an open mind right up to the convention, the Pennsylvania delegation would be split.[72]

As the convention opened, Stevenson was still playing hard to get. "Arvey begged Stevenson to give us some inkling of how he felt about accepting the nomination," said Lawrence. Stevenson refused, because, as discovered later, Stevenson had promised a group of Illinois business leaders to serve out his term as governor. Lawrence recalled, "he would not intimate, even to Arvey, that he would accept the nomination so that we could in turn tell others. That was a tremendous handicap with the politicians who were thinking of their future." Still, without making a "firm commitment," Lawrence indicated he was for Stevenson; Commissioner Kane, Lawrence's political partner in Western Pennsylvania, cited no choice. Meanwhile, James P. Clark, of Philadelphia, demanded the

127

leadership "smoke Stevenson out." After many hours of discussion, Jim Clark insisted on a Pennsylvania delegation caucus, which Lawrence agreed to call on Sunday, July 20, although it had been originally scheduled for Monday, the twenty-first. Some Kefauver people felt Lawrence double-crossed them by calling an early meeting, thus preventing their lining up Kefauver votes. At the caucus, Lawrence, as national committeeman, voted first and for Stevenson. After the meeting, Lawrence went to another gathering, where the people there wanted to elect Lawrence floor leader for Stevenson. Lawrence was afraid that if he accepted, the opposition "would tag me as a city boss." He talked Sen. Frank Myers, Senate whip, into accepting the post. Myers had many friends around the country. "It worked out beautifully and I was very happy to be in on it."[73]

Although things worked out "beautifully" for Lawrence, the Pennsylvania delegation was upset with him. He did not mention that Samuel G. Neff, of Elwood City, a Kefauver supporter, said Lawrence betrayed the New Deal and the Fair Deal by seating Dixiecrats from Texas and Mississippi. Lawrence explained that had they not been seated, "we could have made martyrs of them and given them an issue." At the same time, Dilworth, Joe Clark, McCloskey, and Greenfield people were angry when state chairman Myers called for a polling of the delegates for presidential preference. This had been decided earlier by the Stevenson supporters, and John Kane "was furious" since he had not been consulted. Lawrence, when polled first, said one word, "Stevenson." It was, in effect, over for the Kefauver delegates.[74] Later in the convention, Joe Clark and Dilworth voted for Kefauver on the first two ballots. Jim Finnegan then said to Joe Clark, "Come on now; don't be a damn fool. You and Dilworth turn in for Stevenson." And they did on the third ballot.[75] This effectively removed a Clark-Dilworth group that wanted Lawrence out of power. At the same time, Lawrence recalled, "I have been in politics all my life. My father and grandfather before me were also in politics. I have heard of many so-called drafts, but the drafting of Stevenson was the only completely genuine draft of which I have ever known."[76] But for the Democrats, the 1952 convention ended on a down note. According to Carmine De-Sapio, "We pretty much concluded that when the convention approved Stevenson we didn't have too much chance to win."[77] A Democrat in the White House was eight years away.

One rather discreet event in David Lawrence's campaign for governor gave every indication that Lawrence, win or lose the governor's seat, was to be a significant force in the 1960 Democratic National Convention. When Joseph Kennedy, Sen. John Kennedy's father, made a substantial contribution to Lawrence's gubernatorial campaign, Joe Barr asked, "Why, Mr. Kennedy, would you want to contribute in Pennsylvania?" Barr never tells us what Kennedy's answer was; really, a reply was not expected or needed.[78] The elder Kennedy wanted his son in the White House, and one of the key Democrats who could help Jack Kennedy was David Lawrence. Whether or not Lawrence would support Kennedy's run for the nomination was another question.

Perhaps a bit wiser in the ways of politics than his father, John Kennedy was not sure where Lawrence stood. After speaking in Pittsburgh at a World Affairs banquet in December 1958, John Kennedy said to Jim Knox, Allegheny County Democratic chairman, "What do you think Dave thinks about a Catholic running for president now that he has been successful in being elected governor of Pennsylvania?" Knox replied that he did not know. He related that as Lawrence "analyzed the returns, it was very evident that if he had not had substantial majorities in Philadelphia and Pittsburgh, where he was better known, he might not have been elected." Still, Knox did not feel Lawrence had any hard and fast position on it, and Knox had not heard that Lawrence had changed his mind.[79] This was not good news for John Kennedy, who realized Lawrence's support was crucial. Moreover, Kennedy was aware of Lawrence's enthusiasm for Adlai Stevenson, despite the latter's two successive defeats in national elections.

However, when Adlai wrote to congratulate Lawrence on his winning the governor's chair, he made a passing reference to the '60 presidential nomination, saying, "As for me, I'm for anyone, except Stevenson." If that offhand remark was to discourage Lawrence from supporting or urging Stevenson to make another run for it in 1960, the possibility was not entirely erased from the realm of reality for Lawrence. In March 1959, Lawrence said, "In Stevenson the Democrats have the greatest statesman in either party. But—and it is a big but—he's been defeated twice. And that's a hard thing to overcome. As the convention comes near, we'll have to decide whether the handicap of two defeats by Eisenhower is fatal."[80] Lawrence, for one, hoped Stevenson's defeats were not the end. In 1959, Lawrence truly believed Stevenson could win against a Republican ticket without Eisenhower. He was not so sure the same was true of Kennedy, and one of Lawrence's main objections to Kennedy turned out to be that of religion.

The morning after a 1959 Jackson Day Dinner, Pat Brown, Matthew McCloskey, Richard Daley, Robert Wagner, Jim Finnegan, Carmine DeSapio, and Lawrence attended church together and breakfasted together. Brown recalls Lawrence saying, "Kennedy can't win; he just can't win. Recently districts that have always gone Democratic I lost because I was a Catholic." Brown felt Lawrence was anti-Catholic with respect to Kennedy.[81] But Lawrence was convinced religion would go against Kennedy should he be nominated. Lawrence explained, "When I think of a national campaign I'm sure a Catholic running for the presidency must have an issue so big, so strong, so completely overriding that his religion is never thought of. It's got to be bigger than vicuna coats, oriental rugs, or a golf-playing president."[82] For the Kennedys, then, the thing to do was convince Lawrence that Jack deserved a chance. Robert Kennedy wrote Lawrence in December 1959: " . . . Certainly my brother is not assured of obtaining the nomination, but I think it would be most unfortunate if he was turned down on the grounds that he is a Catholic—by non-Catholics who are bigots or by Catholics who have a fear of 'rocking the boat.' "[83] Bobby's letter stung Lawrence, but he never responded to the "rocking the boat" jibe. Moreover, many years later, Lawrence recalled how he told Joe Kennedy, "Joe, Jack is still a very young man and there's time for him to run. Why push it now?"[84] Until the very month before the convention, the Kennedys were upset with Lawrence over his stand on Jack's nomination. Rose Kennedy recalled "we were all furious" at Pat Brown and Lawrence because they would not declare for Jack. "Their support would clinch the nomination. Joe has worked on Lawrence all winter, but he still can't believe a Catholic can be elected. He has been one of the most exasperating and tantalizing forces. . . ."[85]

What, in their great anxiety, the Kennedys did not see was a carefully orchestrated, subtle barrage of propaganda and rumor concerning Lawrence, Kennedy, and members of the Catholic hierarchy. John Cardinal Wright, then bishop of Pittsburgh, stated for the record he never had any political conversations with Lawrence. Wright said, "I have read that there were many conversations attributed to us on the political aspirations of President Kennedy." Wright referred to a book by Joe Dever that claimed Lawrence and Wright and Lawrence and Cardinal Cushing of Boston discussed Kennedy's candidacy. Dever claimed Lawrence and Wright were opposed to Kennedy. "But the whole thing is made up out of whole cloth."[86] It was this type incident Lawrence feared most, as well as the bitterness he had experienced in his gubernatorial campaign. To his credit, Lawrence later admitted he was too heavy in the matter and he made a poor political judgment. On the other hand, it would be incorrect to say religion was the only ground on which Lawrence objected to Kennedy.

For one thing, Lawrence felt Kennedy was moving up the political ladder too fast. According to Giesey, "Lawrence always thought that one should take his time. He had and others had." Thus, as an experienced politician, Lawrence saw no harm in allowing Kennedy to garner more administrative and political experience. Moreover, in relation to the religion issue, Lawrence was afraid the Democrats would lose Pennsylvania in 1960 without the right national ticket. He felt "Any chance I would have of getting a majority in both houses of the General Assembly would go skimmering if Kennedy was the head of the ticket."[87] Lawrence never really felt obligated to convey his other reservations about Jack to the Kennedys. Whenever he mentioned the question of the 1960 presidential nomination, Lawrence openly acknowledged the religion issue; he never felt it wise to suggest Kennedy's youth or the makeup of the Pennsylvania General Assembly as an intraparty issue.

As convention time neared, Lawrence was watched closely by the Kennedy people. In January 1960, speaking at a Jefferson-Jackson Day Dinner in Springfield, Missouri, and referring directly to John

131

Kennedy, Lawrence said, "It would be a fine thing to elect a splendid Democratic president and slay the dragon of bigotry in the process. . . . The Party must weigh entirely without fear the brilliant public skills and the appealing personality of Senator John F. Kennedy."[88] This was a significant statement for Lawrence. He encouraged party leaders to examine the Kennedy candidacy, and he did it in Truman's backyard. Kennedy people were delighted and saw a possible endorsement in the offing; indeed, Joe Kennedy sought Lawrence's direct help.

Joe Kennedy worked through his friend Matthew McCloskey. In the winter of 1960, when McCloskey went to Lawrence about Joe Kennedy's request for an endorsement, Lawrence said, "It's too early; all you have to do is get all the big political bosses to be for him and you'll ruin him. Let him win a few primaries so that we know that is what the people want and then we can vote for him."[89] That did not satisfy Joe Kennedy. Kennedy asked Lawrence to visit with him in Palm Beach, but due to a tight situation in the Pennsylvania legislature, Lawrence could not get away. Lawrence recalled, "He insisted on coming up. The last thing I wanted was for Stevenson, or any of them, to think I was dealing around with any of the candidates." Still, Joe Kennedy went to Harrisburg and met with Lawrence in the Penn-Harris Hotel. To Lawrence's relief, the press never discovered the meeting. Lawrence recalled, "Of course, he couldn't understand why I wasn't for his boy, Jack. We had a very interesting lunch. He was very vigorous . . . very friendly but very vigorous." When Lawrence held his ground on an endorsement, Kennedy told Lawrence an interesting story, of how the president of a New York bank where Kennedy had invested $9 million was heard saying Jack Kennedy shouldn't be president. Joe Kennedy confronted the man and threatened to remove the $9 million from his bank.[90] Lawrence and Joe Kennedy parted good friends, but Kennedy went back to Florida empty-handed. Lawrence gave no indication whatsoever that he would come out for Jack Kennedy before the convention.

At the same time, Sam Rayburn was after Lawrence to line up for Lyndon Johnson. Rayburn said, "You'll never nominate this Kennedy. He'll never be nominated. He'll never get a stone's throw of

132

a chance. This is the only fellow they could all agree on." Lawrence did not agree. He felt that nominating a southerner in 1960 was out of the question. "Maybe we were wrong," said Lawrence in 1966.[91] Moreover, Lawrence still hoped, as did other party leaders, that Stevenson would agree to run. In the winter of 1960, Richard Daley went to Stevenson and told him, "If you are going to be in on this, you had better get out and into those primaries." Stevenson threw up his hands and said, "Oh, that's terrifying to think of going into those primaries. I am not going to do anything like that." Daley replied, "You won't have a chance if you don't."[92] Lawrence did not feel the same way. At first, Lawrence suggested Stevenson might take the convention by storm, or at least Lawrence hoped such would be the case if the convention deadlocked. But as time passed and Kennedy won West Virginia by a 100,000 vote margin, while getting 176,987 write-in ballots in Pennsylvania, Lawrence changed his mind. "These things convinced me that it was just hopeless for Stevenson and very hopeful for Kennedy. A great many of my best friends in the state were supporting him. But out of respect for me, friendship for me, more or less, they held off."[93]

In the spring of 1960, before the West Virginia primary, Lawrence vacationed in Europe. While in London, Lawrence said, "I'd like to see Kennedy win to get rid of the idea [a Catholic could not be elected President]. We in Pennsylvania are neutral and nothing that I have said should be construed as an endorsement of anyone. You cannot endorse anyone and remain neutral." Lawrence noted further the possibility of a deadlocked convention, with Kennedy and Johnson in a standoff. *Newsweek* saw Lawrence's comments as a position to jump on any evolving bandwagon.[94] Lawrence, however, years later said, "I told Kennedy I would do anything to help elect him if he was nominated and that it was just a question of real practical politics, of nominating a candidate who could win."

A few days later, Lawrence flew to Israel and from Israel to Rome. "When my plane reached Rome, I was met there by an AP man asking my opinion of what had happened" in West Virginia. Lawrence said, "It certainly has enhanced his [Kennedy's] chances." Lawrence would say no more, because Senator Monroney had phoned Lawrence in Israel and asked him to hold the line for Stevenson a little longer. "So I made no further statement until the convention." In Rome, Lawrence visited with Pope John XXIII for fifteen minutes. Lawrence made it clear to the press that he and the pope discussed world affairs in general without mentioning United States politics. Any other indication would have worked against Kennedy in some circles back home. When Lawrence did get back, he privately told his son, Jerry, that he was surprised Kennedy did so well in West Virginia and felt this assured Kennedy's nomination. Moreover, just before leaving for the convention, Lawrence told Andrew Bradley he wished Stevenson could be the nominee because he thought Stevenson would be a better president, but "I think maybe he [Kennedy] has the votes to get elected, but let's see."[95] True to his word, Lawrence took off for California without having endorsed anyone, still privately hoping Stevenson could be the man, although sure Kennedy had the convention sewed up. In effect, Lawrence had reluctantly written Stevenson off as a possible candidate, mostly because of the latter's inactivity and Kennedy's smashing victories in Wisconsin, Pennsylvania, and West Virginia.

Lawrence wasted no time telling Kennedy where he stood. Kennedy arrived in Los Angeles the Saturday before the convention opened, and Lawrence met with Jack and Bobby Kennedy that afternoon. Lawrence told them he would inform the Pennsylvania delegation he was going to support Kennedy and "we would have all but a few delegates for him." However, the public statement would not be made till Monday, because Lawrence wanted to keep his word with the delegates till Monday. On the Thursday prior to the meeting with the Kennedys, John Bailey had met Lawrence at the airport and wanted to know where Lawrence stood, but Lawrence gave Bailey no hint whatsoever. Liberman's suggestion in Bailey's biography that Bailey "played a major role" in Lawrence's swing to Kennedy is without foundation.[96]

On Sunday, Lawrence was invited to attend the Illinois caucus. Lawrence remembered, "When Adlai's home state delegates declared for Kennedy, I was convinced that was the last straw." Stevenson received only four or five votes.[97] That night, following a dinner meeting of the Democratic National Committee, Lawrence huddled with Stevenson and told him the Pennsylvania delegation was going

134

for Kennedy. Moreover, Lawrence was convinced Stevenson did not have a chance. He reminded Stevenson it was a great honor to have had the nomination twice. Lawrence wanted Stevenson to announce for Kennedy. But Stevenson wouldn't budge, saying, "I hate to walk out on those people that are here." Nonetheless, Lawrence was convinced Stevenson was being pressured to stay in the race by Mrs. Roosevelt and Herbert Lehman. They and others held out a stalemated convention as a ray of hope for Stevenson.[98] When Lawrence left Stevenson around 3:00 A.M. on Monday, as far as Lawrence was concerned, the Stevenson candidacy was dead, although Stevenson did let his name be put in nomination.

Back in the Pennsylvania caucus later that morning, Lawrence's announcement for Kennedy met with mixed reactions. Bill Green and Jim Clark were happy. Gen Blatt was not. According to Blatt, Green never liked Stevenson and Clark "who was once proud to have drafted him couldn't stand him afterwards." Blatt felt Lawrence went for Kennedy because he knew he could not win Pennsylvania without Philadelphia. For her part, Blatt said to Lawrence, "Governor, I have to vote for Stevenson and I have to speak for him. And I hope you'll recognize me. I must have my say." Lawrence said, "I know I couldn't keep you from it."[99] Blatt spoke and was the recipient of some catcalls and hissing. After that, Lawrence went to work for Kennedy within the delegation. "The strategy was to get every last one we could get on the first ballot," Lawrence said. Giesey claims Lawrence did not put pressure on the delegates in the caucus. But Lawrence recalled, "Do you remember I was sounding out these fellows on the floor? . . . Oh, yes, we straightened a good many of them out. You see there were a lot of them from Protestant areas upstate and it was local suicide to be for Kennedy." Things went well in the Pennsylvania delegation until Joe Clark told the press during the first ballot that if Kennedy did not make it, "some of us in the Philadelphia delegation would rethink our support of Kennedy." Bobby Kennedy and Lawrence were upset, but the latter figured Clark was getting wires from ADA members back home and had made the statement offhand. "We were pretty provoked at him at the time."[100] As things turned out, Kennedy won on the first ballot and the nomination maneuvers came to a halt.

In retrospect, Lawrence's role in the Kennedy nomination is subject to controversy. Congressman Moorhead was convinced that the vote of the Pennsylvania delegation "was very crucial. They might have been a little bit ahead, but it was that which put him over the top." Richard Daley said categorically, "Without him [Lawrence], John Kennedy would not have carried the '60 convention." Daley admitted Lawrence was not enthusiastic at first, but when Lawrence moved, that was it. Jim Knox felt Lawrence was more effective by not being on the bandwagon. Finally, John Kennedy wrote: "I am so grateful for what Pennsylvania did, what Dave did."[101] The genius of Kennedy in 1960 was that he understood the older politicians like Lawrence. The same was certainly not true for those who moved the Kennedy organization.

Early on in the run for the White House, Kennedy forces demonstrated obvious concern over the "Old party pros" in the Democratic ranks. The whole issue of religion was of particular interest. Kenny O'Donnell admits he was afraid to broach the subject because of men like Lawrence, whose reluctance proved disconcerting.[102] At the same time, it was felt men like Lawrence, as well as McKinney of Indiana and DeSapio of New York, favored men such as Johnson or Symington and, despite Kennedy's success in the primaries, preferred to take uncommitted delegations to the convention in order to be able to "deal" with a compromise candidate.[103] Thus the Kennedy camp seemed, at first, unsure of itself.

Once it became clear to seasoned and green politicians alike that Kennedy had the votes to get the nomination on the first ballot, attitudes began to change. Sorenson felt that rising Kennedy enthusiasm in Philadelphia and other Pennsylvania counties "had finally won over Governor Lawrence and 68 votes."[104] A more straightforward view was that Lawrence made a big show of public fanfare in going through the motions of handing his delegation over to Kennedy at the last minute in Los Angeles. "Kennedy pretended to take the governor's grand gesture seriously. . . . Lawrence had no other choice."[105] But Kennedy knew the price he would pay for Lawrence's support, a proposition that would infuriate the senator's closest associates. Moreover, Eddie Dowling, a personal friend of Lawrence and Joe Kennedy, had, six months before the convention opened, at the request of the elder Kennedy, asked Lawrence to come out

136

for Jack Kennedy's nomination. Lawrence's first reaction was that Dowling and Garry Burns, district attorney of Boston, could return and assure everyone in Massachusetts that Jack Kennedy "doesn't have an enemy at the head of the Democratic party in Pennsylvania." Lawrence wondered, however, whether the Massachusetts people really thought Kennedy could win. "The last time he went, he was defeated for the vice-presidential nomination." Shortly thereafter that same day, Dowling and Burns met Lawrence quite by accident in Pittsburgh International Airport. Lawrence made it a point to talk to Burns and Dowling, and he said directly to Burns, "And you can go back and tell Mr. Kennedy that I wouldn't be surprised at all when the time comes, and I get in there, I will not be the last to declare for Mr. Kennedy; I won't be the first, but I'll be far from the last."[106]

This reaction on Lawrence's part six months before the convention seems to alter somewhat the playing "hard to get" theory. At the same time, Lawrence knew Kennedy could not win a nationwide election on his own. Therefore, the selection of the proper candidate for vice-president was paramount.

Long before the uproar acclaiming John Kennedy's nomination climaxed, convention inner wheels were in motion culling the best possible vice-presidential nominee. Here again the Lawrence role, although challenged by the Kennedy backers, seems to have been a significant one. Quite clearly the many factions at the Los Angeles conclave held contingency plans had Kennedy not gone over on the first ballot. Lawrence forces planned their moves on the assumption of Kennedy's success.

In recalling the 1960 convention, Gerald Lawrence refers to three important points that arose concerning the Johnson nomination: the national ticket, religion, and Pennsylvania's vital role. At the John Bailey meeting in Los Angeles Airport, although Lawrence would not come out for Kennedy, he did discuss with Bailey a vice-presidential nominee should Kennedy win the nomination. Lawrence felt Lyndon Johnson would be a strong vice-presidential candidate. Lawrence knew Bailey would carry that to Kennedy.

After Kennedy's nomination, there were many conferences between Lawrence and the Kennedy people. Jerry remembers, "My father and Ambassador McCloskey spent a great deal of time running

137

back and forth between our location and the senator's suite." Finally, Lawrence returned to his suite and announced that John Kennedy had decided on Johnson and that Lawrence was to nominate Johnson.

Gerald Lawrence helped Walter Giesey gather material for the speech. When Jerry went to Johnson's headquarters, confusion abounded, since a question had developed over labor's support of a Kennedy-Johnson ticket. Also, it appeared there was going to be a floor fight, and Jerry and Giesey were told to stop their speechwriting efforts. Speaker Rayburn was "very upset" over Robert Kennedy's and Kenny O'Donnell's actions. A controversy ensued over whether Rayburn had misinterpreted Bobby's and Kenny's intentions. Some think Bobby Kennedy tried to talk Johnson out of accepting the nomination; others say he merely told Johnson that Jack Kennedy would support Johnson in a floor fight. Rayburn and Lawrence huddled, and Lawrence reported that everything was all right, so Jerry and Giesey went back to work on the nominating speech. Still, since many Johnson supporters had left the convention for good, "it was difficult rounding up someone who had the information . . . needed," according to Jerry.

When the speech was completed, Jerry met Pierre Salinger in Kennedy headquarters. Salinger said no one was available to put the speech in the large type that, due to poor eyesight, Lawrence needed badly. But Salinger later relented and had the manuscript prepared. When Giesey suggested press copies, Salinger retorted they would not be necessary; "No one would be interested." Jerry's general impression was that the Kennedy staff was opposed to Johnson and Jack Kennedy had to make the Johnson decision on his own. Still, the party leadership realized it needed a southerner to offset the religion issue. Some Kennedy people felt the religion issue dead, but Jerry saw evidence of it when campaigning later with Kennedy in Pennsylvania's Bible Belt. "I think my father's support of Johnson was not only the support he would bring to the South, but also the religion factor. And Johnson had a proven record as an administrator, which, I think, was something Kennedy needed at the time."[107]

Jim Tate indicated he knew of no arrangements or disputes about the issue, although he was quite privy to all that went on

138

right up to the nomination of Senator Kennedy as presidential candidate.[108]

On the other hand, Ambassador Matthew McCloskey suggested that Lawrence had a significant role in the selection of Johnson for the Kennedy-Johnson ticket. A few days before the convention began, McCloskey met with Kennedy and Lawrence in Lawrence's suite. Lawrence asked Kennedy who was going to be national chairman and who his running mate would be if nominated. Kennedy mentioned a number of names, including Jackson, Humphrey, and Symington, as possible running mates. Other than Symington, Lawrence told Kennedy none of the men he enumerated would bring anything to the ticket. Then Lawrence said, "Why wouldn't you go for Lyndon Johnson?" Kennedy replied, "Dave, you know there is no way Johnson is going to take that." Lawrence felt otherwise, due to a meeting that had taken place some weeks prior to the convention.

McCloskey had vacationed with Lawrence in Europe, and in their conversations both seemed convinced that if Kennedy won the nomination, a Kennedy-Johnson ticket might win the general election. When McCloskey and Lawrence returned to the United States, Sam Rayburn called McCloskey and asked Lawrence and McCloskey to Washington for a luncheon with Johnson. Of course, Johnson wanted to know how much help he could get from Pennsylvania for the presidential nomination.

Lawrence said, "Well, Senator, I wouldn't fool you; I can't sell you to our delegation. I love you, I think you're a great guy, and I think you have all the qualifications, but it just isn't in the works and there is no way we can do it."

So Johnson said, "Well what do you think I ought to do, drop out?"

"No," Lawrence said, "I think you ought to go in there and stay in there. I am concerned that we have a lot of fellows that are on the Kennedy bandwagon, and if he doesn't get it on the first ballot, I don't think he'll ever get it, and we'll lose it. I don't know anybody else that would be in there swinging but you. You might catch it yourself."

As a result, Johnson said he would stay in the fight.

Then Lawrence said, "I'll tell you what I do think. If Kennedy

139

does get it, I think it would make a great team if you would take the second spot."

Sam Rayburn exploded, "We didn't come down here to talk about the second spot; we came here to talk about the first spot!"

"Now wait a minute, Sam," said Johnson, "I don't want these boys to go out of here and not know where I stand. First of all, I am a Democrat. And I am going to do anything my party wants me to do. Now that's going to be that."

Knowing this, Lawrence and McCloskey told Kennedy what Johnson said.

Kennedy said, "I can't believe it."

Lawrence said, "All we want you to do is promise us if you get nominated you'll ask him, and I'll guarantee you that he will take it."

After Kennedy was nominated, Lawrence was asked to go to the Kennedy suite. Because of crowded conditions there, Kennedy took Lawrence into the bathroom. "Now look, Dave, I don't want to go down there and ask that guy. Are you sure now?" Lawrence assured him and authorized Kennedy to tell Johnson he knew of the luncheon comments.[109] If what McCloskey said was true, the role Lawrence played was quite significant. If not, just what was Lawrence's position in the event?

Carmine DeSapio, then Democratic national comitteeman from the state of New York, is quite firm in his discussion of these happenings. When DeSapio was asked whether or not he knew the story behind the selection of Lyndon Johnson, he replied, "I would have to say that I know as much about it as perhaps anybody." DeSapio then referred to Theodore White's excellent work on the 1960 election, but felt White's description of the Johnson selection is not adequate. In fairness to White, he did suggest the event would bear many interpretations. Nonetheless, Lawrence, Jacob Arvey, Michael Prendergast, Richard Daley, Robert Wagner, and John Bailey "had been assigned" by Kennedy to make a decision as to the vice-president. The group was well aware that Lyndon Johnson had polled over 400 votes in the convention. Moreover, there was a lot of name-calling after Kennedy's nomination, and in DeSapio's opinion the "liberal establishment" was afraid of the concentration of too much power in Texas, where Rayburn and Johnson controlled both houses of Congress. "I wasn't as fearful as they were; neither was

140

Lawrence or Arvey." In the meeting, Kennedy's only comment before leaving was, "You fellows got to help me pick a vice-president." Kennedy left and the others kicked names around like Symington, Williams, DiSalle, Jackson, and a few others. The only initial agreement arrived at was that Lawrence, by virtue of his seniority, should be spokesman for the group.

Meanwhile, "a tornado erupted politically" when talk spread that Johnson might be considered. Bobby Kennedy "initiated or someone else initiated" a movement within the liberal wing of the party to try to stop Johnson's designation. Inside the meeting room, Lawrence and DeSapio felt they "had an obligation to the Party to at least recognize the man who had polled the second highest number of votes, to give him or accord him the courtesy of being recognized and boost the group supporting him by at least making an offer." The others were not enthusiastic, saying they had information that Johnson would not take it. "Lawrence and I [DeSapio] very plainly put it on the table and said whether or not he does isn't the important thing here; I think we have to weld the pieces, eliminate the scars, and put the Party back on track. There is a regional division setting in here in our Party, and if we will ever win we have to breach that gulf and the best way we can do it is at least let them know how we feel. Let Kennedy ask him to be or that he wants him to be his running mate." The rest of the group did not think that had a chance. They had talked to Rayburn, who said, "I'll never talk to this man the rest of my life if he accepts this designation." Lawrence and DeSapio asserted, "What harm in making the gesture?" They finally acquiesced and Lawrence told Kennedy that "it was our feeling that the order of priorities should be Johnson and Kennedy should do it himself, not have us do it." They felt Johnson would be a strong running mate. To win the election they needed Texas. "If we didn't have Johnson on that ticket . . . Kennedy could have never been elected," said DeSapio.

When the news got out that Kennedy asked Johnson to take the spot, "all hell broke loose," but the leaders stood firm. "We pulled all our forces together. We just had a handful of opposition which was nothing, and that was it. I will assure you," said DeSapio, "that's the very way it happened."

DeSapio did not feel sure as to whether or not Lawrence knew

141

ahead of time that Johnson, once offered the vice-presidential nomination, would accept. He felt that Lawrence saw Johnson's selection as a "moral obligation" to a man who had polled so many votes. "I think Jack Kennedy was very happy that he followed Governor Lawrence's suggestion and advice, and maybe Bobby Kennedy was unhappy about it, but it all came out all right and we were all heros."[110]

DeSapio's account, while it does not specifically contradict McCloskey's, is certainly strong in the position that Lawrence had made no significant arrangements prior to the convention. At least, it did not appear to DeSapio that Lawrence was sure Johnson would accept. Still, Lawrence, who had a reputation for playing things quietly, may have sensed the delegates swinging toward Johnson and thus felt no obligation to discuss any preconvention agreements. Lawrence certainly knew the liberals and labor would be upset enough over Johnson's nomination. Why irritate them by exposing preplanned political parleys? For Lawrence, a winning ticket was the major objective. Burdening the ticket needlessly would have been a wasteful impracticality, and Lawrence did not feel he had hoodwinked friends, particularly since they had agreed Johnson would provide the best effort for the entire ticket in the forthcoming campaign.

In stating his views of Johnson's nomination, Lawrence recalled gathering the leaders the Friday before the convention opened and before Kennedy had arrived. Wagner, Prendergast, and DeSapio of New York were there, as were Daley and Arvey of Chicago, David Wilentz and John Kenny of New Jersey, John Bailey of Connecticut, William Coleman of Ohio, and Bill Green, Matt McCloskey, and Jim Clark of Philadelphia. "I took up with them the matter of the vice president: what we would do, who would be able to help Kennedy most. There was just a unanimous, instant agreement among all these powerful political figures on Johnson." They felt Johnson was the only one who would bring Kennedy the votes that he did not already have. Also, they were convinced Johnson would bring in Texas and, being from the South, would probably hold southern and border states for Kennedy. As soon as Kennedy arrived, Lawrence told Jack and Bobby Kennedy of the meeting and its outcome, asking they give it "serious consideration."

After Kennedy was nominated, he asked Lawrence, "Governor, do you feel the same way you felt Saturday about the vice-presidency?"

Kennedy reminded Lawrence he was having problems with Michigan and "some other states." He further got the impression that Bobby Kennedy was pushing Henry Jackson.

Lawrence reminded Kennedy of the meeting the previous week.

Kennedy then said, "I am going down to see that gentleman now. I just wanted to get your views. Do you think the other fellows feel the same way?"

Lawrence assured him there was no question about it.

Later that day, Kennedy called Lawrence and said, "Well, I've seen that gentleman and he's agreed to run and we want you to make the nominating speech." Lawrence was never told why he was chosen, but felt they wanted a northern liberal to offset some of the anti-Johnson feeling coming from leaders like Soapy Williams and Walter Reuther. Immediately, Lawrence contacted Sam Rayburn, whom Lawrence had been friendly with for over thirty years. Rayburn snapped at Lawrence, "I don't know anything about this. What's going on here?" Lawrence explained he needed further information for his nominating speech. Rayburn agreed to meet Lawrence and, in the meantime, secured the services of a man who had been with Johnson for years and could provide top-notch background material. "But old Sam was crabby about it."

When asked in 1966 whether he had any inkling Johnson would take the second spot, Lawrence was noncommittal, saying he felt almost anyone would take it. Too many times he had heard men say they would not take second position, but when the first was gone, "they usually move in. I figured he would." Even when Kennedy protested that Johnson had made some pretty strong statements, Lawrence rejoined, "Don't go for that. He'll take it." Lawrence further explained that he never had any specific contacts with Johnson people. "It was purely Kennedy and myself just as I related it. . . . I was concerned about the South. . . . I had a lot of dealings with the South in previous conventions . . . and I was just greatly alarmed about it."[111]

Lawrence's version of Johnson's designation fails to shed any

143

light on the McCloskey story. It is difficult to say whether Lawrence's memory was hazy or he answered craftily. When asked about his contact with Sam Rayburn prior to the convention, he made a gratuitous, meaningless statement and questioned the questioner. The Lawrence narrative deals with Rayburn after the nomination was a foregone conclusion. That seemed to satisfy the interviewer, and Lawrence never alluded to any preconvention meeting.

What Lawrence, rather uncharacteristically, does confirm here was the well-known dissatisfaction in the Kennedy and Johnson camps. Further, Mayor Joe Barr tells of taking a copy of Lawrence's nominating speech to Abe Ribicoff, who had been handling the convention floor for Kennedy. Ribicoff, in a huffy mood, said, "Oh, yes, if that's the way you want it."[112] Some time later, in a conversation with Andrew Bradley, Lawrence indicated that Bobby Kennedy tried to keep Jack Kennedy from putting Johnson on the ticket, although, according to Lawrence, Bobby had denied this at times.[113] Apparently, the whole affair was something Lawrence talked about with close friends for a long time after the convention. Unfortunately, their recollections do not come together.

When Mayor Robert Wagner of New York was asked if he thought Lawrence knew ahead of time that Kennedy would pick Johnson as his running mate, Wagner replied, "I don't know. I think a lot of people knew they had been talking. I thought it was a good move. I don't know. If he did, he was a good actor." Commenting further on McCloskey's version, Wagner recalled McCloskey was not at the meeting he attended. Still he doubted his recollection. Moreover, Wagner stressed the real problem lay with labor leaders like George Meany, Arthur Goldberg, Alex Rose, and Walter Reuther. "They were very unhappy." But one of the men who "saved the day for Johnson" was David Dubinsky. "Johnson helped him in a particular matter and he was always grateful to him. When they threatened to talk to Kennedy about not endorsing Kennedy if he took Johnson, Dave Bubinsky said, 'Over my dead body.' And that started the thing going the other way."[114] It was Lawrence who put in a call to Dubinsky asking his support for Johnson, and Dubinsky asked Lawrence to convey the above comment to the group.

Again, Wagner doubts McCloskey's position, but does not deny it. And, interestingly enough, Lawrence places McCloskey at the meeting where Wagner claims McCloskey was not present.

Lawrence's executive assistant, Walter Giesey, recalled that the Johnson designation caused dismay for "a hell of a lot of people." He remembers being in Lawrence's hotel room after the Johnson announcement and Mayor Wagner consoling Jackson, "Well, Scoop, you know Bobby and I were for you." Giesey was also present after Kennedy's assassination when Joseph Alsop interviewed Lawrence. Alsop wanted background information on Lawrence, but in reply, Lawrence talked about the selection of Johnson as vice-president. Lawrence mentioned Katherine Graham's husband, who strongly backed a Kennedy-Johnson ticket and had suggested it to Kennedy as well as Johnson before the convention. In Giesey's view, this may explain "why the two principals would be so interested without much hesitation, while their coteries were not." Further, although Giesey admits McCloskey's story could be correct, he feels McCloskey's recollection wrong. "I don't think they would have gone through that charade for five days." Moreover, Giesey just does not know if Lawrence was involved in the Graham meetings. And when Alsop mentioned the Graham tactics as having taken place months before the convention, Lawrence said, "That may well be; I can only tell you what I know of the situation." Finally, Lyndon Johnson seemed to think Lawrence had much to do with his nomination. At the convention when Lawrence went up to make the nomination, Johnson said, "Dave, I'll never forget to my dying day what you have done for me."[115]

Five years after the convention, Lawrence sent his grandson a tearsheet from the *Washington Post* for June 20, 1965. It contained, according to Lawrence, "intimate" coverage of the selection of Johnson as nominee in 1960. "It is very interesting and I thought you might enjoy it."[116] He does not say how accurate the piece was. The tone of the letter seems to indicate that Lawrence is sharing a chuckle with his grandson since they both know something important not contained in the article.

What becomes clear is that by 1960, Lawrence was the man in

145

the Democratic party whose backing presidential and vice-presidential hopefuls sought. More important here was that John Kennedy and Lyndon Johnson were politically astute enough to go with the Lawrence experience rather than the insurgency of liberal youth so characteristic of their devoted, hardworking followers. They were on the same path; their methods were different. And in this Lawrence knew where he stood. As Soapy Williams said in reference to Lawrence's push for Johnson, "He was smart enough not to discuss it with me." Lawrence argued his case in the Kennedy and Johnson minds. When Kennedy won on the first ballot, Lawrence struck with lightning swiftness at the heart of the matter. Kennedy had to take Johnson to win. No threat; that's the way political insight and experience saw it. Kennedy's only retreat, or perhaps hope, that Johnson would not take second spot, was blocked. At the same time, Lawrence doused the labor fires by knowing who to call. Dubinksy's role was the quencher, while Lawrence's long friendship with labor helped pull it off. Today most Democratic politicians are convinced the only Democratic ticket that could have won in 1960 was Kennedy-Johnson, yet as late as 1966, Lawrence would not let it appear that he moved the convention toward that ticket alone. Ever the party man, Lawrence gave credit to the whole group; his orchestration in his mind was unimportant. The maestro bowed only in concert with his colleagues and then campaigned vigorously, for the second and last time supporting a fellow Catholic seeking the nation's highest office.

From the outset of the '60 campaign, Lawrence was solidly in Kennedy's corner. In Lawrence's opening salvo, he noted Kennedy had won the Democratic nomination in an "open contest in which his primary victories were an essential factor; he had the grace, the wisdom and persuasiveness to select as his running mate his principal opponent for the nomination, our great Senate leader, Lyndon B. Johnson." Lawrence predicted that the brilliant Democratic senator would make a great president "of all the people."[117] A few days later, Lawrence, in a private letter, expressed his conviction that Senator Kennedy would "present a much different image for Pennsylvania voters than did Governor Smith. I believe that this will be sufficient to win for him and Senator Johnson the Commonwealth

146

and the electoral vote."[118] Lawrence's reference to Smith again reflects his concern over the religion issue. He was just not sure how the religion thing would evolve. But as the campaign moved on, according to James Knox, Lawrence hopes were bolstered: "He was pleased that Kennedy was forthright about the religious issue and that he met it. He did not cover it up or relegate it to the back burner."[119] Lawrence was never really satisfied that religion as an issue in American politics was dead, yet his elation with the Kennedy approach seemed mostly grounded in the famous Houston speech. That Lawrence was anxious to have the issue out front in '60 is questionable; meeting it head-on when raised is another thing entirely.

The Kennedy forces were as anxious to secure Pennsylvania's thirty-two electoral votes as Lawrence was to deliver them. In 1966, Lawrence talked about Kennedy's crusade. "I campaigned with him through Pennsylvania every time he came in." The Harrisburg Farm Show Arena was jammed for Kennedy's first appearance. It was a $100-a-plate dinner. "Then I was fearful of the religious situation in the Pennsylvania Dutch area, so I thought I might as well hit it hard right off the bat." Lawrence arranged Kennedy speeches in Lebanon, Lancaster, Berks, and York counties, four "dyed-in-the-wool Pennsylvania Dutch Protestant counties. The people there were good citizens, clean, decent, and honest." But Lawrence felt they were anti-Catholic. The crowds that came out surprised him. Later the same thing happened in Montgomery County, but the vote was not there. "Well, they just wanted to look at him, I guess, and then voted against him."

Meanwhile, Lawrence was taken with Kennedy's charm. "I was always very fond of him." He recalled how in Pittston the people just would not let the car move and stood there and cheered for an hour. In Delaware County, a banquet was set up in a tent on a golf course. Kennedy was running late and his people wanted to cancel Kennedy's appearance. Lawrence called Bill Green, who was helping in Delaware County. Green protested, "These people have paid a hundred dollars a plate out here in this tent." So they agreed to go, arriving at one in the morning. It was raining "pitchforks," and the people had been drinking for hours. "They had a singer, but they

147

were singing songs themselves. Here was this Joe Clark, who's about a sixth generation, blue-blood, Main Line Philadelphian out here, and Bill Green. [Clark and Green despised each other]. The two were up there leading these people in songs—the most terrible sight you ever saw in your life." Kennedy tried to speak, but the people, in their cups, drowned him out with cheers every time he opened his mouth.

Pennsylvania voted Kennedy in November, and Lawrence got control of the state legislature. Lawrence was surprised by the size of the Democratic vote in Philadelphia, Pittsburgh, and Scranton.[120] Still, Lawrence proved correct that Kennedy would have difficulty in most of rural Pennsylvania. The Kennedy-Johnson ticket swept only fourteen of the sixty-seven counties, with a total plurality of 116,326 votes. It was Philadelphia's 331,544 plurality along with a 107,485 plurality in Allegheny County and a 30,462 margin in Lackawana County that gave Kennedy Pennsylvania's electoral votes and left the state legislature barely Democratic, but sufficiently so to give Lawrence a working majority for the remainder of his term as governor. It was a far cry from the heated exchanges of the Biltmore Hotel in July, when Bobby Kennedy, on January 3, 1961, in a handwritten note said to Lawrence, "Many thanks to you for your many kindnesses to me this past year. Bob."[121] No doubt Bobby was speaking for his brother as well as for himself, an acknowledgement of the wisdom of political seasoning and experience that contributed mightily to the opening of the New Frontier.

David Lawrence's major role in fashioning a national political ticket was fitting for a man whose approaches in the areas of social action and civil rights had long been recognized in American politics as something new, something refreshing, but sometimes bothersome. Lawrence had long been champion of the underdog. In the twenties, Lawrence, in association with Charles Rice and Majorie Matson, worked to distribute food to striking miners and their families. Rice and Matson were both considered radicals, and Lawrence came in for his share of criticism, although no one ever called Lawrence a communist. Having been born into a lower economic bracket and lived in a depressed neighborhood, Lawrence personally understood poverty. However, in his social action, Lawrence was

148

not a bleeding heart or a "mouther"; his was the more practical approach.[122]

Early in his political career, Lawrence's record in civil rights was average. During the Earle administration, Lawrence was, at first, opposed to the appointment of Paul Jones, a black, as a workmen's compensation referee because he felt white voters would resent it. After much discussion with black Democrats in the state, Lawrence approved the appointment. "After that Lawrence became one of the staunchest supporters of civil rights," according to Andrew Bradley. Moreover, Lawrence forced himself to grow in the knowledge and understanding of Negroes. Lawrence had, for example, many differences with a black legislator, Homer Brown. As a result, Lawrence went to Bradley, a black, for advice. Bradley told Lawrence, "I don't think you understand Homer. You don't understand his background. He was born and educated in the South and you just don't understand his approach to things." Bradley made some suggestions which Lawrence followed, and things worked out much better between Lawrence and Brown.[123] Lawrence continued to study problems Negroes faced in American society, and he eventually led the fight among Democrats in the nation for civil rights. In Pennsylvania, "under Lawrence, the Democratic Party across the state was committed to the principle of social equality and civil rights," according to Senator Clark.[124] Lawrence's major impact on the civil-rights area was in his native Pittsburgh.

There are those who charge that much of what Lawrence did for Pittsburgh accomplished little to improve conditions of blacks. Giesey admitted this to be true, stating, however, that disruption in the Lower Hill affected more Lebanese and Italians than blacks. "The program, however, did not get to the problems of the black ghetto in the Hill District." True, Lawrence fought hard for public housing, although in retrospect, he did not address basic issues.[125] Still, Lawrence was responsible for the thrust that helped upgrade facilities and improved municipal services in the Homewood and Upper Hill areas. He paved the way for the first black councilman in Pittsburgh and appointed the first black magistrate, "which at that time was unheard of." In 1949, Lawrence backed Homer Brown, the first black man to run for judge in Pittsburgh. When the Democrats published their election tabloid that year, they failed to print any photographs of judges because Brown was black. The Republicans put Harry Sherman on the radio. Sherman made a fifteen-minute speech five times a week, the gist of which was, "It isn't because Homer Brown is a Negro; he just isn't the right Negro." Maybe Lawrence and the Pittsburgh Democrats were ready for a black judge, but Pittsburgh Republicans were not. Brown was elected at the same time Lawrence won his second mayoral term.[126] Further, Lawrence advocated the first Fair Employment Practices Commission (FEPC) law ever in any major city, and Pittsburgh's Public Housing Authority became a model. At the same time, Lawrence established a bipartisan Human Relations Commission, appointing only well-qualified people to the commission, people who were willing to work hard to bring about equality of conditions and opportunity for all Pittsburghers.[127] Also, Lawrence set up a Civil Unity Council in Pittsburgh to promote good relations among cultural, racial, and economic groups. In just four years, the council was able to break down many barriers in the professions, industry, and education. Lawrence proclaimed, "For too long a time, the responsibility for bettering human relations has been shunt by one group to another, with very little actually being accomplished. Now local government is becoming aware of its duties in the field."[128]

Yet this was not an easy road to follow. In February 1950, Ida Imhoff, committeewoman in the Sixteenth Ward, wrote Lawrence a five-page letter outlining problems public housing would bring, including that of introducing new elements into the area. Lawrence replied: "Dear Ida: Your letter of February 23rd received. When the Democratic Party ceases to be interested in housing, it ceases to be the Democratic Party."[129] The following year, when Lawrence spoke at a national housing-policy conference, he said, "It would be a national tragedy if any cause except the most stark and compelling problems of survival is allowed to halt the program contemplated in the National Housing Act of 1949." He called for courageous leadership on both the local and national levels.[130] A few years later, Lawrence moved for the establishment of an Urban Renewal Commission to coordinate public and private organizations' efforts in fighting slums. "We have reached the stage where we cannot only

150

deal with slums that exist, but can also direct our attention to preventing the growth of new pockets of blight and squalor."[131] Cardinal Wright observed of Lawrence: "He had a persevering awareness of the needs of the ordinary person, or the things that make the ordinary little fellow laugh, and of the things that are needed to make life more pleasant for very simple and ordinary people."[132]

Lawrence's crusade for the ordinary people went with him to Harrisburg when he became governor. Reviewing the objectives of his administration in the area of civil rights, Lawrence said, "What we seek is the means to insure every resident of Pennsylvania the essentials of human dignity—an adequate education, equal opportunity to work, the right to live in a decent house in the neighborhood of choice, and full use of all public facilities."[133] In June 1961, addressing the problems of the migrant worker, Lawrence wrote Florida's governor, Farris Bryant: "American workers should be offered at least the same facilities and standards as those now being provided for Mexican and British West Indian alien workers. For our government to provide anything less results in a condition of competitive disadvantage for both American workers and American farmers."[134] Finally, one of Lawrence's last acts as governor of Pennsylvania was to establish January 1, 1963 as Emancipation Proclamation Day, "a commemorative day in which our state as a member state of our great union rededicates itself to the application of the principles of freedom and justice under law with which both state and nation were so founded." Lawrence further urged Pennsylvanians to pledge actions that would make freedom a reality everywhere, while, at the same time, learning the "significant advancements and achievements made by the descendents of those freed by the Emancipation Proclamation these past one hundred years."[135]

At the Democratic National Convention in 1948, Lawrence supported the minority civil-rights plank in committee and in the open convention. Arvey feels it was Lawrence's hard line that eventually caused the South to walk out.[136] At the 1956 convention, Lawrence supported the Supreme Court decision on desegregation, but added, "I certainly don't believe in calling out the troops, but there are other ways of establishing compliance." Lawrence suggested it would be unwise for party leaders to ignore southern tradition and society, while, at the same time, he felt it necessary to stress the other important planks in the 1956 Democratic platform—namely, foreign policy, farm supports, and labor. All were significant for national welfare according to Lawrence.[137] By 1957, however, Lawrence had tired of southern reaction toward civil-rights progress. He explained, "We certainly do not want the South to leave the Party, but we have got to stop kow-towing to them. We did not kow-tow in 1948 and we won. We did kow-tow in 1952 and 1956 and we lost. Nobody worked harder than I did to placate the South in 1952 and 1956 but it didn't work out."[138] Thereafter Lawrence never coddled the South. He courageously withstood the assaults of the South as well as northern ultraliberals in the 1964 Democratic National Convention credentials strife.

In January 1965, Lawrence was appointed chairman of a subcommittee of the Democratic National Committee that was charged with developing a plan to help Democratic state organizations more fully open their ranks to Negro participation so as to avoid delegate challenges at future conventions.[139] In just two months, Lawrence, along with John Baily, met with President Johnson to explain the plan. Johnson later wired Lawrence: "I have a very high regard for your judgement, and I'm very glad that you approve of our latest effort to achieve equal opportunity for all citizens." At the same time, a series of activities were slated to carry out the objectives of the national committee. Johnson wrote Lawrence: "I agree with the outline of activities. . . . You and the Equal Rights Committee of the National Democratic Committee have every right to expect success with the program that you have outlined."[140] Lawrence's work here was one of his last major contributions to the Democratic National Committee.

Meanwhile, when Lawrence left the governor's office, President Kennedy asked him to chair the president's Commission on Equal Opportunity in Housing. The AFL-CIO wrote President Kennedy commending him for appointing Lawrence. "We pledge our fullest support of the Commission in its vital task of assuring equal opportunity in housing to all Americans without regard to race, creed, color, or national origins."[141] As national spokesman for fair housing,

Lawrence told the National Civil Liberties Clearing House Convention, "There is no reason we can't help move a man into a house he wants and can afford, while, at the same time, we are exerting the maximum energies to get some other man up on the moon."[142] Again, he told the Conference of Committees for Human Rights, "I suspect I am the only person in this nation who has signed a city fair housing ordinance and a state fair housing ordinance into law. In a long lifetime in public affairs, I can think of no two actions in which I have greater pride."[143] In 1963, Lawrence told the United States Conference of Mayors there was nothing he could devote himself more conscientiously to than "this unsettled problem." The solution of fair housing would, according to Lawrence, "raise new horizons for our nation's integrity and prestige."[144] Further, using very strong and direct language concerning housing and the Negro, Lawrence told the Women's Association of the University of Pittsburgh, "The most prevalent myth is that the presence of a Negro family in a white neighborhood would reduce the value of property, wipe out savings, and invite the end of the world. Time and time again this notion has been proved to have no foundation in fact."[145] It was this direct, hard-hitting language and philosophy that marked Lawrence's crusade for civil rights. Still, Lawrence the compromiser also proved diplomatic when a civil-rights dispute called for tact. Such was the case at the 1964 Democratic National Convention.

As convention time drew near in Atlantic City, it became clear to President Johnson that seating, particularly for Mississippi, was going to be difficult. Johnson wanted to prevent a floor fight. He called Lawrence and asked him to chair the Credentials Committee. There were over 100 members on the committee, and as the Freedom Democratic Party of Mississippi put forward its claims, committee members endured three tough days of hearings. At times, Lawrence seemed to resent some of the wild, militant rhetoric. But as Governor Hughes observed, "He [Lawrence] was preeminently a reasonable, fair man, so obviously fair." Lawrence first asked for patience and for people to recognize the higher nobility of their own character. He suggested reasonable men and women ought to sit down and discuss things reasonably. Moreover, Lawrence did not want to see anybody lose face.[146]

153

However, the Freedom Democratic Party wanted the issue on the convention floor. They needed eleven votes to bring the minority report before the convention. Paul O'Dwyer, New York City councilman, who had worked with the Freedom Democratic Party in Mississippi, tells how he pleaded with the New York delegation to instruct their representatives to the Credentials Committee to vote for the minority position. Averill Harriman shook his fist at O'Dwyer, saying, "Paul, you are acting in an irresponsible fashion and you are placing burdens on the president. You are totally irresponsible." O'Dwyer replied, "Governor, had you shown that kind of spirit when you were Governor, you would have been reelected. . . . Look, Lyndon Johnson can't lose; and if Harry Truman could take a position and lose the South in 1948, Lyndon Johnson can do it in 1964."[147] It was these kinds of positions and considerations that convinced Lawrence to call the party leadership together with the most powerful black Democrats in the country in order to work out a compromise. At first, the Freedom Democrats rejected what came to be called the Lawrence compromise, saying they did not come from Mississippi to ride in the back of the bus in Atlantic City. But when Lawrence explained how the compromise would work, and at the urging of Martin Luther King and Al Lowenstein, the Freedom Democrats agreed. The plan recognized the Freedom Democratic Party and the blacks by seating two as delegates at large. When this happened, the whites in the Mississippi delegation refused to appear and Freedom Democrats took their places on the convention floor. Lawrence had a hunch that would happen and used it as his selling point for the compromise with the Freedom Democrats. In the end, nearly all agreed that the master stroke of the convention was allowing Lawrence to work out the compromise.[148] Personally, Lawrence felt "we were very fortunate in effecting a settlement that bridged the emergency. Neither side was wholly pleased with what happened, but it was generally accepted as the best way out. I had great help from both Senator Humphrey and Walter Reuther in working out the solution." Further, Lawrence observed, "It was tough, but I didn't mind. Because a problem is difficult, it shouldn't deter anybody."[149]

With the issue resolved and the convention sustained, it was Johnson's show. For vice-president, although Richard Daley sought

Lawrence's backing, Lawrence favored Humphrey. There was general agreement on Humphrey, while "some Catholics and others" were for Bobby Kennedy, according to Lawrence. In addition, Lawrence observed, "Hubert's generosity in going about the country so often in the past won him many leaders. Also his ability and capacity for work qualified him to take over the presidency if need be."[150]

With the Johnson-Humphrey ticket set, Lawrence was questioned about the Republicans. He admitted he had no idea who would run against Johnson, "and while I have treated the Republican situation a little facetiously, I don't mean to joke about the importance of their actions and the seriousness with which I am sure they will go about their task." Lawrence thought the presidency too vital an office for the United States and the world to be treated lightly and hoped the Republicans would put forward their best man. However, after the Republicans met, Lawrence suggested Eisenhower and Nixon had failed to exercise "any kind of leadership" in the state primaries and conventions: "It was a sad spectacle for the Republican Party."[151] With Barry Goldwater and William Miller on the Republican ticket, Lawrence was sure the Democrats would win.

Yet Lawrence campaigned in Pennsylvania as if Johnson might lose and was elated with the results, saying he never thought he would see Delaware, Montgomery, Chester, and Bucks counties voting for a Democratic president. At the same time, Humphrey wrote Lawrence: "The President and I are very grateful for your efforts on our behalf. It was through work such as yours that the Democratic party was so successful this year."[152] Lawrence too had much to be grateful for, especially Johnson's civil-rights record, which enabled Lawrence to work more effectively for civil rights in his twilight years.

Notes

1. Fuller, p. 48.
2. Shames, pp. 17–18.
3. Lawrence to Roosevelt, March 29, 1932, FDR Library, Personal File, under "Governor Lawrence."

155

4. Fuller, p. 48.
5. Jones, p. 1.
6. Dent, p. 5.
7. Fuller, p. 49.
8. Ibid.
9. Ibid.
10. Lawrence to Roosevelt, October 7, 1932, FDR Library, Personal File, under "Governor Lawrence."
11. Selby and Selby, p. 80.
12. Stave, pp. 32–33.
13. *New York Times*, June 21, 1936, p. 27.
14. Ibid., June 24, 1936, p. 13.
15. Ibid., June 26, 1936, p. 1.
16. Lawrence to James Farley, July 17, 1937, FDR Library, Personal File, under "Governor Lawrence."
17. *New York Times*, August 19, 1936, p. 12.
18. Lawrence to Roosevelt, October 5, 1936, Roosevelt to Lawrence October 6, 1936, FDR Library, Personal File, under "Governor Lawrence."
19. Jones, pp. 1–2.
20. Shames, p. 41.
21. *New York Times*, Feb. 4, 1940, p. 2.
22. Lawrence (HST), pp. 2–3.
23. Memo, General Watson to FDR, October 17, 1940, FDR Library, Personal File, under "Governor Lawrence."
24. Farley, p. 2.
25. Lawrence (HST), pp. 3–6, 9–11.
26. Bradley, pp. 7–8.
27. Tate, pp. 11–14.
28. Lawrence (HST), pp. 6–9, 11–14.
29. *Pittsburgh Post Gazette*, November 22, 1966, p. 4.
30. Bradley, pp. 8–9.
31. Barr, pp. 6–7.
32. Lawrence (HST), pp. 16–18.
33. *New York Times*, November 4, 1944, p. 12.
34. Ibid, December 17, 1947, p. 34.
35. Ibid., July 13, 1948, p. 4.
36. Shames, p. 43.
37. Dent, pp. 5–6.
38. Lawrence (HST), pp. 26–27, 30–32.
39. Ibid., p. 24.
40. Ibid., p. 25.
41. Ibid.
42. *New York Times*, December 11, 1934, p. 5.
43. *Pittsburgh Post Gazette*, May 21, 1940, p. 1; Shames, p. 135.

44. Lawrence to FDR, August 2, 1940, Memo, FDR to General Watson, August 2, 1940, FDR Library, Governor's File, under "Lawrence."

45. Fenrich, p. 6.

46. Shames, p. 105.

47. Farley, p. 6.

48. Tate, pp. 21–22; Barr, p. 2.

49. *The Reminiscences of Carmine DeSapio,* (1974), pp. 1–2, 7, in the Oral History Collection of La Salle University, hereinafter DeSapio.

50. Ibid., pp. 3–4.

51. McCloskey, p. 10.

52. *The Reminiscences of Governor Richard J. Hughes,* (1974), p. 3, in the Oral History Collection of La Salle University, hereinafter Hughes.

53. Williams, p. 4.

54. Arvey, pp. 5, 8.

55. Arvey, p. 5.

56. Truman to Lawrence, July 22, 1959, PSA, Lawrence, General File.

57. Ibid., George Rock to Tracy McCracken, August 14, 1959.

58. Ibid., Lawrence to Hartke, September 15, 1959.

59. Ibid., Clark to Lawrence, September 14, 1959.

60. Lawrence (JFK), pp. 92–96.

61. Ibid.

62. Lawrence to Michael F. Doyle, Esq., February 26, 1960, PSA, Lawrence Papers, Subject File.

63. Saxe, p. 14.

64. Joseph Clark to Lawrence, October 2, 1963, PSA, Lawrence Papers, Correspondence.

65. Memo, James Jones to Marvin Watson, November 22, 1966, LBJ Library.

66. *New York Times,* February 16, 1950, p. 10.

67. Saxe, pp. 1–2.

68. Sloan, p. 3.

69. Saxe, pp. 2–3; Blatt, p. 6.

70. Lawrence (HST), p. 32.

71. Shames, p. 45; Lawrence (HST), p. 34; Blatt, pp. 6–7; *Pittsburgh Press,* July 9, 1952, p. 10.

72. *The Reminiscences of Senator Joe Clark,* (1974), pp. 6–7, in the Oral History Collection of La Salle University, hereinafter Clark.

73. Fuller, p. 51.

74. Shames, pp. 48–49; Saxe, p. 3.

75. Clark, p. 7.

76. Shames, pp. 53–54.

77. DeSapio, p. 12.

78. Barr, p. 3.

79. Knox, pp. 12–13.

80. Stevenson to Lawrence, December 30, 1958, private collection; Selby and Selby, p. 78.

81. *The Reminiscences of Governor Pat Brown*, (1974), p. 1, in the Oral History Collection of La Salle University, hereinafter Brown.

82. Selby and Selby, p. 78.

83. Robert Kennedy to Lawrence, December 4, 1959, PSA, Lawrence Papers, General File 24.

84. Letter to author, Rabbi Seymour Cohen, September 17, 1975.

85. Rose Fitzgerald Kennedy, *Times to Remember* (New York: Doubleday, 1964), pp. 370–371.

86. *The Reminiscences of Bishop John Wright*, (1974), pp. 2–3, in the Oral History Collection of La Salle University, hereinafter Wright.

87. Giesey, pp. 17–18; Lawrence (JFK), pp. 9–10.

88. PSA, Lawrence Papers, press release, June 30, 1960.

89. McCloskey, pp. 2–3.

90. Lawrence (JFK), pp. 17–21, 19–21.

91. Ibid., pp. 67–68.

92. Ibid., p. 71.

93. Ibid., p. 11–13.

94. *Newsweek*, May 16, 1960, p. 32.

95. Fuller, pp. 51–52; *New York Times*, May 15, 1960, p. 3; Gerald Lawrence, I, pp. 4–5; Bradley, p. 16.

96. Lawrence (JFK), pp. 14–15; Fuller, P. 52; Lieberman, pp. 253–254.

97. Lawrence to Arthur M. Schlesinger, Jr., December 30, 1965, PSA, Lawrence Papers, Correspondence.

98. Lawrence (JFK), pp. 58–60; Gerald Lawrence, I, pp. 5–6.

99. Blatt, pp. 7–8.

100. Lawrence (JFK), pp. 62, 74–75; Giesey, p. 18; Clark, pp. 5–6.

101. Moorhead, p. 4; Daley, p. 1; Knox, p. 13.

102. Kenneth P. O'Donnell, David F. Powers, and Joe McCarthy, *Johnny we Hardly Knew Ye: Memories of John Fitzgerald Kennedy* (Boston: Little, Brown and Company, 1970), p. 165.

103. Theodore S. Sorenson, *Kennedy* (New York: Harper, 1965), p. 124.

104. Ibid., p. 161.

105. O'Donnell, pp. 173, 175–177.

106. *The Reminiscences of Eddie Dowling*, (1963), pp. 290, 293, in the Oral History Collection of Columbia University.

107. Gerald Lawrence, II, pp. 1–4.

108. Tate, p. 21.

109. McCloskey, pp. 2–6.

110. DeSapio, pp. 5–7.

111. Lawrence (JFK), pp. 15–16, 21–23, 63–67, 81–83.
112. Barr, p. 7.
113. Bradley, p. 14.
114. Wagner, pp. 4–5.
115. Giesey, pp. 35–37.
116. Lawrence to David Donahue, June 21, 1965, PSA, Lawrence Papers, Correspondence.
117. Ibid., Lawrence Papers, press release, September 15, 1960.
118. Ibid., Lawrence Papers, Subject File 30, Lawrence to John P. Broderick, September 27, 1960.
119. Knox, p. 13.
120. Lawrence (JFK), pp. 24–33, 54–56.
121. Robert Kennedy to David Lawrence, January 3, 1961, PSA, Lawrence Papers, General File 53.
122. Giesey, p. 14.
123. Bradley, pp. 6–7, 9–10.
124. Clark, pp. 1–2.
125. Giesey, pp. 11–13.
126. Ibid.
127. Knox, p. 6.
128. New York Times, September 6, 1950, p. 26.
129. Giesey, p. 15.
130. The American City, April, 1951, p. 145.
131. Shames, pp. 253–254.
132. Wright, p. 7.
133. PSA, Lawrence Papers, press release, March 1, 1960.
134. Lawrence to Farris Bryant, June 16, 1961, PSA, Lawrence Papers, Subject File 26.
135. Negro History Bulletin, January 1963, 26:141.
136. Arvey, p. 4.
137. Shames, p. 88.
138. Ibid., p. 104.
139. New York Times, January 20, 1965, p. 19.
140. Memo March 2, 1965, wire, LBJ to Lawrence, March 22, 1965, memo Watson to Lawrence, September 16, 1965, LBJ Library, Personal File, under "Governor Lawrence."
141. PSA, Lawrence Papers, Correspondence, Report of AFL-CIO Housing Committee, 1963.
142. Ibid., speeches, March 28, 1963.
143. Ibid., May 23, 1963.
144. Ibid., June 10, 1963.
145. Ibid., October 8, 1963.
146. The Reminiscences of Walter Mondale, (1975), p. 2, in the Oral History Collection of La Salle University, hereinafter Mondale.

147. *The Reminiscences of Paul O'Dwyer,* (1975), p. 2, in the Oral History Collection of La Salle University, hereinafter O'Dwyer.

148. Ibid., pp. 4, 5.

149. Lawrence to John Robin, September 21, 1964; PSA, Lawrence Papers, Correspondence; speech, Sloan Collection, 1964.

150. Ibid.; Giesey, pp. 26–27.

151. Ibid.; speech, Sloan Collection, 1964.

152. Humphrey to Lawrence, November 13, 1964, PSA, Lawrence Papers, Correspondence.

V
Davey

David Leo Lawrence was born on June 18, 1889, in a house built by his grandfather on Penn Avenue and Greentree Alley, in the Point section of Pittsburgh. The Allegheny and Monongahela rivers meet there to form the Ohio River, the site of an Irish colony in 1889. Emigrants from Ireland settled there in boarding houses, biding their time till they could secure their own homes. It was a busy area. Boats of every description lined the wharves on the Allegheny River. Exposition Hall, hard by the Allegheny, contained a large outdoor balcony for strollers. Inside were Mechanics Hall, where a variety of exhibitions took place, and Symphony Hall, which hosted musical performers from around the world. On the Monongahela side of the Point, a horse auction operated several days a week in good weather. Horses were run up and down cobblestoned Front Street before bids were made. In summertime, youngsters from other sections of the city journeyed to the Point to swim in the rivers' cooling waters.

Most of the homes in the area were quite modest. As for the Lawrence home, specifics are unrecorded, although the lot contained a "large house, with a smaller four-room dwelling in the rear."[1] The premises were quite respectable when one considers that Isaac Lawrence, David's paternal grandfather, emigrated from Ireland during the famine of the late forties. Eventually, Isaac worked his way to ownership of a shoe shop on Penn Avenue in the downtown area. His expertise in carpentry helped expand the family dwelling once he secured a steady financial footing.

It was not surprising that David's maternal grandfather, Charles

Conwell, immigrated for the same reason as did Isaac Lawrence. Conwell was first employed in Pittsburgh as a stonecutter before he was appointed county assessor. David Lawrence rarely discussed his grandparents, except to say at one time that all four grandparents were born in Ireland—two in County Cavan and two in County Donegal. Moreover, Lawrence admitted there was some Scots blood on his father's side. Other than that, little is known of the Lawrences and the Conwells. It may have been that Lawrence never knew his grandparents personally, although he did say they were involved in politics.[2]

David's father, Charles Lawrence, was a "mild-mannered" individual. Charles had little if any education and worked in various capacities as a navy corpsman, hauler, and warehouseman. Charles, a Democrat, was very active in the labor movement and politics. A teamster, the elder Lawrence became the Democratic Third Ward chairman, a cog in William Brennan's faltering Democratic organization. David was, as a young man, well aware of the poor working conditions and discrimination his father experienced and fought.[3] To what extent David and his father communicated is not recorded. David, in his later years, seemed to talk only of his mother.

Catherine Conwell Lawrence was one of nine girls. Apparently, Catherine, like Charles, had little formal education. She was a hard worker, who took boarders into her modest home on Greentree Alley, decorated and cleaned the sanctuary of Saint Mary of Mercy Church, and worked in many areas of the Rosalia Foundling Home. Many old-timers in Pittsburgh recall Catherine Lawrence soliciting contributions on the streets of Pittsburgh for Rosalia. Catherine's zeal, hard work, and homely philsophy had a very definite impact on her son. "He idolized his mother," according to Andrew Bradley. Lawrence said his mother was a source of great strength for both him and his brother Isaac. She was one of the main reasons David did not drink. Catherine Lawrence always reminded her boys how drinking was a frequent cause of fighting and trouble among the Irish. Moreover, Lawrence was impressed by the fact that his mother, on a very limited income, was able to raise her four children while providing a stable and happy home life.[4]

David was the third boy welcomed into the happy Lawrence home. He was preceded by Isaac and Charles. Mary Lawrence, who died in her early twenties, was the last child born to Charles B. and Catherine C. Lawrence. Sister Irenaeus, who lived just a few doors from the Lawrences, remembers David as a "lovely fat baby. As a baby he seemed to react to every smile."[5] As David grew older, he participated in the usual boyhood activities of his day. To say the least, David, although somewhat impaired by poor eyesight, actively engaged in sports and other youthful pastimes. Along with the members of the "Irish gang," who were his constant companions, he frequented Exposition Hall and its many activities. David took advantage of the influx of Exposition Hall visitors into the neighborhood by setting up a newspaper stand. In later years, David recalled a fellow vendor, an old woman who sold candy in front of the Pittsburgh Blockhouse. The waters provided excellent fishing and swimming opportunities. Of course, the Irish lads always swam apart from the Italians, who lived on Washington and Webster Avenues. On a few occasions, there were confrontations, and David was not one to back away, although his mother disapproved of such encounters. But in everything he did, David was "very enthusiastic, a live wire," according to Art Rooney. On the less active side, Lawrence played the piano quite well and Sundays found him as an altar boy in Saint Mary's. Even from his youngest days, David had a bit of flair about him. He became widely known as the "cart boy." Every time there was a parade, which according to Leonard Stabile, a boyhood friend of Lawrence's from Washington Avenue, seemed to be quite frequent at the turn of the century, David would be in the parade, riding in a two-wheeled cart pulled by two white Angora goats. David would wave and smile to the people, almost as if a candidate for office. It is not known whether the Lawrences owned the goats and cart or whether they belonged to neighbors. Still, Pittsburghers began to expect the "cart boy" at every such event.[6]

Each summer, some time was spent on a relative's farm near Wilmerding, Pennsylvania. In 1965, Lawrence recalled, "This corner of Pennsylvania has always been dear to me. It was here . . . that I used to spend a good deal of time as a lad on vacation and where

163

I enjoyed myself so well that the memories are still vivid."[7] Other than trips to Wilmerding, the Lawrences rarely left the Point, except for schooling.

Since Saint Mary Mercy Church had no elementary school, David was enrolled at the city's Duquesne School. Tom Joyce remembers David as an intelligent "young fellow who was always at the top of his class." David left Duquesne School after eight years and enrolled at Saint Mary's High School, on Tunnel Street. His was the first class to graduate from the then two-year commercial curriculum, where Lawrence acquired skills in typing and stenography. David was proud of Saint Mary's, having said in 1965, "I would prefer being recognized, rather, as one of the first graduates, more than sixty years ago, of St. Mary's High School, the first Catholic high school in the Pittsburgh Diocese."[8]

In a more informal way, much of David's education was received at home and in the Point neighborhood. Lawrence remarked, "My family was always Democratic. . . . They always talked politics at home." In addition, William Jennings Bryan had long been a hero in the Lawrence home. Also, Lawrence recalled how when he was very young, his grandmother "told me to make friends with bankers and people with money."[9] It was not surprising that David eventually became involved in politics.

Outside the Lawrence household, David was exposed to the deeply involved emotions of the Irish emigrants over Ireland's fights and aspirations, "the fights more than aspirations. To these Irishmen of that day the past was real and vivid and they made it come alive to me." David became deeply concerned with the struggle of the Irish for freedom and independence. He belonged to Friends of Irish Freedom and the Association for Recognition of the Irish Republic.[10] David listened, studied, sifted information, tested theories of elder Irish spokesmen, and learned much of Irish politics. He appreciated the Irish problems and determined to become involved politically at home in order to preserve the civil rights of which the Irish were deprived in their native land.

At age fourteen, in 1903, David went to work for William J. Brennan as a clerk-stenographer. Brennan and David's father were close friends in politics, which, no doubt, helped David obtain his

164

position. Charles Lawrence knew his son would be well instructed in the basics of the American political system while in Brennan's employ. Brennan, while a machinist for Jones and Laughlin Steel Corporation, studied law at night under the direction of J. K. P. Duff. In 1883, when Brennan was admitted to the bar, he moved into labor law, becoming one of the first labor lawyers in Western Pennsylvania. A Democrat, Brennan served as alderman, councilman, member of the Democratic State Committee, and Allegheny County Democratic treasurer, as well as delegate to nearly every Democratic national convention, starting in 1876. Young David then had a wealth of experience within reach in the person of William Brennan, and David took advantage of a mutual friendship and respect that grew daily. As Brennan's work increased, James P. Kirk was hired, and he and David began what was to be a long-standing friendship and, eventually, a business partnership.[11]

In 1915, Lawrence left Brennan's office and started an insurance business with Sen. Frank Harris. A short time later, Lawrence and Kirk went into the second mortgage business, and later still, Kirk joined Lawrence and Harris in the insurance business. During the twenties, Lawrence bought out his two partners, and although Lawrence had an associate run the company, he remained its president till he died.[12]

With the advent of World War I, David Lawrence, already launched on a business career and active politically, wanted to answer his country's call to arms. Due to poor eyesight, David was passed over by the draft. So he enlisted on September 17, 1918. As Lawrence entrained for Fort Myer, Virginia, a large delegation was on hand from the David L. Lawrence Club, an informal group of Democrats who held Lawrence as their spokesman, to bid him farewell. In the army, Lawrence served under Enoch H. Crowder in the justice adjutant general's Office in Washington, D.C. Lawrence did not like his desk job, and at war's end, Second Lieutenant Lawrence refused to wear his American Legion pin, since he did not help conclude the war.[13]

After the war, Lawrence returned to his business, where, in the early twenties, Lawrence and a group of associates loaned money in pool to purchase stock in the Guffey-Gillespie Oil Company.

Lawrence and his friends had to sue E. N. Gillespie for the loan and in 1929 were awarded $107,919.40 in relief. Shortly thereafter, Lawrence suffered severe setbacks on the stock market, and as a result, he remained conservative in his investments, sticking to public utilities and municipal bonds. Other than the Harris-Lawrence Insurance Company and his personal investments, David Lawrence was not involved in any other enterprise. Allegations that Lawrence owned Allegheny Asphalt and had interests in Cleveland and Virginia racetracks were absolutely false.[14]

David Lawrence must have learned the lessons of politics well from his mentor, William Brennan, and his friend, Joe Guffey. But Brennan always warned Lawrence that marriage and politics mix poorly, if at all. For fourteen favorable political years, Lawrence stood fast by the no-marriage suggestion. Who is to say why Lawrence, at age thirty-two, finally decided to abandon bachelorhood for matrimonial domesticity? Lawrence never told us.

It is not surprising that David Lawrence married a woman from Pittsburgh's North Side. He frequently played ball and managed other sports in the area. It was not unusual for the young men of the Point and Lower Hill sections of Pittsburgh to cross the Allegheny River for physical as well as social recreation. It is generally thought that Lawrence met Alyce Golden in the winter of 1920 at a dance in a North Side social hall. We know little of their courtship except that it included many dances. On June 8, 1921, David Lawrence and Alyce Golden were married in Saint Andrew's Roman Catholic Church, in Pittsburgh. Saint Andrew's has since been disbanded. Anna Mae Lawrence Donahue, Lawrence's second oldest daughter, thinks the couple honeymooned on a boat trip up the Saint Lawrence River.

Alyce Golden Lawrence was born on April 21, 1897. Her parents, John and Anna Golden, native Pittsburghers, ran a liquor business on the North Side. In 1901, John Golden died and his wife was left with nine children, eight girls and one boy. A few years later, Alyce Golden's brother died. Anna Golden, who was reputed to have been a woman of very strong character, carried on her husband's liquor business while rearing her eight surviving girls. Some time before Alyce married, Anna Golden had died, but it is not clear where Alyce made her home after her mother's death and during her courtship with David Lawrence.

After their honeymoon, David and Alyce Lawrence settled in a new home on King Avenue near Highland Park, Pittsburgh. A few years later, Lawrence purchased a farm in Ross Township. It was about twenty acres with a little house on it. Lawrence acquired the farm for his mother and father's use on weekends and as a summer place for the family. The farm remained in Lawrence's possession until his death. In the meantime, as more Lawrence children came, another home on Evaline Street, near Friendship, was purchased. Some time later, a duplex on Winebiddle Street, between Friendship and Harriet Streets, was acquired. Both homes were in the Bloomfield area. Finally, in 1938, a commodious, fourteen-room house on Aiken Avenue, in the Garfield section, became the hub of Lawrence family activities. This home was not sold until six months before Lawrence died.[15]

Just one week after their first wedding anniversary, David and Alyce welcomed their first child, Mary, who was born June 15, 1922. Mary was named after Lawrence's sister, Mary, who had died at the age of twenty-one. Anna Mae Lawrence was born the following year on September 15. She was named for Anna Golden, although it is not clear where her middle name came from. On December 12, 1925, William Joseph Brennan Lawrence arrived. Eventually the William Joseph was dropped and Lawrence's oldest boy was called Brennan in honor of Lawrence's first employer and political mentor. Another boy, David Leo, joined the family on August 28, 1928. Between 1929 and 1939, Alyce Lawrence lost two children at birth. Finally, on March 18, 1939, Gerald Lawrence, the last of the Lawrence children, arrived. Jerry's birth, according to Anna Mae, caused much family discussion over the name. Finally, "Gerald was the name my mother picked out of the blue because she liked the name."

It should be kept in mind that just two years after the Lawrence marriage, a relative moved into the Lawrence household. Gerald Lawrence explains that since his two sisters were born fifteen months apart, Alyce Lawrence asked her sister Helen to help with the babies. Helen stayed for forty-two years. Another sister of Alyce's,

167

Mary, lived with the Lawrences for several years after her policeman husband was killed in the line of duty. Jerry's cousin Jack Fitzgerald, whose parents died when he was twelve or thirteen, was raised by the Lawrences, living with them in the thirties and early forties. "Throughout nearly my mother and dad's whole married life, there were one, two, or three people from the Golden side of the family living in the house."[16]

What is particularly striking here is Lawrence's kindness and generosity toward Jack Fitzgerald. Mr. Fitzgerald once remarked that he owes everything to David and Alyce Lawrence. This is all the more interesting in light of the fact that Lawrence educated two other relatives, Lawrence and Robert Dawes. However, contacts with relatives on the Golden side of the family seem abundant, while contact with those on the Lawrence side appear less frequent.

Gerald Lawrence recalls, "We didn't know his side of the family well at all." In addition to his deceased sister, Mary, Lawrence had two brothers, Isaac and Charles. Charles, a plumber, was not seen too much by the Lawrence family. Isaac, or Ike, was a maintenance man for the county and used to do a lot of work around the Lawrence home. If a fuse blew, David called Duquesne Light. Lawrence used to say his "mechanical ability stopped at winding his watch." He paid dearly for this lack of mechanical skills when he saw the repair bills, which visibly upset him. But he always wanted his home in good order.[17]

Anna Mae saw the family contacts with relatives much the same way. The Lawrence side of the family rarely visited. Isaac, a widower, "used to bring his little boy to play frequently" while he worked. When Lawrence's mother was alive, she was there quite a bit, but she never stayed at the Lawrence home. Even when she broke her leg, she refused to move in, saying no house was big enough for two families. Lawrence was very upset with her, but she was very strong in her beliefs and convictions. "Daddy was much like that too. He was very strong in his beliefs."[18]

Not only was David Lawrence strong in his beliefs, but he also was strict in raising his children. It certainly was not rigor without love and kind provision, however. Whereas David might have been demanding, Alyce struck a fine balance. More sensitive children would find amelioration with Alyce when David's more stringent view was exercised. And there is no doubt Lawrence provided well for his children. According to Anna Mae, her father was frugal man, but where something worthwhile like education was involved, Lawrence was ample in providing for his family's needs.[19] Lawrence arranged for Anna Mae's education at prestigious Trinity College, in Washington, D.C., a city Lawrence knew he would often spend time in. Mary was sent to Marywood College in Scranton, Pennsylvania. Both Mary and Anna Mae completed their college education in Pittsburgh as a result of the untimely deaths of Brennan and David. Lawrence, because of political demands, was absent a great deal, and he wanted the girls close to their mother.

Even before he lost his two sons, Lawrence was aware of the inroads his absence due to politics made on his family. Thus he always planned the holidays at home. When the children were young, Thanksgiving always found Grandmother Lawrence and Alyce's two sisters and brother-in-law present for the great feast. Alyce Lawrence was an excellent cook and closed her kitchen to outside culinary help. As older family members passed away, just the immediate family, which included Helen Golden and for a time Jack Fitzgerald, was present. After the girls married, the crowd began to swell once again. Easter was celebrated in about the same fashion, but Christmas was something very special.

Anna Mae remembers Christmas at home as a festive occasion with an early-afternoon dinner. The youngest child opened presents first. Lawrence opened his last and was delighted with specially chosen "funny" gifts. Following dinner, Lawrence would take his gifts upstairs "like a little boy" and try them on or examine them.[20]

Gerald Lawrence, sixteen years younger than Anna Mae, gives us a glimpse of Christmas on Aiken Avenue in the later years. It was a very special day because the whole family gathered. But it was always a very sentimental time for Alyce Lawrence, and sometimes her emotions dampened the festivities, although not frequently. Decorating the house was a big thing for her. There were five Christmas trees; every tabletop, mantlepiece, and chandelier was covered with ornaments. Doorsills were ringed with Christmas cards, and every bedroom was adorned. Alyce Lawrence loved giv-

169

ing, and everyone had to get ten or twelve packages to open on Christmas Day. She always spent more money than she was given, planning to pay the overages with money David always gave her for Christmas. David loved sharing his wife's generosity.

One year, Jerry and his father decided Mrs. Lawrence's Christmas gift would be a formal picture of President Kennedy and Mr. and Mrs. Lawrence, taken in the Kennedy limousine at the Army-Navy football game. Jerry recalls how Alyce, positioned next to her husband during the gift exchange around the dining-room table, would graciously accept her usual money gift under the table from Lawrence. "So, he reached over and handed her this box and she got a look on her face, what the hell is this; where's my money?" It was a father-and-son joke, but Mrs. Lawrence loved the picture and later received the usual cash to pay off her Christmas debts.

As time passed, numbers at the Lawrence Christmas dinner grew. The Lawrence children and grandchildren would be there, along with other relatives and some Christian Brothers when Jerry was in high school. Dinner was followed by the traditional trip to the cemeteries, where Lawrence placed wreaths on his sons' and parents', brother's, and grandparents' graves, as well as those of Jimmy Kirk, his former business partner, and Judge Primo Columbus.[21]

David Lawrence loved his children dearly. The gruff exterior hid from outsiders his deep and abiding affection for his family. Lawrence literally boiled with bitterness and resentment when Alyce or the children suffered public humiliation because of his political involvement. And the personal tragedy that struck the Lawrence household separated the surviving children. Both girls were much older than Jerry, and although there was love and care among them, the girls married and moved out. Anna Mae recalls how shortly before her wedding, she went to her father's office. They got to talking, and Lawrence began to cry. Anna Mae was really hurt by her father's reaction, but ascribes her dad's emotion to their unusual father-daughter relationship, which she described as "extremely close." However, once Lawrence composed himself, he accepted the situation, saying he realized Anna Mae had to make a life for herself. From then on, Lawrence was "great" about the wedding.[22]

Within a very short period of time, both Lawrence daughters were married. Thus, over a span of about four years, the immediate family was reduced to four: David, Alyce, Jerry, and Helen Golden. Jerry was starting school and David and Alyce were, in effect, beginning over again with Jerry. They were both near their fifties, and Jerry's youth spanned David Lawrence's most significant public, political years. Jerry talks about those years as lonely times for him. As the only living son, he felt overprotected. For the first five years of schooling, Jerry was enrolled at Mount Mercy Academy, a private school on the campus of Mount Mercy College. Since the students were transported back and forth from school, Jerry had little contact with neighborhood children of his age. After five years at Mount Mercy, Jerry was sent to Saint Paul's Cathedral Grade School. His aunt taught in the high-school division at Saint Paul's. This time he commuted by trolley. Again, he was, in a sense, out of the neighborhood activities. By the time he was ready for high school, he had few acquaintances, although after four years at Central Catholic High School, the situation was somewhat improved.

Jerry had the impression that his father regretted not having spent more time with the two sons he lost. "So, he made a great point of taking me along with him, not only to public affairs around the city, but traveling with him as much as possible." They went to the racetrack, ball games, dinners, picnics, and trips. "In the early stages I didn't realize what I was doing or where I was going because I was so young." Jerry attended Truman's inaugural at age nine and was to Europe twice, once at age eleven and again at age twelve.

At home, Lawrence rarely if ever discussed politics, especially when Jerry was young. Lawrence's workday was over when he went home. He never carried a briefcase home, would not take business calls except in case of emergency, and did not make business calls. On a rare occasion, he might rehearse a speech. He usually arrived home around six-thirty after a steam, shower, and some sunlamp at the Y. Jerry remembers calling Lawrence one day when he was in the seventh grade. Jerry wanted to discuss General MacArthur's firing. Jerry had been impressed with the nun's argument that Truman was wrong: "I don't remember his exact words, but he let me know in very short order that Truman was right and MacArthur was

171

wrong, and that's all there was to it." Lawrence never minded Jerry calling him at the office as long as it was not for something silly. "He had no time for silliness." This did not mean Lawrence was serious or that you had to be formal with him all the time. He liked to joke, but never to the point of aimlessness.

Once Lawrence finished dinner at home, prior to the advent of television, he read widely and listened to the radio. "He did a great deal of reading in history." Lawrence felt this a good way to supplement his education, which he always considered somewhat lacking. On radio, he loved Jack Benny, Charlie McCarthy, and Fibber Magee and Molly. With the advent of television, Lawrence became somewhat of a TV fanatic. But every night, before going to bed, Lawrence would read. His light was out, however, by eleven o'clock. Sometimes, if he had no appointments, Lawrence would not rise till nine and would then have a very light breakfast and get to the office a little before ten. This routine was about the same in Harrisburg, except Lawrence missed the card-playing cronies who used to gather in the late afternoon before going to the Y. And Harrisburg was a more confining place, because of the absence of professional sports. "Harrisburg is a pretty desolate place to live, especially Indiantown Gap."

In his first year as governor, Lawrence lived in the old governor's mansion in Harrisburg. The house was ancient and hardly functional. Lawrence determined to do something by eliminating an appropriation for a new mansion that dated back to the James administration, in 1941, and appointing a commission to study the question. Meanwhile, the old mansion was sold and Lawrence removed to Indiantown Gap. The commission first suggested an apartment be built in one of the new state office buildings then under construction. Lawrence was miffed at this, feeling the commission chose an expedient because it was an election year. He probably would have been more satisfied if they had decided to build a new mansion and get it over with.

Lawrence's interest in the mansion was out of character. "He had no personal desires to live pretentiously or have a big car." When the Lawrences purchased a family car, Lawrence wanted a "Ford or Chevy," whereas Alyce preferred a Cadillac or an Oldsmobile convertible. "She had a fixation for convertibles." Lawrence won the argument and simplicity in auto acquisition prevailed. When Jerry was graduated from college, Lawrence said, "Buy yourself a new car; that car is getting pretty old. . . . Get a Ford and get a black one." Jerry kept the new car just a year and then purchased a convertible. His father "loved it." Jerry would drive his dad between Harrisburg and Pittsburgh, and the elder Lawrence wanted the top down all the way.

In addition to being a person with a simple life-style, Lawrence was a very religious man. Lawrence regularly attended Saint Mary's at the Point, in the parish where he was baptized. It was always the twelve o'clock mass, and Lawrence ushered: "That's one of the things I recall, the screaming on Sunday mornings because we were going to be late. He could not stand being late."[23]

In 1957, the Lawrence household was reduced once more when Jerry left for college. Anna Mae points out that it was a very difficult time for Alyce Lawrence and the family empathized with her. However, "we all felt that this was very good for Jerry. We felt he needed to get away. She was very possessive of Jerry. When Jerry graduated from college he remained out of Pittsburgh. He's never really come back since."[24] Jerry attended La Salle University, in Philadelphia, which was not that far away. Moreover, he kept in contact by phone and spent the holidays and summers at home.

During Jerry's college days, David Lawrence was nominated and elected governor of Pennsylvania. Through the campaign and after, Jerry was somewhat active in politics insofar as his situation allowed. At other times, some of his activities, although normal for college students, drew much public comment because he was the governor's son, and Lawrence was certainly aware of this. Still, he worried about Jerry, but was not condemnatory. He used to say, "I wish Jerry would straighten out. I wish he'd meet some nice girl and get married." He thought marriage would solve all Jerry's problems, which were really not that significant.[25] Actually, Lawrence became very concerned when any of the children were in trouble.

Once, while Lawrence was visiting Israel, Jerry was given a speeding ticket by a Pennsylvania state trooper. When Lawrence returned from Israel, there was still discussion of Jerry's speeding ticket. A technicality involving a required check on the police vehicle that was used to clock Jerry's speed had arisen. The charges could be dropped. But Lawrence interrupted and said, "He violated the law, he will get no license, and there will be no interference to get him anything. He will just do without his license."[26] And that was that. Jerry mailed his license to the Motor Vehicle Bureau, another opportunity for media comment, and went without the permit, although it did not cramp his style.

As Jerry moved through college, an abiding interest that Lawrence fostered in Jerry's younger days continued apace. Just before the Fall semester examinations in 1960, Lawrence wrote Jerry: "I certainly hope you are bearing down for the mid-year exams and not letting the trip to Florida, basketball and all those other collateral things, take up too much of your mind space."[27] One month later, with examinations over and the second semester just underway, Lawrence wrote Jerry that he heard the Penn-La Salle game on the radio and thought of Jerry. "I was assuming you were there and eating your heart out." In Lawrence's opinion, La Salle "had thrown the game away."[28] Lawrence had a way of twitting his son so that Jerry's ego would not inflate. This was part of the reality he felt his son needed as he moved through his formative years.

On June 6, 1961, Lawrence's fondest hopes for Jerry were realized. Lawrence, speaking at Jerry's graduation, told how he went to the chapel in Mercy Hospital the night Jerry was born. He thanked God that both mother and baby were healthy. "I said another prayer that night. I prayed that God would let me live to see my youngest child through college. He has answered my prayer today. I can only hope that those of you whose sons are degreed with my son have as much happiness and gratitude in your hearts as I have in mine."[29]

While in college, Jerry met Rita Duffy of Willow Grove, Pennsylvania, whom he would eventually marry. Meanwhile, he began work in the Philadelphia area, which may have been a disappointment for Lawrence. Jerry at one time was very interested in getting involved in politics. Lawrence's friend Frank Ambrose mentioned this to Lawrence, and his reaction was, "Well, Frank there's no vacancy. He's too young anyhow." In 1966, State Sen. Joseph Sarraf died and his place had to be filled. Again Ambrose suggested

174

that Jerry run. "Jerry has been dying to get into politics for a long time. This is a great opportunity for you to run Jerry. He would be running from this ward . . . he couldn't lose." Lawrence answered, "The SOB just transferred his registration to Philadelphia."[30] With Jerry seemingly out of Pittsburgh for good, new directions appeared in the Lawrence family experience.

Two years after Jerry went to college, David and Alyce moved to the Harrisburg area for the duration of Governor Lawrence's term. Still, the house on Aiken Avenue was kept within the family. Since Helen Golden was now alone, Mrs. Lawrence hired a couple to live in an apartment that had been set up on the third floor. Alyce returned home frequently, and the entire family was there for Thanksgiving, Christmas, and Easter. When the Lawrences came back from Harrisburg for good, Mrs. Lawrence, who had developed osteoporosis, had to spend a lot of time in bed. As a result, a house-keeper was hired.

When Lawrence accepted a position in the Kennedy adminis-tration, Mrs. Lawrence did not go to Washington. Since she was alone most of the time, Alyce wanted to sell the house; David ob-jected: "But she was very vehement, and he finally conceded. . . . I really think mostly for her." The Lawrences then moved to Chatham Center, where they occupied a three-bedroom apartment.[31] The Aiken Avenue home was sold in June 1966, and the following November David Lawrence died.

Gerald Lawrence, around 1960, wrote of his father as he saw him while home. Jerry said his father was a self-sufficient man who liked people and, at the same time, enjoyed solitude, especially with a good book. Mrs. Lawrence used to say, "He'll eat anything you put in front of him," although his favorite dish was chicken and dumplings. He bristled with energy and personality when with young people, and he loved to romp with his grandchildren. He got a lot of mileage out of everything. Jerry remembered his using "the same old Gilette safety razor" as long as he could remember. Every election night, Jerry remembered his father saying over and over again, "It looks good . . . it looks good." Finally, Lawrence enter-tained very little, seemingly reserving most of his social life for his family.[32]

At one time, Lawrence said he purchased the big house on Aiken Avenue to entertain. At the end of the Earle administration, he thought he would have a lot of social obligations. But something changed his thinking. Perhaps his indictments, the trials, or the deaths of his sons made him rethink his social obligations. He never had parties at the house, and people would stop by to visit very, very rarely. Some might stop if they saw Lawrence on the porch, but other than that, his friends and political colleagues respected his domestic sanctuary.[33] Even with those very close to him in politics, there was little in the way of social contact, and this may have been by design. Genevieve Blatt, a Lawrence protégé, had few social contacts with Lawrence. Friday night was family dinner night, and Saturday David and Alyce usually went out for dinner and dancing. No one ever intruded. On Sundays Lawrence went from Mass at St. Mary's directly to City Hall or the State Office Building, and he would see people all afternoon.[34]

Even when Lawrence was out of town, his family was included in his social life. When in New York City, Lawrence frequently dined with Mayor Robert Wagner. He impressed Wagner as a man who loved his family. "He was the kind father and grandfather that you would expect of David Lawrence, which would be loving, almost doting over his grandchildren. He was proud of his family and happy to be with them."[35]

Despite his many favorable and strong characteristics, Lawrence was a human being with needs. And for a man whose political life took him away from the family circle so frequently, it would be foolish to suggest that Lawrence totally abstained from socializing or relaxation outside his home. Moreover, Lawrence spent time with nonpolitical organizations that provided a social outlet. As early as 1912, Lawrence was associated with the Fraternal Order of Eagles, and he was one of the organizers of Eagles in Pennsylvania.[36] He had almost a passion for card-playing, according to Frank Ambrose. "The first time I played with him I beat him the first two games, and I didn't want the half-dollar. He said, 'When you play me, when I lose I pay, and when you lose you pay.' So that's the way it was from then on."[37] Huck Fenrich remembers Lawrence once told Patsy McGheen, "Your mind is not on the game and you are no competition at all. I don't have any fun if you are not any competition."[38]

Walter Giesey states that Lawrence would relax after a difficult day by playing cards with friends like Frank Ambrose, the Fagenbaums, the Danas, and the Kirks. These were Mrs. Lawrence's friends also. "Still, Lawrence never mixed his social life with his political or governmental life."[39]

Lawrence, then, was able to meet his social needs outside the family in such a way that the political demands on his time mixed well with his few, relatively simple recreational forms. A Dutchtown "sluggfest" was both a night out and political fence-tending wrapped in one, a seeming contradiction to Giesey's assertion about not mixing politics and socializing. At the same time, a card game could be initiated with little trouble in any available time: while waiting for a meeting to begin; on a train or plane; while waiting for a late delegation; or during some extra minutes while secretaries cleaned up final correspondence for the day. Enjoying these respites the way he did enabled Lawrence to take a generous slice of weekend time at home, while, at the same time, remaining on top of things at the office. And even as Lawrence became more and more involved in national politics, his simple social needs could be adequately met and family devotion maintained.

Family concerns became an even higher priority for Lawrence following his vindication in the courts. He seemed to turn more toward his family, almost as if to make it up to them for the humiliation suffered. But whatever dreams he had for his two daughters and three sons were shattered on April 19, 1942. His sons—Brennan, sixteen, and David, thirteen—were killed in an auto accident. An Associated Press wire-service report from Portersville, Pennsylvania, stated. . . . "when they tried to pass another car on a downgrade on Route 19, 30 miles north of Pittsburgh, their car spun around in the road, headed backward into a tree, and overturned. George G. Allenbaugh of Wordsworth, Ohio, driver of the other car, summoned an ambulance and notified State Motor Police. The dead were removed to a Zelienople funeral home, where Edward McCabe, Pittsburgh undertaker and cousin of Lawrence, made the identification."[40] For the second time in his career, Lawrence's family had been thrust into the public eye, this time in a sorrow that would mark Lawrence till his last days.

Joseph Barr was in the Lawrence home immediately before the accident and was still there when the news arrived. He recalled that the Lawrence boys and a group of friends came in from a ball game and that Mrs. Lawrence fed them "all the things kids like." The boys went to the Lawrence third floor after eating to relax. Mrs. Lawrence had allowed Brennan and David to build a sort of clubhouse there. The Lawrences and their friends went out to dinner and, upon returning, played cards, thinking the boys were upstairs. A call came from the business manager of the Saint Francis Hospital, who told Barr he heard the Lawrence boys had been in an accident. At first, it appeared the Lawrence family auto was outside; actually it was Barr's car. He had the exact same model. Mrs. Lawrence then realized she had given the boys permission to go for a ride. Then Lawrence called the state police, who confirmed the accident and reported two killed. Lawrence asked the names of the living. "I remember he turned to his wife and told her the boys were gone." For a while, pandemonium prevailed, but soon things calmed and Lawrence, Barr, and James Kirk went to the hospital in Zelienople and checked on the living. One of Lawrence's greatest concerns on that trip was to determine whether or not one of his boys was driving. Neither had been driving. The auto rammed backward into a tree after going out of control and down a steep incline. The Lawrence brothers, seated in the rear of the auto, caught the worse of the impact.[41] The lives of David and Alyce Lawrence and their surviving children were inexorably changed.

Anna Mae Lawrence feels that her mother never got over the shock, but that her father "threw himself harder into political life than I had ever known him to do." Things, according to Anna Mae, "were rough at home." However, one "saving grace" was Jerry, who was then three years old. Still, it remained difficult for Alyce Lawrence to cope with a young child. Her daughters had to argue with her to allow Jerry to do normal things for boys his age. Later, when it came time for him to drive a car, the memory was revived.[42]

Lawrence wanted his sons waked at home. The bodies of David and Brennan reposed three days and nights in the large family

178

residence on Aiken Avenue. Flower tributes covered every wall and floor of the fourteen rooms, and over three days, about 2,000 people paid their respects. Lawrence stayed upstairs most of the time. About twelve-thirty at night, he and a few close friends would go for a short walk in the neighborhood. But "he never did come down to meet the public." Hundreds of people stood outside the jammed Saint Lawrence O'Toole Church during the funeral service. When the Lawrence family returned home from the cemetery, they discovered a strange thing. People had gone into the house and taken the flowers, and "there were petals strewn all up and down the street."[43]

That afternoon, accompanied by a few close friends, Lawrence left his home and went downtown to Democratic headquarters. Lawrence went into his office alone, while the others remained in the outer room. James Kirk suggested that they go in and ask Lawrence if he wanted to play cards. The others were shocked at the thought, but Kirk insisted, so they asked Lawrence if he wanted to play. He did not reply, but after a short time he came out of his office with a card deck and the score card. "And we played four hours that afternoon, and never a word did he say about the kids, and, of course, neither did we mention it."[44]

In the months immediately following the accident, Mrs. Lawrence was despondent; she frequently wept and talked about the accident. Lawrence, although he would mention the boys' names from time to time, rarely mentioned the accident. Even though Lawrence buried himself in work, he found the pervading sense of loss at home very difficult to bear. David and Alyce were marked for life, and their future would never allow them to forget their misfortune.

Naturally, Lawrence's friends and colleagues saw the impact in a different way. Art Rooney remembers Lawrence worked harder and traveled more around the state, "going places that maybe he wouldn't have gone had he not been pushing himself at the time."[45] Eddie Leonard recalled being out with the Lawrences one evening and Mrs. Lawrence's saying since she was a woman, people understood how she felt, "but she didn't think anybody ever knew how Dave felt, how he brooded, but no one ever saw him that way."[46] Here the relationship between Alyce and David comes to light.

179

Alyce, of all people, knew the intensity of David's suffering, yet only in this instance was this depth of understanding recorded during those sad days.

Fr. Woody Jones tells how Lawrence would mention the incident in passing from time to time. "It was usually if some nut was driving like maniac to pass him. 'Nobody knows better than I what radar might do. Because we had some recalcitrants in the State Senate like the late George Wade who was opposed to radar.' Little passing remarks like that."[47]

Many years after the accident, Lawrence was talking with Genevieve Blatt, who had just suffered a deep personal tragedy. "He had a picture of the two boys on his desk; and he alluded to the picture and said, 'Just work, Gen; Just keep at work.' And I know that's what he did with those two boys. He almost worked too hard just to crowd the thought of it out."[48]

In the late fifties, while campaigning for Adlai Stevenson, Lawrence chatted with party worker Rosemary Plesset, who was driving him to a political gathering. "He talked about the event that night, that occasion, and how he felt about this and about the vagaries of accidents. They were sitting in what he considered the safest part of the car, yet they were the ones who were killed."[49] A few years later, when he was governor, he attended a wake in the Zelienople area. He pointed out the tree that was struck by the auto in which the boys died. This was uncharacteristic of Lawrence, but as he grew older, he may have found it easier or a source of relief to mention the incident. Finally, David and Alyce did not let an opportunity go by without offering condolences to other parents who had lost children in accidents or illness. From 1942 till they died, the Lawrences sent hundreds of messages of sympathy and empathy to distraught parents across the United States, encouraging them and suggesting means to assuage their grief. On August 12, 1963, Lawrence wrote President Kennedy; "Years ago, Mrs. Lawrence and I lost two of our sons and we came to know how deeply such tragedy can affect parents. It is with this knowledge that we express to you and your wife our sympathy and remember you in our prayers."[50]

Tragedies have a way of seeming simple to those not affected, but of becoming deep-rooted and complex for those immediately involved. The latter was true for the Lawrences. The return from college of her daughters and the presence of a surviving son were not sufficient to eliminate the dejection that Alyce experienced. Even in retrospect, it is difficult to judge how a person should survive the assault on one's senses and feelings in such an eventuality. But that Alyce Lawrence was not able entirely to cope with her misfortune is really not so unusual. Still, as weeks and months dragged by after the funeral, it became painfully evident to David that in addition to the loss of two sons, he would have to carry a distraught, somewhat changed spouse. It was a double burden for him. And indeed it became a part of his life. As he pushed himself to forget, his home life was a constant reminder of what the children's death did to their mother. Inevitably, these changes affected Lawrence's daily affairs with party and public. His staff could sometimes sense upset, yet over the years Lawrence remained intensely loyal to his Alyce.

It was not too long after the boys died that Mary and Anna Mae were married. Gerald Lawrence, the only remaining child at home, grew up in a difficult situation. Mrs. Lawrence developed a drinking problem. This really disturbed David. It was a weakness he couldn't stand in anyone, and as a result, they had "vicious" arguments. Still, Lawrence remained intensely loyal, and he would not tolerate anyone talking about Alyce's problems. He was very devoted to her. Jerry remembered that one night someone was pestering Mrs. Lawrence at the Pittsburgh Athletic Club when Lawrence was mayor and "he decked the guy." However, once these two strong-willed individuals argued, they were difficult to get back on track.

As time passed, the public became aware of the Lawrence predicament. Some people, particularly in the Garfield section where the Lawrences lived, "were always trying to protect her [Mrs. Lawrence] if they found out she was out someplace."[51] Moreover, no one ever attempted to take political advantage of the situation. According to Frank Hawkins, "It was just one of those unfortunate things and nobody saw any reason or purpose to try to exploit it. . . . I think it would have been in bad taste to try to exploit her."[52]

Nonetheless, the problem at times created a substantial strain on David. Sometimes he would become so exasperated he would pack a bag and go downtown to the William Penn Hotel. On some occasions, Mrs. Lawrence would go down to City Hall. Frank Ambrose remembered, "When she came into the building I took her out the back door, put her in a cab and brought her up here. And my wife would sit here with her a couple of hours and that was it."[53] Evidently, the people of Pittsburgh and Lawrence's many friends and acquaintances provided sufficient support in a delicate situation. Actually, it may have been easier on him, given the nature of his public, had he been more open and patient with the condition.

There were many who felt Lawrence should have been more understanding. Mrs. Lawrence's problem admittedly puzzled, annoyed, angered, and occasionally embarrassed him. From a woman's point of view, "in his singlemindedness," Lawrence sometimes inconvenienced others unintentionally and "his wife was one of those who suffered from his total involvement in politics." Mrs. Lawrence was left almost seven nights a week with the responsibility of raising a family. Rosemary Plesset felt "she was probably not equipped to do so." Lawrence dated Alyce's problems from the time of the tragedy, but others felt the difficulty existed before that and "broke out more severely at that time." Her loneliness was difficult to manage, and although Lawrence wanted his wife to become more active in some of the charities he was interested in, as well as some facets of his political career, Alyce Lawrence did not get involved.[54]

If there was ever an alter ego in David Lawrence's life, it was his secretary—executive assistant, Walter Giesey, who worked closely with Lawrence from 1950 through 1966. Giesey remembered, "You would know something was going on at home." Anna Mae was usually the intermediary, and Giesey had the impression that the settlement involved acting as if nothing happened when Lawrence returned home. At the same time, Giesey contrasts David as outgoing and forward-moving, whereas Alyce was "shy and retiring. The compatibility that existed became strained at best . . . although I always had the feeling that there was a deep affection between the two."

When these domestic problems flared, they affected Lawrence's disposition. His somewhat gruff nature would become more pronounced. His office staff knew when this was going on. "It was always something you would prefer you didn't have to go through. Whatever kind of cordiality he had vanished during those periods." Naturally, people coming in for appointments did not notice the storm warnings, but coming out of Lawrence's office, some would say, "Gee, he is in a hell of a bad mood today, isn't he?" Of course, staff would nod or wink agreement, but never felt explanations were in order.[55]

It is important to understand here that David and Alyce Lawrence shared a heavy burden in their domestic difficulties. Despite this, both within and without the family circle, the two were able to provide substantial contributions to their respective occupations—Mrs. Lawrence in the home and Mr. Lawrence in his party and public offices. Moreover, in the evolution of their family relationships, an abundance of happiness came to the Lawrences in their later years in the persons of their grandchildren.

When Gerald Lawrence was asked if the grandchildren in any way assuaged his mother's grief, he surmised, "I think they did to a degree. My mother used to say that when my brothers were killed, my sister, Anna Mae, supposedly said to her 'I'll get married someday and bring you two boys. . . . ' They loved having the kids around. And they looked forward to it, my dad particularly." Eventually, the Lawrences and Donahues would share dinner every other Friday in each other's homes.[56] Once the grandchildren were on the scene, the weekly family gathering again was a significant event for Lawrence. Cronies tell of his making the stoutest efforts to be in Pittsburgh on Fridays or Sundays so that he could participate in these family celebrations. It was a time when he could forget the burdens, responsibilities, disappointments, and bitterness that were frequently his fare in public and political life. These celebrations were a tonic for Lawrence and helped strengthen a family circle taxed with many pressures. That these were happy times for Lawrence, his wife, and the grandchildren is revealed by David Donahue, a Lawrence grandson.

David, admittedly the favorite grandson, was impressed in his early days with the pomp and circumstance surrounding his grandfather. Later he grew to appreciate the positions Lawrence held. Frequently, Lawrence would have the grandchildren to his office; then they would be off to a sports event or some other appropriate entertainment. Nearly every other weekend, one or more grandchildren would visit the Lawrence home. Saturdays would be spent with Mrs. Lawrence. Sundays all would go to Saint Mary's at the Point for mass. A big dinner usually followed. Mrs. Lawrence's sisters were always in the house. "They were a lot of fun—there was always great laughter in the home when we went there as children." Before her illness, Mrs. Lawrence was very active, taking the grandchildren swimming and horseback riding. Mrs. Lawrence loved horses; it was not till later that her grandson found out she also bet on them. David remembers, "Always the accent was on enjoying yourself and getting the most out of life that you could." Lawrence was, of course, limited in his availability to the grandchildren, but when he was home he would sit and converse with them and play as best he could.

David Lawrence's big day with his grandchildren was Christmas. "He had an amazing love for Christmas." The grandchildren used to buy presents for him—a difficult job, since he had everything he needed. Lawrence was watched anxiously as he opened the gifts, and at some he would "sort of scowl, saying, "What am I going to do with this kind of thing?" This was all in fun, and Lawrence enjoyed himself immensely. Gifts for the grandchildren were piled to the ceiling. Dinner would follow opening the gifts and the inevitable trip to the cemeteries to "remember those people whom I [David Donahue] never knew, but whom you sort of felt a sense of closeness to because of those visits."

As David Donahue grew older, his relationship with his grandfather matured. Whereas in the early years they would talk mostly of athletics and family, later they would discuss politics, what was happening in school, and what young people were thinking, and their attitudes, "some of which he could not understand." Both David and his grandfather enjoyed musicals and would always attend a few in New York. "Since I was not interested in athletics as he was, he sort of bent over backwards to find things that I was interested in, including books we both read and T.V." Finally, when David spent a lot of time with the elder Lawrence in Washington, they discussed David's future, as well as Pittsburgh's and the nation's. "He was always thinking ahead and trying to visualize what would come even after he was gone, both for the family, and for the city, state, and nation that he worked for all those years."[57]

For Lawrence, then, the warmth and happiness that were his grandchildren to a degree dispelled the chill of his sons' deaths and filled a void that enabled both him and Mrs. Lawrence to secure mutual happiness, love, and affection in shared relationships with their grandchildren. It is difficult to say whether both David and Alyce Lawrence were ever fully at rest over the loss of their sons. Each in a sense went a different way; Mrs. Lawrence settled into domesticity, whereas David occupied himself with politics, friends, and goals.

Almost to a person, Lawrence's acquaintances verbalize their memory of him as an individual large in body, mind, and spirit. It was the latter two qualities that seemed to motivate the great force and power that was David Lawrence. If on the surface, Lawrence seemed almost cocksure of himself in advancing toward political goals, it was because his mind had already absorbed insights, perceptions, understandings, analysis, argumentation, and decision. Lawrence, in a word, had developed an attitude of mind that was his politics, a philosophy he believed in strongly, convinced it would best serve his country, state, county, city, and party.

In the politics of party, Lawrence was firmly attached to the American two-party system. For Lawrence, the foundation of the two-party system was cooperation, and where some of his most devoted followers were unsteady, Lawrence stood firm in the belief that a viable, dual-party system was good for the body politic. "The Republicans will not surrender their identity or wipe out their differences with Democrats by helping Pennsylvania to develop a sound fiscal program any more than John Foster Dulles destroyed his political career by serving in the State Department of Harry Truman and Dean Acheson." Lawrence saw political differences as basically American, which in his mind constituted a religiously, ethnically, and economically diverse society. "But that diversity does not separate us from one another. Rather it provides a freedom to have differing views while we are united in a common citizenship and a common allegiance."[58] Lawrence, then, saw party politics, particularly the challenge phase, as essential to the American system as well as the American community. Without the tension between the

185

two or among several parties, politics was emasculated.

This element of distinction readily demonstrates why Lawrence was such a strong partisan Democrat. It was his duty to bring all his powers to bear toward advancing the Democratic cause, and as Lawrence understood it, you had to be partisan to get elected. Once elected, Lawrence believed he was obliged to serve all the people. "First, I am concerned with what is best for my community, my state, my country. Secondly, I am concerned with what is best for the party."[59] But Lawrence did not believe this applied only to himself and his political colleagues. The very basis for good citizenship in the United States was active interest in the affairs of one's party. This meant every citizen should be well versed in government at all levels as well as international affairs, maintain a "full and active" interest in government, vote at every election, share the burden of government through taxes, respect all public authority, be active in community functions, and be an active church member regardless of denomination.[60] Good citizenship was a full-time job for idealist Lawrence.

Another idealist and a longtime friend of Lawrence, Msgr. Charles Owen Rice, tagged Lawrence a "pragmatic idealist." Lawrence always served well the causes he believed in. "He . . . believed in power politics and was a frank partisan. Within Democratic ranks, Lawrence had a special group of followers," which he tended with care and some stern disciplne." Ever the party man and "a compromiser of ambitions," Lawrence would pull himself and his faction back for the good of the organization at large. Quick to reward the faithful, he was equally as swift in blocking those who tried to "move up" without serving their time. "Enemies within the party were objects of his private scorn, but publicly he observed the amenities as well as the realities. . . . He coexisted with men who hated him and whom he certainly did not love."[61] As a practical politician, he looked with disfavor on boat-rockers, yet extended himself to the utmost for party people. Moreover, in his belief that good politics involved the community's welfare, Lawrence "was able to rise above the drudgery of City Hall when it came to improvement of the Commonwealth."[62] This was the primary reason for government, the common good. *Government* and *commonweal* were synonymous in the Lawrence dictionary. Thus we see his abiding attention to and concentrated care with the politics of government.

Speaking before the Deborah Grand Chapter, Order of the Eastern Star, Lawrence reminded his listeners, "Government is everyone's concern today and the payment for government every one's obligation." The obligation was different in degree depending on one's station in life. Involvement in politics had to be pursued on the ward and district, the township, borough, and city levels. "Politics becomes a good, strong, effective instrument for decent government only when it is given these qualities at the lowest possible level." Local government was the key that opened the door to effective government for the community's benefit, while, at the same time, serving as the focus of political power. Lawrence constantly hammered away at the significance of participation in local politics and government, ". . . . for there is the strange idiosyncrasy in American life that whereas everyone ought to care about government, the field of politics is somehow beneath the dignity of the spiritually elevated and the socially inclined." For Lawrence, good government was rooted in good politicians and the latter were simply good citizens "who are determined that good government and good citizenship are the opposite sides of the same coin."[63]

Pragmatist that he was, Lawrence recognized that talent in government had to be equitably rewarded. "Government employees, on the average, are not paid the type salary that would create an incentive for able young people to enter government service." A major step toward relieving the situation would be a change in the direction of American education whereby young people were trained for civil service "at all levels of government."[64] This was a constantly recurring theme in the Lawrence philosophy. Without decrying the past, Lawrence urged the people to look into the future of government by encouraging the nation's youth "to involve themselves in politics." He believed that such youth interest and involvement were the "best assurance of a better politics, better government, and a better America." Wherever Lawrence went in the country, he took every opportunity to address young people. The message was always the same: get interested; get involved in politics. On one occasion, when Lawrence was not quite sure whether or not

187

he could secure tickets for the 1964 Democratic convention that his grandnephew had requested, Lawrence reminded the boy's father "that should not deter him from making the effort to crash the gate."[65] Lawrence was deadly serious. He never wanted to discourage any interested young person and gladly offered them a challenge. Moreover, Lawrence saw that out of an active, highly motivated youth the future nation would cull its leaders.

If Lawrence was staunch in his conviction that the liturgy of American government and politics involved total community participation, his creed in the gospel of leadership was perhaps firmer. As he saw the system, Lawrence was convinced that the multitudes expected elected officials "to exert political leadership as well as administrative direction." The art of politics and the science of administration were, in the minds of the people, to be well blended through leadership exercising the commandments of good government for the common good. Admittedly, according to Lawrence, the practice of leadership demanded courage, and he was nonplussed over the fact that "men often act more rapidly out of fear than they do out of hope." The Lawrence experience was that things men most often feared seldom happened. "I have always found that the ability to make hard decisions and to provide resolute leadership, even in matters of great arguments and disagreement, had far less risk to it than the consciousness of contentious uncertainty and inaction itself."[66] Competence in public office, in the Lawrence view, called for a significant measure of leadership input. Coupled with competent business leaders, the limits to which leadership within the community can be exercised for its own good are without bounds. With counsel from labor, education, and church as guides, bolstered by a determination to see the undertaking through, despite time, risks, petty politics, temporary disappointments, and harassments, the combined political and business leadership are enabled to accomplish the most grandiose goals. However, since leadership in the United States is exercised in a free society, it is necessary that all citizens "engage in a continuing dialogue with their elected officials." In this way, although more often than not this colloquy proves difficult for both parties, freedom and the highest common good are achieved for the community.[67] Moreover, Lawrence was convinced that the United States during its history, was singularly blessed in the great recorded examples of individual and group accomplishments, a chronicle of singular importance for the young American mind.[68]

The Lawrence stress on youth should not be construed as narrow. If anything, for Lawrence, experience was the basis for learning our political and governmental system well. He did not accept the adage of discarding the old. This, in the Lawrence philosophy, was a tremendous waste of commonwealth resources. The elder statesman, the experienced politician, had much to offer the community. "It is said that one is as old as he feels. I would rather say that you are as young as your faith and as old as your doubts. You are as young as your self-confidence and as old as your fears. You are as young as your hope and as old as your despair."[69] Just two years before his death, Lawrence chided Richardson Dilworth, former mayor of Philadelphia, for referring to Lawrence as a "retired politician." He said, "I am sure that regardless of the years, you will, like myself, never cease to have a full-blown interest in life and politics. It would be ridiculous otherwise."[70] The individual or the body politic must not stop contributing to and participating in its own government. Should the majority thus give up their birthright, then, according to Lawrence, the people would suffer inexorably.

After leadership, Lawrence saw the politician's duty to his people as the essence of the art of government. Concern "about our fellow citizens, an interest for their rights and opportunities, and a commitment to human and community progress" were elemental in the complex institution called politics. Moreover, in the Lawrence view, it was in local government that the politician had the "grass roots advantage of being close to the people. You can see the problems with your own eyes and measure your progress in solving them right on the scene." At the same time, Lawrence indicated, local government, compared to state and federal government, had a "more direct impact on everyday activities of our citizenry." In addition, the local unit of government was more manageable, although there were complexities.[71]

Even in local politics and government, Lawrence recognized that there were differences among the people. In many instances,

Lawrence felt, people who needed lobbies, lawyers, and associations lacked them. Thus those in politics should be charitable in assisting the more needy segment of the community. A favorite saying of Lawrence's was "Government should help those that need it most." Aware of his humble origins, Lawrence evolved a political philosophy of action whose enlightened characteristics were "service to people; helping people out." And those who knew Lawrence as a politician experienced the results of the pragmatic political philosophy that was his own. "He brought . . . a sensitivity and a bit of poetry and a huge shot of humanity to his work."[72] At the same time, Lawrence was always quick to remind the people that action on their part was essential. It was a throwback to his concept of dialogue. "You must be vocal at all times on political matters, pro or con, voicing your opinion so that it may be heard by those who govern. Governors and legislators alike are guided in their decisions by the desires of the electorate."[73] The people must not fail to give their leaders direction, voice their concerns, demand legislation where required. Lawrence felt the people's will constituted the true issues for the politician and the questions that elected officials must make the objective of their primary concern.

Lawrence believed one of the main purposes of a political party was to educate the people. Every election provided an opportunity to discuss issues as well as candidates. After attending a political rally one evening where one of the speakers proved inept, Lawrence complained, "My God, it was awful, just awful. Couldn't even tell a story. And a good story has its place. You just do not stand when you are running for office and tell numerous jokes. This is serious business." Another favorite expression of Lawrence's was "Let's get the truth."[74] Further, Lawrence, in admitting his desire to win elections, warned that political victory without "positive programs and progressive performance" was hollow. "It is not just enough to win. We must make certain that every voter understands fully what is at stake. We must make certain they know the issues and they comprehend the consequences of their ballots." The Lawrence methodology in all this was development and presentation of an accurate and realistic assessment of the situation at hand. Intelligence and imagination worked in bringing about the evaluation; "prideful

190

emotion" had no place. "Often there is a wide gap between what must be done and what, at the moment, seems possible of achievement. Even so, the goal should not be shortened nor the solution diluted merely because the odds are against total success."[75] It was this conviction on Lawrence's part that was most severely tested in his regard throughout his political life over the issue of religion and the separation of church and state.

Lawrence's political career, spanning as it did the twenties through the sixties, was, in retrospect, marred by Lawrence's deep conviction that Catholics had little chance of securing a high elective public office. As times changed, Lawrence admittedly did not keep pace on the issue. At the same time, Lawrence never tried to hide his religious convictions as he moved in political circles, and this was not always an easy situation for Lawrence. In September 1956, the Rev. Joseph S. Altany, a Roman Catholic priest serving in Munhall, a Pittsburgh suburb, wrote of his disappointment with Lawrence for not having backed then Senator John Kennedy in 1956 as the party's vice-presidential nominee. Altany felt Catholic hopes, sequestered since the days of Al Smith, had been dashed by Lawrence and the Pennsylvania delegation. "You and Pennsylvania sold us out; it will ever remain a blemish on your record . . . oftentime we do not consider the common good which should be the measure of our activities and interests—you missed the boat, Dave." Lawrence replied that he was shocked at "your undated letter." He could not believe that a man of Altany's educational background could write such a letter. "For you as a Catholic priest, to write the following, 'Dave, I wonder if you are not first a POLITICIAN and only then a CATHOLIC. . . . I am sure the majority of the clergy and Catholic laity feel the same.' I resent your judging me and especially a false judgment. As a Catholic priest you should know better." Reminding Altany that he voted for Al Smith 103 times in 1924 and helped nominate and voted for Smith again in 1928, Lawrence said "I make no apology to you or anyone else for my attitude in public life or as a practical Roman Catholic." Lawrence explained further that he and other Pennsylvania delegates were pledged to Kefauver "long before we went to Chicago or ever knew Senator Kennedy would be a candidate." Moreover, Lawrence explained, "you, like

191

a great many others, who have not studied the problem, were fooled by the fact the southern states were temporarily voting for Kennedy only for the purpose of blocking Kefauver's nomination and causing a deadlock." In closing, Lawrence reminded Altany that "Reckless letters such as yours can do more damage to the Church and to young Catholics trying to make their way in this country than anything else I know of."[76] Even when under attack from his coreligionists, Lawrence stood firm, because he disagreed with those who suggested "that unswerving adherence to Christian principles and ideals is the shortest route to political failure. If failure has come, its cause was not Christian principles but rather something else, most probably inexperience or lack of knowledge and understanding."[77] Here again, Lawrence's passion for truth, particularly in matters dealing with religion, was most effective for Lawrence and his party.

In 1958, Lawrence was questioned about Senator Kennedy's position on certain important matters resting within the sphere of church and state. Lawrence instructed the questioner that a Catholic's loyalty to the Church is in the spiritual realm. "He freely accepts the Church's teachings in matters of faith and morals . . . 'freely accepts' for the Church has no police force." Further, on the question of loyalty to one's country, Lawrence indicated, "the more thoroughly he accepts his faith, the more completely he accepts his responsibilities as an American citizen." For the Catholic, loyalty to the United States was a "responsibility before God." Catholics in public office who would violate their oaths "would be guilty of a most serious sin." At the same time, Lawrence noted, there was no "Catholic line" and a study of political, economic, and social issues would demonstrate no unanimity among Catholics or indeed the hierarchy.

Lawrence then turned to the specific question. "Would a loyal Catholic favor the public schools above the parochial schools?" He felt it an unfair question. Lawrence stated any religious group has the right to educate its children "according to the dictates of their conscience." As a public official, he was aware of his duty to provide the best possible public education. Neglecting such would be "un-American" and, for a Catholic, "a violation of God's law." Lawrence said that because many public officials, judges, statesmen, and leading citizens sent their children to private and parochial schools, he did not therefore assume that they were disloyal. Concerning the related issue of the separation of church and state, Lawrence said: "I am absolutely opposed to the union of Church and State. But further I would like to point out that union of Church and State is not the teaching of the Catholic Church. . . . I would violently fight against any union of Church and State in America. . . . Finally, it should be made clear that no Catholic is expected to pay political allegiance to a 'foreign power.' The allegiance which the Catholic gives to the Holy Father is spiritual and it is not incompatible with his national loyalties whatsoever they may be." In concluding, Lawrence recalled that most of his life was in public service, during which period he held many positions, while, at the same time, attempting to live a Catholic life. "My faith has never, even remotely, suggested anything which would violate my oath of office nor our constitution." Moreover, Lawrence was convinced he was responsible before God for every duty accepted and obligation assumed.[78] Pre–Vatican II churchmen may well have considered Lawrence a liberal in his church and state stance, but most saw it merely as a complement of his liberal politics.

In 1950, *Commentary* magazine editorialized the notion that the political bosses of the New Deal and Fair Deal after twenty years were still very much in the picture. These bosses, including Lawrence, their recognized leader, were liberalism's strong allies on nearly every public issue in the fields of labor, law, housing, welfare economics, and civil rights. It was said that without liberal support, Roosevelt and Truman would not have achieved the White House.[79] David Lawrence never denied his liberal philosophy. In 1963, he told an ADA dinner meeting, "I am proud to be associated with all of you in the continuing effort to advance the liberal concepts of American government and American life." Moreover, Lawrence asserted that his being a politician "in no way infringed upon my liberal tendencies, my liberal commitment." Instead, his position helped bring into being ideas and proposals, all the while converting liberal platforms into law. At the same time, as a liberal, Lawrence saw a distinct advantage in having had the opportunity to formulate

193

public policy and select party candidates.[80]

Yet Lawrence, the liberal, although a potent force for constructive liberalism, did not rush headlong into problem areas of government and community that had no visible solutions. His was a calm, steady pressure ever moving forward with liberal ideas and programs. Lawrence saw, for example, prejudice as the "Berlin wall of American Society." He considered the 200,000 people who marched from the Washington Monument to the Lincoln Memorial on August 28, 1963, not as a pressure group, but as having exposed a basic truth that Americans believe "openly or somewhere deep within them, that so long as inequality is imposed upon any of us, we are none of us free." Lawrence saw injustices in the United States rooted in restrictions in employment, education, housing, public accommodation, and rights of citizenship. American society, according to Lawrence, had to expand its best efforts to overcome "these evils and injustices, which is what I have devoted myself to do over the years, as I shall continue to do without unreserved conviction." These were not just empty words for Lawrence. His public career contributed to breaking down barriers, bringing divergent groups together, striving for equal opportunity. Lawrence in his later years liked to tell the story of how he, a Catholic, asked a Protestant, Frank Denton, to intervene to ask a Jew, David Kurtzman, to become the chancellor of the University of Pittsburgh. For Lawrence, that would have been impossible in the early fifties.[81]

As a man of high public office in Democratic national politics, Lawrence tried to bring peace to the world. In the turbulent sixties, Lawrence felt peace was beyond the grasp of governments and endorsed the People-to-People program. "No matter how peaceful the intent of governments may be, peace itself will be the result of the honorable determination of human beings to understand one another and live together in the communion of common dignity and human progress."[82] These sentiments, however, were not enough for the liberal cause. Action was called for. Lawrence continued to preach his message in the ordinary forum; he never took to the streets. Moreover, many fellow liberals dubbed Lawrence "elderstatesman," which implied "semiretired." And as the sixties moved by, some, like G. Mennan Williams, no longer saw Lawrence as a liberal. "He was what I would call a moderate whose mind was not closed to progress, although I did not recognize him as a progressive or liberal." Williams felt Lawrence vitiated his liberalism through his association with "the American business environment" in Pittsburgh.[83] Moreover, Williams was angered with Lawrence's pushing Johnson for vice-president in 1960. In the long run, Williams admitted Lawrence was correct in that instance, since Johnson's civil-rights record proved acceptable to the liberals. So even though his pace may have slackened just a bit, Lawrence was ever the student of the liberal cause and advocate of a progressive philosophy.

In understanding Lawrence's philosophy of politics, it should be noted that Lawrence considered education and a sense of humor as two very necessary ingredients not only for the public servant, but also for the entire community. It was obvious to Lawrence's colleagues that he had a great deal of respect for education and the educated. Some saw this as a reference to Lawrence's fairly brief formal education. Later, as a successful insurance man and Allegheny County Democratic chairman, Lawrence felt his public-speaking ability lacking, so he attended a public-speaking academy. Lawrence never admitted this, but close friends used to tease him about it. Apparently, however, Lawrence's schooling proved effective. William Block testified, "I noticed over the years fantastic development of Dave's ability with the English language in his delivery of speeches. He learned a great deal and could ad lib very effectively." Columnist Charles Owen Rice remembered, "His way of talking, grammar, vocabulary, and pronunciation was that of an educated man no matter whom he was talking to, and, amazingly, it sounded right whether he was conferring with the lads from the wards or the drawling members of the establishment." His accomplishments aside, Lawrence continued to admire the Dilworths, Clarks, Stevensons, and that type. In trying to get the best for the Democratic party, he wanted those kinds of people in the party. At the same time, Lawrence found it difficult to accept failure in an educated man. On one occasion, a public official was indicted for failure to file an income-tax return. Lawrence said, "Why, that's impossible. That man is a lawyer. He's an educated man!" When the same party pleaded nolo contendere, Lawrence was flabbergasted.[84]

Despite similar shocks on a number of occasions, Lawrence's faith in and dedication to education never faltered. Speaking at the Institute for Politics in Harrisburg, Lawrence said, "When I mention education first, you might conclude that I attach the highest priority to that area and you would be right." Lawrence said education was the foundation for everything man seeks in an "enriched society," as well as a necessary basic element in working toward an economically viable community.[85] And education had to be available to all people—young, old; rich, poor; healthy, and handicapped. For this reason, Lawrence pushed educational television. He was aware that Frieda Hannock, a Federal Communications Commissioner, had won a battle to get certain television channels set aside for education. "I was President of the Council of American Mayors and she told me that I must do something to cause the cities to implement these educational television channels." Lawrence, in response, appointed a committee of educators, headed by Dr. Alfred W. Beattie, and Lawrence turned to the Allegheny Conference. The conference "gave its blessing in principle to the project," and out of this came WQED—the first community-sponsored educational television station in America.[86] For Lawrence, educational television closed the circle in providing educational opportunity in society. Only death would still the Lawrence rhetoric urging his fellow citizens to seize every educational experience proffered.

In spreading his homespun theories and formulas of politics, Lawrence laced his rhetoric with a healthy dose of humor. Colleagues remember him as an outstanding storyteller, with a great sense of humor. Sometimes in the most serious negotiations, the Lawrence humor would lighten the tensions. Mayor Robert Wagner of New York recalled Lawrence injecting humorous asides in the "tough" negotiations carried on by Pennsylvania and New York over the problems related to the Delaware River. This same humor shone through when Lawrence spoke on public occasions. He constantly gathered material and was a great friend and admirer of Harry Herschfield and Myron Cohen. When these two attended affairs sponsored by the Eagles, Lawrence always asked Maurice Splain, Eagles national secretary, for copies of the comedians' remarks.[87] John Cardinal Wright reports that Lawrence was not a stuffy person and that he found Lawrence's "corny" jokes charming. "The humor was clean and innocent and usually turned on some silly situation." The night Lawrence collapsed during the 1966 campaign, as he was being put in the ambulance, a roll of papers fell from his pockets. The attending priest, Fr. Tom Ferris, picked them up. "It was twelve or thirteen pages containing all these corny jokes which Dave carried around with him to meetings so he would have a story with him when the story was needed." The Lawrence family allowed Wright to keep the papers "as a souvenir of what I mean when I say he was a very simple, very ordinary, and very wonderful man."[88] Wright neglected to say Lawrence was the complete man and politician.

"One versed or experienced in the science of government; one addicted to or actively engaged in politics as managed by parties" is the way Webster's defines *politician*. This definition fits David Leo Lawrence. Still, the public appreciation and understanding of *politician* in the twentieth century is admittedly different. Diversity in its highest degree prevails when the modern American tries to portray the concept "politician." Americans want more than Webster's classification in their politicians. A certain flair, a jaunty style, a happy appearance, and acceptable TV showmanship designate our politicos. And, except for the proverbial cigar, Lawrence had it all, according to his contemporaries. Even to the point of fashion, Lawrence seemed to ape mentor Brennan's Beau Brummel style. This was enhanced by the huge, brilliant, toothy smile that Lawrence showed to his public. In 1942, he told a press photographer on election night while his picture was snapped, "Take it with a smile. We'll get them next year."[89] Always the professional, Lawrence epitomized the politician's politician.

As a politician, Lawrence knew he could not do it all himself. He relied heavily on those who worked with him. In considering candidates for public office, Lawrence seemed to possess a sixth sense for quality, yet Lawrence saw candidates as merely a fraction of the political structure. He made ward leaders feel they had an essential role in the party. If anyone ever approached Lawrence with a problem or request, he would say, "See your ward chairman." And while many good workers contributed to the success of each ward, not all held title or position. Lawrence saw to it that these

197

were aware of their important role or contribution to party organization. In thus gaining the loyalty of his co-workers, Lawrence kept in contact with every level of his party. No facet of organization politics escaped the Lawrence scrutiny. But he played his role of leader with a light hand as long as underlings did their job. Lawrence never told anyone how to do a job; once told what had to be done, one was expected to accomplish the task or step aside.[90]

In addition, Lawrence continually updated his organization's information. Ward leaders, party workers, party faithful—all knew they had an open line to Lawrence at Democratic Headquarters in the Benedum Trees Building. There political strategy was discussed, appointments made, speeches prepared and scheduled, and party homework done.[91] When anyone in the organization died in office or retired, Lawrence replaced the individual with one of the same caliber, nationality, and religion. Moreover, like many politicians, Lawrence was superstitious about elections. He insisted Democratic campaign windups in Western Pennsylvania be held in Carnegie Hall, North Side, Pittsburgh. "You get that Carnegie Hall. We have won there continuously for years and we're going to go there no matter what happens." In 1956, when the Democrats moved their headquarters, Lawrence ordered, "You hold one little room in the Benedum Trees Building and mark it 'Democratic Headquarters' and don't break the lease until after the election." All that was in the room was one chair.[92]

The Lawrence superstition seems the more unreal when one considers the almost infinitesimal knowledge he had of precincts, districts, and wards. Some felt his information so complete that Lawrence always knew how each election would come out beforehand. His computerlike understanding of voter patterns covered every ward in Pittsburgh and Allegheny County. Thus he insisted on a large dose of spadework at the grass-roots level. During voter-registration campaigns, Lawrence kept a practiced eye on every ward. If he saw some problem, he would ask a ward chairman in to see him. "How come you had only 115 registrations? You had 115 kids that turned twenty-one last month—how come?" He posed the same type question to every ward chairman in the county.[93] Even when out of town, Lawrence kept tabs on things back in the wards.

198

One time Frank Hawkins and Bill Block met Lawrence and Philadelphia backer Albert M. Greenfield at the Democratic national convention. Hawkins recalled, "Lawrence reached into his pocket and pulled out an envelope. On the back he had scribbled figures showing increases in Democratic registrations in wards back in Pittsburgh. This was his great concern; this was his method of operation. He always kept in touch with political realities at home."[94] Following the election of 1942, President Roosevelt and other Democratic leaders were shocked by the Republican sweep in Pennsylvania and asked Lawrence what he felt should be done. Lawrence said he wanted to correct any false impressions that may have arisen concerning election outcomes in Pennsylvania and the resultant delegation to Congress. It was Lawrence's view that this challenge from the Republicans would help keep the Democrats more vigorous in their efforts. Further, Lawrence said he did not feel there had been a wholesale change in voting patterns, but more of a slackening in Democrats' zeal. He felt the latter could be obviated through greater cooperation among the national committee, the various state committees, and their congressional delegations.[95] Realist that he was, Lawrence realized that his people had to be told in an off-year situation to get things together or else, and Lawrence kept the entire matter out in the open for the public to view. It was his personal conviction that when you wanted the party to get moving, you told the rank and file and they would prick any lethargic organization standard-bearers.

In every political endeavor, Lawrence tried to determine how new ideas or policies would be accepted—not only at the leadership level, but also throughout the rank and file. As mayor, Lawrence would not start a program in Pittsburgh "without careful, primed conversations and commitments with people who were in a position to help him." The press would be called in, and Lawrence would try to persuade them that his program was a public undertaking worthy of support. Moreover, Lawrence's keen understanding of how to use the power he had enabled him to evolve a careful mix of information and thrust in dealing with the public on matters of new and pending legislation that he felt was needed for the community's welfare. Frequently, when on a speech-making circuit, Lawrence would drop a "bombshell" in order to get the people's reaction. After his talks, he would have his driver visit the men's room to garner comments and reaction about the proffered ideas. At general meetings, Lawrence listened attentively to what was being said on the elevators, sometimes riding them more to listen than of necessity. Sometimes he asked questions of his captive elevator audience. Back home, he consulted the barbers in the City Hall area, lawyers were questioned on the street, and students were interviewed at every opportunity. Lawrence wanted to know what the "little" people as well as the professionals were thinking, especially in reference to his proposals. [96]

In meeting the public the way he did, Lawrence, besides getting information, received many requests for help. "He was willing to help anybody that needed help, and he knew how to do it and he did it." One former assistant secretary claims Lawrence never fired anyone. Once, when he had fired a policeman, Lawrence discovered the officer had only a few years to go before receiving his pension, so he rehired him. [97] Wanting the best for his people, Lawrence would not tolerate running an unqualified candidate. He wanted the Democratic party to look good if it got elected. Once you received the Lawrence stamp of approval, he placed you in a position so that you could move up the ladder as you gained experience. Always backing the Democratic ticket, Lawrence would "walk the extra mile and sacrifice himself for you" once he was convinced you were good for the party and community. [98]

Since Lawrence understood how complex politics could be, he realized that as he was a leader of a large metropolitan area, there would be times when some individuals on the ticket might not meet his standards. Still, Lawrence managed to convey the impression that he was for the entire ticket without indicating he was for or against any particular individual. Once, as Democratic national committeeman, Lawrence felt it a duty to speak at a fund-raising testimonial dinner in an adjacent county, even though he detested the individual honored on the occasion. After the speech, Lawrence quipped, "Well, I made the whole speech and never mentioned his name once."[99] On another occasion, a group calling itself the Mid-Penn Block organized opposition to the state organization when

200

Lawrence was still chairman. They held a dinner meeting one night in Canoe Creek and made the mistake of inviting Lawrence. When the meeting was over, the Mid-Penn Block was defunct. Driving back to Pittsburgh, Lawrence remained silent for a long time. Finally, he said, "Well, Mauri, my boy, we taught them a little politics tonight."[100] But that was the end of the affair. No heads rolled; a lot of people understood the art of politics better after that night, and Lawrence was satisfied. No need for bitterness or revenge. Lawrence had a great ability to fight people on the political level while, at the same time, respecting them as persons. Morever, there were some people he got on well with in politics, but "he couldn't stand them at all and wouldn't want to be with them any longer than necessary."[101] Of course, the opposite was also true, so that in handling people in matters political, Lawrence knew his place and kept it. Once, when Lawrence was governor, David Kurtzman suggested Lawrence knock some legislative heads together because of faltering tax legislation. Lawrence reminded Kurtzman, "You forget this isn't Pittsburgh. I had something to do with each of the Councilmen. Here we have 251 members. . . . Some districts that I didn't carry as Governor they carried as Democrats. They'll come along but it will take a little longer than it would take back in Pittsburgh."[102] The legislators in question were aware of Lawrence's sentiments, and they appreciated his deference for their positions. By knowing how long to wait, Lawrence usually got what he wanted. Practiced politicians had to maintain a long-range view, yet this had to be supported with "practical day-to-day achievements." The politician and his party had to accept the responsibility and govern well without instigating divisions. Broad-based common agreement was a worthwhile objective to be sought in concert with men and women of goodwill, while, at the same time, being careful not to crush opponents or dissenters accidentally or intentionally.

His fellow politicians on both sides of the aisle saw Lawrence as an example to be imitated. Jacob Arvey recalled Lawrence never used his power in office to hurt or besmirch anyone. He would compromise rather than destroy, but on the question of principle, "you couldn't move him." Lawrence believed in fighting his way to the top, but for the good of the party or community, he would slide all the way to the bottom. Instead of viewing public office as a power source, Lawrence saw it as a focal point around which the citizenry could rally to do something for the commonwealth. In this attitude, Richardson Dilworth admitted emulating Lawrence. Mayor Richard Daley recalled that one always knew where David Lawrence stood. "His word was his bond." Sen. Joe Clark remembers that when Lawrence was asked for help, he was always ready and willing, but "very cautious, very slow to make a commitment." Once made, the promise was as solid as Gibraltar. Mayor John T. Gross of Allentown, Pennsylvania, wrote Lawrence: "I tried at all times to follow your advice and guidance and apparently it paid off on November 5th." That day Gross was reelected mayor. James H. J. Tate, once mayor of Philadelphia, recalls his first contacts with Lawrence, when Tate was a "first-termer" in Pennsylvania's House of Representatives. "Dave Lawrence would attend all the sessions and would sit on the side of the House and whenever we would have any real problems, we could go to him. And this was very good for me, because I did not know too much about politics." Later, Lawrence would meet with House Democrats in Davenport's all-night cafeteria. He was able to instill a sense of unity among the thirty-six–member delegation from Philadelphia. After 1945, "when he wasn't around they always seemed to have a lack of unity. He was a great fellow for reconciling differences." Finally, in the very delicate area of intra-party disputes, Lawrence in his middle and later years put into practice the knowledge gained in his personal party battles. "He is skilled in the arts and sciences of making sure that, in intra-party disputes nobody loses and everybody wins."[103] Joe Barr described the political Lawrence as having a dynamic personality and keen political mind. He wanted results and "he knew where and how to get action when he wanted or needed it. But he was no boss. A man of action yes, but not a boss."[104]

Over the years, Lawrence never accepted the glib appellation "boss;" nor did he ever admit to that position personally. Even so, many considered him such. Robert Ryan, Pittsburgh financier, recalled Lawrence as one of the last city "Bosses," who was powerful locally and nationally. For Ryan, Lawrence was "one of the Kingmakers in the Democratic Party . . . we still do not have any individual who stands above the crowd politically to the same extent that Lawrence did. . . . Lawrence compensated for the fact that we haven't had a United States senator from Western Pennsylvania."[105] Aside from the use of the terms "boss" and "Kingmaker," Lawrence would not have been too uncomfortable with Ryan's view. According to Charles Owen Rice, the Democrats under Lawrence had to convert an "old style political machine to modern usage." To get the power they needed as a party, Democrats had to be elected. Of course, party faithful "had to be fed, but they could not be allowed to gorge themselves" at the public trough.[106] In this, Lawrence was the enforcer who determined how much for how many. In such a role, Lawrence appeared to be the "boss," but was enforcing needed discipline for the organization's welfare.

Many who worked closely with Lawrence in his organization deny the "boss" allegation. James Knox, Allegheny County controller for twenty years, who also served as a member of the Democratic Policy Committee and the Democratic State Executive Committee and was Democratic county chairman, allowed that he considered Lawrence a political boss at first, but "I found he wasn't what I had come to know as a political boss at all." Knox admits Lawrence did "exert tremendous qualities of leadership" in bringing Democrats together and instilling pride in themselves, their party, and their city. When Knox first ran for county controller, friends advised him he would not be allowed to make his own appointments to the over 140 positions in that office. They were wrong. Lawrence never asked for one position. All Lawrence ever said was, "Who are you going to appoint as your legal counsel, because you are going to be elected." When Knox mentioned a name, Lawrence said, "He's a fine man; I know him by his work and reputation." Other than answering that question, Knox ran the county controller's office completely on his own.[107]

In a broader countywide context, Lawrence guided the Democrats in day-to-day political activities with a seemingly light hand. He constantly sought cooperation. "If your vote was in question and he somehow found out that the question could be resolved by your Aunt Nellie being given a job as a clerk in some office where she had applied but had not yet been hired, if she could do the work he would make an effort to see that Aunt Nellie got the job." Lawrence wanted his people contented and happy working for the organization. When there were problems without explanation, Lawrence would ask the involved parties to come see him. "Have them come in; let's talk to them, because those people are probably 98 percent for us Democrats, the party and everything. What's ailing them? Get them in." Obviously, people were happy to see someone interested in their problems. As long as the matter could be settled legally, Lawrence happily obliged. If it involved conspiracy or illegality, Lawrence would simply say, "Out!" Then he would tell his people to beat that individual at the polls the next time. Frequently factions would come in very angry with one another. "I have seen them come through the door cursing each other . . . and within forty-five minutes to an hour, agree to support the party, the ticket, and get their workers together." Always the great mediator, Lawrence could be quite frank. Once, two factions from one of the cities visited Lawrence. He tried to get them together, but to no avail. One city councilman was very stubborn and would not agree to any suggestion. Lawrence began to twiddle his fingers, a sign he was getting impatient. He turned to the reluctant councilman and said, "You know I have wondered for a good number of years what has been the matter with the Democratic party in your city. Today I found out. It is you, you son of a bitch; you won't agree to anything." He turned to the other people and said, "Sit down and work out your problems. And get a good ticket, the best you can get, and go out and beat the hell out of them." Lawrence left; the people responded and the councilman was defeated and out of public office for good. Finally, Lawrence, as an intensely loyal individual to the party, expected the same from organization membership, resenting individuals who put themselves before the party. Anyone who bolted the party could not be trusted, and Lawrence was "unforgiving to people who were not loyal to their colors."[108]

The basis of the Lawrence discipline within the party was that everyone was expected to carry his or her share of the burden in promoting the Democratic party, even if this meant, at times, self-effacement. It was this Lawrence discipline that seemed to be the source of organization success. Admittedly, many people confused *discipline* with *boss* and *machine*. According to Rep. William S. Moorhead, who admits he never would have been elected without Lawrence's support, he was never put under any stress by Lawrence. In fact, the first year Moorhead was in Congress, a very "sticky affair" materialized with "good" Democrats on both sides. Moorhead was in a stew, and someone suggested he call Governor Lawrence. When Moorhead finished explaining, Lawrence said, "Bill, I don't envy you the decision you have to make." That was the only advice Moorhead ever got from the "boss." Moreover, when Lawrence moved to Washington during the Kennedy and Johnson administrations, there was "never a situation where he even suggested something that I considered unreasonable." Moorhead explained further, "He had great breadth of vision and judgment, and particularly when you are new in this venture as I was, I sought out his help rather than his imposing it on me."[109]

Not all Pensylvania Democrats were as enthusiastic about Lawrence. Gov. Milton Shapp saw Lawrence as epitomizing the "era of the political boss" in Pennsylvania politics. Shapp alleged that there was never any doubt about who ran things in Allegheny County, suggesting that Lawrence called the shots for Barr while he was mayor of Pittsburgh. What Lawrence affirmed as to appointments was it.[110] Shapp also claimed to have broken the Lawrence organization when he successfully secured the Democratic nomination for governor in 1966. Other Democrats argue this was not so.

On the national scene, the press and media covering the Democratic national conventions took it for granted Lawrence was the "boss" of Pennsylvania and made no apology for their portrayal of him as such. Carmine DeSapio, a New York leader also classified in the same category, said that there was no arrogance or cynicism in Lawrence's style. Lawrence would caucus the Pennsylvania delegation and say, "Here is what we are planning to do, and this is what we have in mind. This is what we feel is good for the country, state, and party. How do you feel about it?" Since Lawrence acknowledged he was dealing with individuals who represented party rank and file back home, he frequently asked delegates if they would support him if he took certain positions. The main objective here was to win, and Lawrence and other leaders wanted to "win with good candidates, good issues, and good organization." According to DeSapio, that is how the party's aims could realistically be achieved. "If you want to call that bossism, then that's bossism."[111]

In evaluating Lawrence's role in the Democratic party, particularly in Pennsylvania, it is more correct to say that Lawrence was an enlightened leader, possessed of an unusual understanding of people and politics. Moreover, his qualities of intelligence, fairness, dedication, loyalty, and willingness to work hard enabled Lawrence to direct his organization in such a fashion that the labels "boss" and "bossism" were shabby misrepresentations. Withal, Lawrence retained the power of the proverbial "boss" and, in most instances, achieved what the boss-controlled machine accomplished in other metropolitan areas.

If Lawrence was unlike other big city bosses in his political methodology, in one sense Lawrence seemed to fail himself and his political posterity since he neglected to prepare a successor. Whether or not death caught Lawrence unawares, no one knows. Suffice it to say Lawrence did not prepare a successor, and although one may speculate on the reasons for this, there is no definitive explanation. As far as the future of the Democratic organization in Pennsylvania was concerned, Lawrence seemed satisfied to prepare for its tomorrow by stressing the active involvement of youth. He may have been convinced that in time his successor would arise out of the Young Democrats.

Some Allegheny Democrats felt that Lawrence saw Joe Barr as his successor, while others feel either Lawrence wanted no successor or hoped matters would take care of themselves without his tapping a protégé. The Barr speculation is interesting in view of Lawrence's association with Barr. Barr stuck with Lawrence in politics from 1928 on and was involved with Lawrence in organizing the Young Democratic Club of Allegheny County. It was Lawrence's decision to form the organization in 1935, once the Democrats had elected George Earle governor. An organizational meeting was held at the home of Mrs. J. Wood Clark, vice-chairlady of Allegheny County. Joe Barr became the Young Democrats' first president, "and from that day on I can say that instead of politics just being a hobby, I also made a living from it."[112]

As secretary of the commonwealth under Earle, Lawrence continued to push for the development of Young Democratic clubs throughout the state. He believed in them and by his support and presence gave the clubs a needed spark. Judge Blatt recalls how impressed she was that Lawrence would take time to spend several hours with the Young Democrats. "So many others wouldn't take the time, and he didn't seem at all stuffy or pompous." At the same time, he had little patience with youngsters who wanted to sit around and theorize. He would jolt them into reality by saying, "Well, now, what you have to have is more people registered. They can never get registered either if you don't get some concrete programs to take them. And with young people, what kinds of programs would appeal to them?"

Further, when Lawrence saw young people in the clubs jockeying for position or looking to launch themselves, he became very impatient. He constantly harped on the idea of service to party first rather than individual promotions. Moreover, he reminded them that good government did the job better. "If you just run a job right, that will be the best kind of politics. People want to see the government run right; that's the way to get elected again."[113] Moreover, Lawrence conveyed to Young Democrats his fondness "for the type of democracy we are." Lawrence constantly urged the youngsters to be active, Democrats or Republicans, and contribute something worthwhile to one's government. "He didn't think you should complain unless you made an effort to try to make it better."[114] Finally, toward the end of his career, Lawrence recalled how he first became impressed with John Kennedy because of Kennedy's willingness to help out with the Young Democrats. It was through the Young Democrats that Lawrence first met Kennedy in 1946,[115] an interesting fact in view of the Kennedy-Lawrence relationship in 1960. Moreover, although Lawrence moved out of the state chairmanship and on to the Democratic national committee in 1940, he remained active with the Young Democrats. That Lawrence in his new position took such a grass-roots interest in the Young Democrats was a factor in providing the Democratic party in Pennsylvania with practiced political wisdom from the top echelon of the party.

Any consideration of David Leo Lawrence lacks the spice of a

207

"backstairs at the White House" type. There was little about the man in Pittsburgh, Allegheny County, Harrisburg, or Washington that was not right out front for scrutiny by friend and foe alike. Lawrence was a simple, honest, well disciplined, hardworking, rock-ribbed, personable individual. This was Lawrence in public and seemingly in private. People spoke of only one Lawrence, no matter what facet of his life is considered. Even the media and rank and file etched positive portraits of the man.

Lawrence has been portrayed as one who could get along well with people, "the highest and the lowest." Convinced that the lifeblood of society was the availability of jobs, Lawrence courted the corporate structure, which provided work opportunities, while, at the same time, assisting those who needed jobs most. Lawrence, without extolling, could convince one to accept a task in the public interest that ordinarily one might not have considered. Still, it was never an assignment Lawrence would not do himself, and in this respect he could make himself do almost anything. Here Lawrence is faulted for his level of criticism focused on colleagues who did not perform to his standards. On the other hand, his criticism was blunted by the fact that "he worked harder than anyone else that worked with him."[116]

For those who worked very closely with Lawrence in day-to-day operations, Lawrence seemed a hard taskmaster. John Robin called Lawrence a "nicer Lyndon Johnson." Yet, a very simple man in his personal needs, Lawrence had a great depth of sympathy for the underdog, the down-and-outer, and was intensely loyal to those with whom he collaborated. He gave himself to his colleagues. But if one turned away or severed the bond of loyalty, such an individual was finished. Men like Irwin Wolf, president of Kaufman's, or county commissioner Howard Stewart, who resigned without consulting Lawrence, experienced the complete communications shutdown.[117] Still, he could get along with people. One Pittsburgh Democrat who did not always agree with Lawrence on policy said, "He can work with Stevenson and John L. Lewis, Democrats and Republicans, the North or the South, the American Legion and the Pittsburgh Symphony. Anyone."[118] Moreover, over his sixty-plus–year political career there were very few individuals Lawrence turned off completely. Lawrence's energetic approach to life inspired rather than discouraged, and few were tempted to abandon this hardworking leader.

For the most part, Lawrence's colleagues saw him as tireless. Always on the move, the Lawrence mind never seemed at rest. One would never catch Lawrence just sitting around. According to Congressman John Dent, "He would be going to a meeting, coming from a meeting, setting up a meeting, or on the phone. I don't ever remember seeing Dave that his mind wasn't working on something."[119] At the same time, Lawrence was extremely efficient and punctual in his personal habits. One of his drivers, Robert Aiken, remembers, "You could set your watch by him. If he said 'Pick me up at a quarter of nine,' he would walk out of the house at a quarter of nine." Lawrence used to joke about his sleeping habits and his office-arrival time, saying that once you got the reputation for being an early riser, you could sleep till noon and everybody thought you were an early riser.[120] Still, no matter where Lawrence scheduled himself to be, he was always on time, God and the weather permitting.

When one considers all the public appearances, civic functions, political meetings, and day-to-day personal contacts Lawrence had, there is little physical evidence today of what Lawrence said or thought. He was, according to Walter Giesey, a "non-verbalizer." Lawrence used to say frequently, "Old Mr. Brennan taught me never write a letter and never destroy one." Lawrence followed that dictum religiously. His correspondence, such as it is, is really of little value. Lawrence was a telephoner. Giesey thinks, "If you could have taped all his phone calls you would have gotten some measure of the man." Moreover, his collected speeches contain some of his ideas, but the words were not his. Lawrence always spoke from the heart once he finished the prepared text. Here was the true Lawrence, but, sadly, an unrecorded Lawrence.[121] Finally, most of his political work not accomplished on the phone was done on a one-to-one basis in his office.

At his desk, perhaps more so than anywhere else, we see the highly disciplined man Lawrence was. He did not waste time. "Have your say, hear the answer, and get the job done." Appointments were scheduled for fifteen minutes. "Things that took time to think through would be attended to after the meeting. His phone manner seemed gruff, somewhat in the style of a 'what do you want?' " He gave people the impression that he was a busy man. Yet those who worked with him daily found this to be a facade. Lawrence believed a political leader could operate three ways, "out of love, respect or fear. I don't think he ever sought the love; he sought respect and, in certain instances, fear."[122] Lawrence changed somewhat when he went to Washington. Here he was no longer in a position of power, or did he have to maintain the image of mayor or governor. The transformation was amazing. Lawrence then came across as a very warm individual, something he had always hidden since it might be interpreted as weakness. Lawrence was very cordial and congenial with his Washington staff, whereas in Pittsburgh or Harrisburg it was never much more than "Good morning" or "Good evening." Now he wanted the staff birthdays remembered with special dinners and similar little kindnesses.[123]

Even in his earlier years, in his own quiet, unassuming way, he had allowed his kindness to shine through. Those who felt Lawrence was hard to work for realized he was a kind and thoughtful man. While governor and working in the Pittsburgh area, on cold mornings he would pick up women who were waiting for buses. One day a young lady said to Lawrence, "Don't I know you?" "Yes," he said. "I am one of the county detectives." This was his way of providing a service without recognition. Lawrence did not like to be noticed going from place to place—he would never use the siren, and unless he was with Mrs. Lawrence, he always sat up front with the driver.[124] He was not a pretentious individual.

One day, motoring between Greensburg and Bedford, Lawrence asked his driver to stop at Saint Xavier's Convent. "One of my old schoolteachers is here." An elderly nun came out and rapped Lawrence across the back, almost upsetting him. They chatted at length, and Lawrence finally got in the car while the nun was still talking and said, "Let's get the hell out of here; she's going to talk forever."[125] He used to ride the "Ham and cabbage special," sponsored by McMannus' Restaurant, to the Kentucky Derby, prizefights in New York, and Steeler games. Art Rooney remembers Lawrence on those trips. "He was such a human being. Even when he was mayor or governor he was down to earth; he never changed. He stayed just the way he always was." Once Governor Lawrence attended an Eagles-Steelers game in Philadelphia with Jim Clark and Joe Donahue, both Philadelphians. Clark said, "Now that you are governor, you have to be neutral." Lawrence replied, "Like hell I'm neutral; I'm for Pittsburgh."[126]

Lawrence never sought privilege, nor would he let it be exercised in his regard. An eye affliction required frequent visits to the doctor. He would "sit down like any other patient, pick up a magazine or make small talk with others and wait his regular turn."[127] Finally, Lawrence hated to see people embarrassed, especially his friends. In 1945, when Margaret Truman was to make her concert debut in Pittsburgh, Lawrence discovered little had been done to advance the concert. Lawrence contacted the booking agent and asked the price of the cheapest ticket, which was a dollar-twenty. "I'll take a thousand," said Lawrence. He divided the tickets among student groups and asked a women's organization to promote the recital and hold a postconcert reception. As a result, a crowd of 4,000 heard Miss Truman. President Truman remarked some time later, "You turned a concert into a political rally. I'll always be grateful for what you did. You know, she's all I got."[128] Lawrence was singularly impressed with Truman's statement about his daughter. Despite Truman's high position, family pride and affection came first; that was for Lawrence a valuable object lesson in the way things should be for people in public office.

Again, Lawrence was always quick to go to the aid of those he felt falsely accused. On one occasion, Lawrence voluntarily went before a special committee of the Allegheny County Bar Association to defend an assistant district attorney who had been suspended because of alleged communist associations. Moreover, Lawrence defended Roy Harris, composer-musician in residence at Chatham College and a former foe of Dave's, whose alleged sympathies were under attack by Pennsylvania supreme court justice, Michael A. Musmanno, a Democrat. Also, Lawrence was a character witness for Republican governor John H. Fine at his tax-evasion trial. Lawrence likewise took the stand, when the governor, in favor of assistant

211

police superintendent Larry Maloney at his embezzlement trial.[129] Further, when Lawrence testified in someone's behalf, his was not a token appearance. The Lawrence recital was accomplished professionally.

There seemed to be a connection between the man as a professional politician and Lawrence's deep-seated enjoyment of contests in the sports arena. His love for and participation in athletic events were essential facets of his being. He was very active in all the organized athletic teams in Pittsburgh's Point area, but his poor eyesight forced Lawrence to assume a supervisory role, managing and coaching football and baseball teams. Art Rooney classified Lawrence's teams as "sandlot and semipro."[130] Lawrence also managed boxers. "I managed Pat Connors, Kid Hogan, and a fellow from Columbus named Dick Coy in 1910. We fought in old City Hall, usually on Saturday nights, and the admission was one dollar. The biggest purse any fighter of mine ever received was $350, the night Connors fought Buck Crouse at Duquesne Gardens."[131] Commenting further on his athletic interests, Lawrence recalled, "Tommy Davies, Howard Harpster, and Marshall Goldberg were my college favorites. And Bill Dudley was my favorite football back. The best coach I ever saw was Dr. Jock Sutherland." Speaking of baseball, Lawrence called the Pirates' 1935 and 1960 teams tops on his list. "Bill Mazeroski gave me the thrill of thrills with his dynamic home run," said Lawrence, referring to the 1960 World Series. Overall, Lawrence felt Honus Wagner was the best athlete he ever saw. "Honus and I were good friends. I waited at the gate at old Expo Park and he always took me in to see the games. He was my idol."[132] Lawrence also played with and managed teams in the same park. Today the site is occupied by Three Rivers Stadium. Art Rooney observed, "I thought they should have named this stadium after him because he was responsible for all this. I don't know of anything that would have been more appropriate . . . because he was so active and played on these grounds. He's responsible for the stadium."[133] Lawrence's love for sports stayed with him till the end. When he grew older and became actively engaged in politics, Lawrence became Pittsburgh's most notable and avid fan.

When he was in town, Lawrence always had a ringside seat at the *Pittsburgh Post Gazette* Dapper Dan Club Golden Glove boxing bouts. Lawrence loved boxing and took in amateur and professional boxing contests as he moved about the country. Next to boxing, Lawrence liked baseball. Even when he had one, two, or three previous engagements in a single evening, Lawrence tried to get to old Forbes Field after nine o'clock to catch part of the Pirates game. Box 208 was Lawrence's, and if he was out of town, the tickets were always used by friends and cronies. Once when the Pirates were in last place, Lawrence went to a twi-night doubleheader, the last two games of the season. In the second game, with the Pirates down 11–2, Frank Ambrose suggested they leave because it was getting chilly. Lawrence snapped, "The game's not over yet!" And he remained until the bitter end. [134] Attending sports events was a passion with Lawrence, and he just loved being out with the people and, as a public official, made no attempt to hide or isolate himself. According to Lawrence, Pittsburghers and Pennsylvanians had a right to see the man who governed them. Moreover, Lawrence was convinced his public presence was a way of communicating with rank and file who might never get a chance to see a public leader. Effective communications was an important characteristic of the man Lawrence, and he made it work.

Accordingly, Lawrence usually had good press. Reporters were always welcome in the mayor's or governor's office. One reporter remembers Lawrence would usually have two or three stories a week about city activities. "I found him to be very candid, and he could give me a good story almost every day and he leveled with me and I respected his confidence." Sometimes, when office pressures slackened, Lawrence would play pinochle with City Hall reporters, answering any questions they might have or discussing civic situations. When he held formal press conferences, Lawrence would frequently answer questions before they were entirely formulated. He seemed to be able to read the questioner's mind. Generally, these sessions went well, and Lawrence never overused the "No comment" response. Frequently, however, when he gave a "No" answer and was asked why, Lawrence would say, "I don't have any 'why'; the answer is no." Or if asked for an elaboration of a "Yes" answer, Lawrence replied, "No explanation; the answer is yes." Lawrence never let himself get trapped. [135]

An avid newspaper reader, Lawrence had a special light in his car for night reading. Every day he read the three Pittsburgh papers, the *Wall Street Journal*, the *New York Times*, a Washington paper, and a Philadelphia paper. In Harrisburg he added the local dailies. There were times when Lawrence did not like the way reporters set down his views, but Lawrence understood that you get "smacked" once in a while, and he learned to take it. There were, however, few reporters that Lawrence did not get on with. As for Washington correspondents, Lawrence felt the writings of men like David Lawrence, Walter Lippman, Marquis Childs, Merriman Smith, and Ernest Vaccaro would be none too useful for scholars, whereas the works of Edward Folliard were worthwhile. Generally, Lawrence respected the press corps, except for a *Pittsburgh Post Gazette* reporter, Raymond Sprigle. William Block recalled Lawrence "felt that Ray Sprigle had done some rather bad things to him over the years, and he had a genuine dislike for Sprigle." However, once Sprigle had to have a detached retina operation, something Lawrence had had himself. Another reporter, John Thomas, told Lawrence that Sprigle was in Doctors' Hospital for the operation. Lawrence phoned William Block right away and asked if Block knew Sprigle was in for the operation. Block did not. Lawrence said, "Well, I think you ought to look into it, because I don't think it is a very good place for him to be operated on." Block arranged with Mrs. Sprigle for a transfer to Eye and Ear Hospital, where it was discovered Sprigle had diabetes and was in no condition to undergo the surgery. Block was impressed with Lawrence's character here. "Now there was a case where Lawrence had every reason just to ignore it. He disliked the man intensely. . . . I had a lot of reason to respect him for that and for other things."[136]

This respect covered almost the entire Pittsburgh newspaper industry. Frank Hawkins recalled, "From the beginning of his career as mayor, he showed an ability to take hold of things and make them happen." Every year Lawrence would hold a dinner meeting for the officers of the various newspapers. Close associates and department heads were also invited, "and we would kick around civic problems, urban renewal . . . industrial development." This was good for the press and good for the city government.[137] In addition, when Lawrence had a new budget or program, it would be sent to the newspapers and questions answered. "This would help us in our understanding what they were trying to do and their motivation." City Hall would then ask what the press thought as to the reaction and response the program would get. On the other hand, despite the mutual respect between Lawrence and the press, the former never took advantage of his favored position. Rarely did Lawrence publicly criticize the press, particularly newspapers, and he never called to intervene in an editorial discussion.[138] Moreover, at the Democratic national conventions, the press corps, aware of the Lawrence character and insight, sought him out. This was the man in the Democratic party whose word was his bond, for the press, the party, and the public. The American political arena could ask no more of any man.

Notes

1. Joseph Veres, "David Lawrence: A Psychologial Biography." Washington and Jefferson College, unpublished paper, 1975, p. 9; *The Reminiscences of Arthur Rooney*, (1974), p. 1, in the Oral History Collection of La Salle University, hereinafter Rooney; *The Reminiscences of Leonard Stabile*, (1975) p. 1, in the Oral History Collection of La Salle University, hereinafter Stabile.

2. Lorant, p. 40; *The Reminiscences of Anna Mae Donahue*, (1974), p. 1, in the Oral History Collection of La Salle University, hereinafter Anna Mae Donahue; Shames, p. 11; PSA, Lawrence Papers, speech, September 1963.

3. Veres, p. 7.

4. Veres, p. 7; Plesset, p. 5; Bradley, pp. 2–3; *The Reminiscences of Sister Irenaeus*, (1974), p. 1, in the Oral History Collection of La Salle University, hereinafter Sister Irenaeus.

5. Sister Irenaeus, p. 1.

6. Veres, p. 10; Shames, pp. 11–12; *The Reminiscences of Thomas Joyce*, (1974), p. 1, in the Oral History Collection of La Salle University, hereinafter Joyce; Rooney, p. 1.

7. PSA, Lawrence Papers, speeches, Italian Social Club, Wilmerding, 1965.

8. Ibid., Saint Matthew's High School, Conshohocken, Pennsylvania, 1965.

9. Shames, p. 14; Stave, p. 15; Lawrence to Frank G. McCartney, March 2, 1965 PSA, Lawrence Papers; Bethany College, June 17, 1964.

10. PSA, Lawrence Papers, speeches, March 17, 1963, U. S. Chamber of Commerce, September 1963.

11. Shames, p. 12; Veres, p. 16.

12. Shames, p. 13; Gerald Lawrence, II, p. 14.

13. Shames, p. 13; *Pittsburgh Post Gazette*, September 17, 1918, p. 1.

14. *Pittsburgh Post Gazette*, April 10, 1929, p. 1; Gerald Lawrence, II, pp. 15–16.

15. Gerald Lawrence, II, p. 2.

16. Ibid., p. 4.

17. Ibid., pp. 2–3.

18. Anna Mae Donahue, p. 9.

19. Ibid., p. 2.

20. Ibid., p. 7.

21. Gerald Lawrence, II, pp. 10–11.

22. Anna Mae Donahue, p. 4.

23. Gerald Lawrence, II, pp. 4–8, 17.

24. Anna Mae Donahue, p. 6.

25. Plesset, p. 11.

26. *The Reminiscences of Thomas Hooper,* (1974), p. 2, in the Oral History Collection of La Salle University, hereinafter Hooper.

27. PSA, Lawrence Collection, General File, letter to Gerald Lawrence, January 14, 1960.

28. Ibid., letter to Gerald Lawrence, February 19, 1960.

29. Ibid., press release, June 6, 1961.

30. Ambrose, pp. 11–12.

31. Anna Mae Donahue, pp. 6–7.

32. PSA, Lawrence Papers, General File, 1960.

33. Gerald Lawrence, II, p. 12.

34. Blatt, p. 16.

35. Wagner, p. 6.

36. *The Reminiscences of Maurice Splain,* (1974), p. 1, in the Oral History Collection of La Salle University, hereinafter Splain.

37. Ambrose, pp. 1–2.

38. Fenrich, p. 5.

39. Giesey, pp. 23–24.

40. *Evening Bulletin*, Philadelphia, April 20, 1942, p. 1.

41. Barr, pp. 8–9, 10.

42. Anna Mae Donahue, pp. 2–4.

43. Ambrose, p. 2.

44. Ibid.

45. Rooney, pp. 3–4.

46. Leonard, p. 4.

47. Jones, p. 4.

48. Blatt, p. 17.

49. Plesset, pp. 11–12.

50. David Lawrence to John F. Kennedy, August 12, 1963, PSA, Lawrence Papers.

51. Gerald Lawrence, II, pp. 1–2.

52. Hawkins, p. 4.

53. Ambrose, p. 10.

54. Plesset, pp. 5–6.

55. Giesey, pp. 18–20.

56. Gerald Lawrence, II, pp. 8–9, 11.

57. *The Reminiscences of David Donahue*, (1975), pp. 1–2, 3, in the Oral History Collection of La Salle University, hereinafter David Donahue.

58. Shames, p. 68; PSA, Lawrence Papers, speeches, New Kensington American Italian Club, November 23, 1963.

59. Knox, pp. 2–4; PSA, Lawrence Papers, speeches, Beaver County Democratic Dinner, April 13, 1964.

60. Lawrence to Liza Holmes, March 12, 1963, PSA, Lawrence Papers.

61. *Pittsburgh Catholic*, November 10, 1966, p. 8.

62. *The Reminiscences of John Mauro*, (1974), p. 3, in the Oral History Collection of La Salle University, hereinafter Mauro.

63. PSA, Lawrence Papers, press releases, July 4, 1959, April 27, 1961, October 19, 1961.

64. Ibid., Lawrence to Governor Scranton, February 23, 1965.

65. Ibid., speeches, Pennsylvania Young Democratic Convention, June 6, 1964, Lawrence to Charles J. Lawrence, Jr., August 14, 1964.

66. Shames, p. 200; PSA, Lawrence Papers, speech, U. S. Conference of Mayors, June 10, 1963.

67. PSA, Lawrence Papers, press releases, June 11, 1959, November 16, 1961.

68. Lawrence (HST), p. 38.

69. PSA, Lawrence Papers, press release, July 4, 1959.

70. Ibid., Lawrence to Richardson Dilworth, August 17, 1964.

71. Burns and Mulvhill, p. 179; PSA, Lawrence Papers, speeches, U.S. Conference of Mayors, June 10, 1963.

72. Arvey, p. 6; *The Reminiscences of Richard Daley*, (1974), p. 2, in the Oral History Collection of La Salle University, hereinafter Daley; Wright, p. 9.

73. PSA, Lawrence Papers, press release, June 1, 1959.

74. Knox, p. 17.

75. Sloan Collection, speech, House Caucus Room, Harrisburg, July 25, 1964; PSA, Lawrence Papers, speech, Harvard-Yale-Princeton Club, 1965.

76. Rev. Joseph Altany to David Lawrence, n.d., David Lawrence to Rev. Joseph Altany, September 4, 1965, private collection.

77. PSA, Lawrence Papers, speech, Pittsburgh Theological Seminary, November 5, 1965.

78. Lawrence to Virginia Nielander, February 10, 1958.

79. *Commentary,* October 1950, p. 301.

80. PSA, Lawrence Papers speeches ADA, March 8, 1963, Roosevelt Day Dinner, ADA, February 19, 1966.

81. Robin, pp. 5–6; PSA, Lawrence Papers, press release, September 8, 1962; speech Philadelphia Federal Bar Association, September 24, 1963, Lawrence to Dr. Helene D. Mayer, September 13, 1966; *The Reminiscences of Saul Weisberg,* (n.d.) in the Oral History Collection of the University of Pittsburgh.

82. PSA, Lawrence Papers, speech, People-to-People Program Delegates, October 26, 1962.

83. *The Reminiscences of G. Mennan Williams,* (1975), p. 2, in the Oral History Collection of La Salle University, hereinafter Williams.

84. Blatt, pp. 4–5; Block, p. 5; *The Pittsburgh Catholic,* November 10, 1966, p. 4; Plessett, pp. 12–13.

85. PSA, Lawrence Papers, speech, Institute of Politics, December 4, 1965.

86. *Pittsburgh Post Gazette,* November 22, 1963, p. 10.

87. Barr, p. 10; Wagner, p. 7; Splain, pp. 4, 5.

88. Wright, pp. 5–6.

89. Fuller, p. 47; Shames, p. 161.

90. McCarthy, p. 7; Rooney, pp. 2–3.

91. Robin, p. 1.

92. Fenrich, p. 7.

93. Ambrose, pp. 10–11.

94. Hawkins, p. 1.

95. Lawrence to FDR, November 6, 1942, FDR Library, Governor's File, under "Lawrence."

96. Hawkins, p. 1; Aiken, pp. 3, 6.

97. *The Reminiscences of Stanley Noszka,* (1974), pp. 1–2, 3, in the Oral History Collection of La Salle University, hereinafter Noszka.

98. Humphrey, p. 4; Blatt, p. 9.

99. Plessett, pp. 9–10.

100. Splain, p. 3.

101. David Donahue, p. 6.

102. *The Reminiscences of David Kurtzman,* (1971), p. 14, in the Oral History Collection of the University of Pittsburgh.

103. Arvey, pp. 3–4; Saxe, p. 5; Daley, p. 1; Clark, p. 12; PSA, Lawrence Papers, Mayor John T. Gross to Lawrence, November 14, 1963; Burns and Mulvehill, p. 48.

104. Burns and Mulvehill, p. 175.

105. *The Reminiscences of Robert Ryan*, (1971), pp. 5–6, in the Oral History Collection of the University of Pittsburgh.

106. *Pittsburgh Catholic*, November 10, 1966.

107. Knox, pp. 2, 4.

108. Knox, pp. 6–7.

109. Mauro, pp. 5–6; Moorhead, pp. 1–2.

110. *The Reminiscences of Milton Shapp*, (1974), p. 5, in the Oral History Collection of La Salle University, hereinafter Shapp.

111. DeSapio, p. 8.

112. Barr, p. 1.

113. Blatt, pp. 1–3.

114. *The Reminiscences of Judge Richard Conaboy*, (1974), p. 4, in the Oral History Collection of La Salle University, hereinafter Conaboy.

115. David Lawrence (JFK), pp. 1–2.

116. Barr, pp. 2,3; Blatt, p. 10.

117. Robin, p. 3.

118. Joseph Kraft, "Pennsylvania's New Breed of Politician," *Harper's*, October 1958, p. 49.

119. Dent, p. 4.

120. Aiken, p. 2.

121. Giesey, p. 15.

122. Giesey, pp. 15–16.

123. Giesey, pp. 16–17.

124. Sloan, p. 3; Aiken, pp. 1, 2.

125. Aiken, p. 5.

126. Rooney, pp. 7, 5.

127. *Pittsburgh Post Gazette*, December 7, 1966, p. 18.

128. Ibid., November 22, 1966, p. 4.

129. Splain, p. 5; Hawkins, "Lawrence of Pittsburgh," p. 61.

130. Rooney, p. 1.

131. *Pittsburgh Press*, November 23, 1966, p. 22.

132. Ibid.

133. Rooney, p. 8; Block, p. 3; Fenrich, p. 5.

134. Ambrose, pp. 9, 10.

135. Barr, p. 11; Aiken, p. 4; Mauro, p. 1; Knox, p. 5.

136. Lawrence (HST), pp. 35–36; Block, pp. 5–6.

137. Block, p. 4.

138. Hawkins, p. 4; Block, p. 8.

VI
In Harness

On January 2, 1963, a few weeks before Lawrence was scheduled to leave the governor's office, President Kennedy wrote Lawrence suggesting he consider accepting the chairmanship of the President's Commission on Equal Opportunity in Housing. The commission was constructed in such a broad manner that the chairman was to be a special assistant to the president. In this way, the chairman would be his own man and would control the commission. Kennedy wanted someone with political knowledge and experience, and, given the civil-rights implications of the commission's start-up, particularly with the South, Lawrence was, for Kennedy, a palatable answer to a very difficult problem. In 1963, Kennedy was still very cautious about pushing too hard on the civil-rights issue, since he did not want to lose the South.[1] As a result, according to Lawrence, Kennedy had trouble getting "anyone to take the job. . . . I had certain standing in the Democratic Party that would be helpful with some of the southern Senators and so forth."[2] The situation was quite delicate. As Governor Hughes points out, Kennedy, although committed to a civil-rights program, was aware of how this brought the states into "severe confrontation" with old-line labor. Hughes saw Kennedy using Lawrence "around the country to spread the gospel of civil rights, while, at the same time, giving him position in Washington."[3] Mennan Williams agrees with Hughes. "It was quite evident that David Lawrence was one of the people that Kennedy looked to to carry his fortunes. I think that Kennedy had a kind of wistful admiration of those of us who were more liberal than he. . . . I think perhaps he felt more comfortable with some of the more traditional leadership."[4] Conversely, Congressman Moorhead saw Kennedy selecting Lawrence because of the latter's knowledge of politics in a large industrial and ethnic state "and his ability to deal with the South and get a maximum job done for the blacks in the Democratic Party."[5]

Lawrence met with President Kennedy on the afternoon of January 10, 1963, to discuss the position. After a twenty-minute conversation, Lawrence emerged from the president's office and Walter Giesey asked, "Well, how did it go?" Lawrence said, "Well, I told him I would take it if I could bring you along!" Lawrence had never discussed that possibility with Giesey.[6] On February 1, 1963, Lawrence was sworn in. He set as his first task recruitment of the public members of the committee, indicating he wanted broad representation of labor, business, the clergy, and other fields. In issuing his appeal for talented public members, Lawrence said, "Desegregation is engulfing continents. The United States has to show an enlightened response."[7]

The move to Washington was a difficult transition for Lawrence. He was used to making decisions. Things were different on the New Frontier. When asked how he liked his job, Lawrence replied, "I like it all right, but it is about to drive me up a wall. In all my life I have been in jobs where I called the orders. I have to sit here and wait."[8] Apparently, Lawrence spent much of his waiting time on a bench outside the Sheraton Park Hotel, where he lived. In addition, some business was conducted there. There seemed to be no reason for his doing this other than he felt the confinement of his hotel suite and preferred to be out of doors.

Another aspect of the Washington scene that irked Lawrence was poor communication with things back home. Pennsylvania and Pittsburgh newspapers were always late, and Lawrence did not have unlimited use of the phone. Finally, in political matters, Lawrence indicated how much easier patronage issues had been in Harrisburg, "because there I had the final say. There is so little Federal patronage now and such a wide area to serve that it becomes quite a problem."[9] Despite these minor inconveniences, Lawrence performed well in his position, making himself as helpful as possible to Kennedy.

Beyond his role as chairman of the President's Committee on Equal Opportunity in Housing, Lawrence, according to his contem-

221

pories, played an additional part on the New Frontier in 1963, as an advisor to the president. The president's official appointments list shows, however, that Lawrence met with Kennedy only four times in "off record" circumstances after being sworn in as committee chairman. In 1961, Lawrence and Kennedy met alone only once, and they met twice in 1962, although Lawrence met Kennedy twice with Joe Clark present in 1962. Still, indications are that Kennedy sought Lawrence's advice on other occasions. Lawrence admits that in 1960, shortly after Kennedy's election, the governor mentioned Matthew McCloskey for the post of ambassador to Ireland and John Rice for the post of ambassador to the Netherlands. Both men were so appointed. Again, Kennedy asked Lawrence about appointing Robert Kennedy attorney general. Lawrence told Kennedy if he wanted Bobby as attorney general, he should appoint him based on the Lawrence philosophy that any elected official should have his lawyer and his secretary as his own people. "They were in the intimate recesses of the workings of whatever he was doing. They ought to just be part of his conscience, thinking, and direction all the time."[10] Lawrence was not arguing cause-effect in discussing his advice to Kennedy, but Bobby became attorney general.

Hubert Humphrey asserts that Kennedy needed people of seasoned political judgment, who knew how to implement ideas. "There is no doubt that David Lawrence was a man that Kennedy would talk to very openly and know that he had a man that was loyal, that would never in any way divulge the conversation, and would talk very frankly to him. . . . I know that John Kennedy looked upon him as a kind of sage." Further, Humphrey declared that both Kennedy and Johnson knew they needed Lawrence, "a very capable, seasoned, experienced politician, statesman in politics, in affairs of government."[11] Others testify along the same lines. According to Jim Knox, "Lawrence used to tell me about some of the trips when he would ride along with the President and they would talk things over." When the president reached his destination, Lawrence then returned to Washington.[12] Carmine DeSapio saw Lawrence's role as more personal. "They were seeking the benefit of his experience and his advice and contacts and relationships with a lot of other people whom they didn't have access to on a friendly level." Further,

222

DeSapio saw Lawrence's chairmanship as an umbrella "that was a help to Lawrence to make his contacts legitimized in the sense that they weren't using a boss to twist any arms."[13] Congressman John Dent suggests that Lawrence's role in the Kennedy administration was an important one, since Lawrence knew so many people in Congress, the states, and the Democratic national committee, while, at the same time, he had a reputation for keeping his word.[14] Gov. Pat Brown asserts, "I know that Kennedy had great respect for him, because John Kennedy and I talked about Lawrence."[15] Colonel Arvey agreed with Brown, but observed further, "I don't think he used him as much as he should have." Arvey suggests the reason for this may have been the so-called Irish Mafia that surrounded Kennedy. "Dave was not in that inner circle." Moreover, some of them Lawrence had little use for. "He didn't like their methods."[16]

Lawrence, in his recollections, never tells us just how close he was to Kennedy. Lawrence recalled flying from Philadelphia to Washington one evening with Kennedy, when the latter asked Lawrence if he remembered the old knock-knock jokes. Kennedy said, "This is one in your department." Then Kennedy said, "Knock, knock." Lawrence replied, "Who's there?" Kennedy said, "Izha." Lawrence replied, "Izha who?" Kennedy said, "Izha your next-door neighbah!" Lawrence noted that Kennedy, in the civil-rights issue, was leaning toward "kissing the southern states goodbye." Lawrence told Kennedy he would have to make a stronger pitch in the northern states. Also, "he was so much stronger now that the first brush of voting for a Catholic was out of the way. . . . He could definitely corral the Negro vote, win it by his sincerity and what he was doing in pushing these laws and the Meredith case." Finally, on another occasion, Kennedy asked Lawrence to ride with him to a luncheon at the Mayflower Hotel. Kennedy wanted to discuss a patronage problem involving Joe Clark and Bill Green. Lawrence took Green's side, and as he explained the situation, Kennedy was getting provoked at Clark. When Kennedy got out of the car, he turned and said about Clark, "When does that guy run, in '66?" Lawrence said, "No, Mr. President, he doesn't come up till '68." Kennedy retorted, "Well, probably neither you nor I will be here then." Lawrence related how a chill went up his back and he said, "Wait a minute;

wait a minute. That might apply to me at my age, but not to you." Lawrence said later, "I have thought of that a hundred times since, you know. He must have had a premonition he wasn't going to live long in any event. You know, I didn't like him to pick me."[17] These incidents reflect the free and easy relationship between the president and the governor. In addition, it seems that in the New Frontier, Lawrence was something more than chairman of equal opportunity in housing. In the Lawrence-Kennedy encounter, there was definitely a broader dimension, one that a clever Kennedy used to his advantage.

Lawrence recalled, rather wistfully, that the last time he was with Kennedy was the night of the knock-knock story. Kennedy's assassination was a shock for Lawrence. David Donahue said, "I remember he was greatly shaken by it, perhaps more so than I had ever seen him." Lawrence felt the country had been robbed of a man who really had not reached his potential as president. In a political sense, he felt the United States had lost an individual who had roused the enthusiasm of the nation.[18] Moreover, Lawrence was impressed with Kennedy's charm. "I don't think I ever knew anyone who had the natural charm he had. . . . His was so real." Kennedy had the knack for making people feel important and Lawrence liked this. He told how the day Lawrence was sworn in, Kennedy picked out of the crowd one of the office women who had worked in his campaign and said, "Peggy, I didn't know you were with the governor." Peggy was walking on air for months after that. Further, Lawrence realized he and Mrs. Lawrence were in the "upper age bracket" at Kennedy's social affairs, but Kennedy would always "wend his way around and pick Mrs. Lawrence out to say something nice to her."[19] Truly David Lawrence liked young Kennedy and had high hopes for his future role as party leader. That ended on November 22, 1963, and in less than twenty-four hours, Lawrence found himself closeted with President Johnson.

During Lyndon Johnson's administration, Lawrence retained his commission chairmanship. At first, it was not clear what direction Johnson would take in the civil-rights field, but as it turned out, Johnson was more liberal and effective in his efforts on behalf of minority interests than Kennedy had been. This, of course, made

Lawrence's task in Housing easier and enabled him to move several programs forward in that area. On the other hand, Johnson was clearly anxious to have Lawrence present as a resource person. When Johnson made his first address to a joint session of Congress, on November 27, 1963, Lawrence, along with Wagner of New York, Carl Sanders of Georgia, and Daley of Chicago, were with the Johnson family in the gallery. Congressman Dent said there was a much closer understanding and relationship between Johnson and Lawrence than there had been between Lawrence and Kennedy. There was much greater rapport. Andrew Bradley, who was privy to suggestions Lawrence made to Johnson, saw things happening that resulted from Lawrence's suggestions. Art Rooney suggests that Lawrence had "a lot of faith in Johnson." David Donahue adds that Lawrence felt President Johnson was an extremely capable individual in terms of the American system of government. Donahue remembers how Lawrence was frequently called to the White House by Johnson and people who had nothing to do with Housing were often in and out of Lawrence's office and hotel suite. Hubert Humphrey testified that Lawrence was asked by Johnson to work with cabinet officers, to work with the labor movement, "all sorts of major assignments." Further, Humphrey asserts, "Johnson respected his judgment very, very much, and I remember very distinctly how he many times bounced off an idea on David Lawrence." But what impressed Humphrey most of all was the way Johnson dealt personally with Lawrence. "I know Lyndon Johnson, who was very overpowering with many people, always treated David Lawrence with the greatest of respect, almost with humbleness, asking him about this or that. And really listening to him."[20] Finally, Johnson's official appointment record evidences Lawrence and Johnson meeting many more times than Kennedy and Lawrence met. Moreover, Humphrey tells of the many, many times Johnson would go to Lawrence's office, call Lawrence on the phone, stop him in the White House corridors, or order some staff member to check with Lawrence.

Despite Lawrence's responsibilities to Presidents Kennedy and Johnson, as a matter of course he continued to follow through in his role as Democratic political leader in Pennsylvania, remaining a significant political power in the Keystone State till the very end.

Nothing would have pleased Pennsylvania Democrats more in 1963 than to have a fellow Democrat succeed Governor Lawrence in Harrisburg. With Lawrence at the head of the party and in control of the governor's chair, it seemed only natural the Democrats could effect such a succession. However, since Lawrence could not succeed himself, there was a question as to who was going to be the candidate. In February 1962, Lawrence complained, ". . . . our Philadelphia friends are raising a strenuous opposition to Dilworth as a candidate, although a check over the slates shows that about thirty-five of the county chairmen prefer him to anyone else."[21] Bill Green had an intense dislike for Dilworth, while at the same time, he felt Dilworth incapable of carrying the state. At first, Green would not budge on the matter.

In the meantime, Natalie Saxe and John Robin suggested rigging a primary fight between Green and Dilworth, convinced that such a battle would enhance Dilworth's chance of winning, "because Dilworth was then genuinely becoming an anti-organization candidate." Saxe and Robin asked Lawrence to close his eyes while they did this, but Lawrence would have no part of it, saying he did not want a primary fight.[22] Instead, Lawrence went to President Kennedy and asked the president to suggest to Green that he accept Dilworth. Green, through Kennedy's persuasion, finally gave in. "Bill Green didn't want to be for Dilworth for governor. As it turned out, Bill was right and we were wrong because we took a terrible lacing."[23]

With his choice secure, Lawrence campaigned for Dilworth on the records of the Lawrence and Leader administrations. He boasted of 37,345 new jobs that had opened through the Pennsylvania Industrial Development Authority; 225 new industries and plant expansions that had taken place in six years; diversification of Pennsylvania's industrial complex; improved education, for the first time introducing education for the handicapped; 700 new public schools; new facilities and higher enrollments at state universities; elimination of the teacher shortage; development of the interstate highway system in the commonwealth; and "we have completely eliminated a 177 million dollar deficit left over from years of Republican fiscal irresponsibility."[24] Further, Lawrence spoke of Dilworth's "tremendous qualifications," called Senator Clark "a magnificent senator," Steve

McCann "the best house majority leader in Pennsylvania history," and Genevieve Blatt "the state's brilliant secretary of internal affairs." Moreover, Lawrence claimed that the election of Dilworth and Clark would "assure the continuance of humane, progressive government for the people of Pennsylvania."[25] However, Pennsylvania Republicans, aware that the Democrats were split over the Dilworth candidacy, ran their campaign in such a fashion that William Scranton had little difficulty defeating Dilworth. A month later, Lawrence wrote, "The election was really a nightmare and it's too much to put in writing. . . . Needless to say, it was one of the most peculiar elections that I have ever seen and the results point out that fact very strongly."[26] Dilworth lost by over 500,000 votes, Senator Clark won by over 103,000 votes, Genevieve Blatt won by a margin of only 1,410 statewide, and Steve McCann lost the lieutenant governorship by just over 171,000. This strange pattern confused and upset Lawrence, although he did take hope in the Clark and Blatt victories. Lawrence felt the Democrats still had a strong position in the commonwealth despite the fact that they had lost control of the state government. At the same time, Lawrence was convinced Kennedy's candidacy would help Pennsylvania Democrats in 1964, not realizing that it would be a Johnson candidacy. What is more, Lawrence never dreamed the Democrats would split over the state's United States senatorial candidate.

Republican senator Hugh Scott had to stand for reelection in 1964, and as the Johnson administration progressed, Lawrence, along with many Pennsylvania Democrats, felt Johnson would help them elect a United States senator. At first, no one candidate surfaced. In early considerations, Lawrence had dismissed Supreme Court Justice Michael Musmanno's running. "Oh, my God, we'll never take him and I can get him out." Senator Clark also felt the party would reject Musmanno, who Clark, much to his regret later on, called contemptible.[27] At the same time, many Democrats felt Genevieve Blatt should try for the candidacy, since in '62 she received more votes than any local Democrat. Blatt, who had run with Raymond Shafer in 1963 for constitutional revision, felt too drained physically to even consider the race. Blatt recalled feeling in 1963 that her running would be out of the question because running two

227

Catholics, Kennedy and herself, would have meant sure victory for Senator Scott. But when Kennedy died, Blatt thought maybe she would have a chance, but never proposed herself to Lawrence. Blatt wanted George Leader to run, but he was unavailable. Then Lawrence told Blatt that Frank Smith and Albert Greenfield wanted to draft Michael Musmanno and Musmanno was anxious to run. Musmanno had told Lawrence he was unhappy on the Supreme Court and wanted to get back to the hustings. When Blatt heard that, she said to Lawrence, "Oh, he wouldn't do it; he would never resign." Lawrence replied, "Well he would resign when he was nominated." Blatt countered, "I don't believe he will resign even if nominated. He won't resign until he is elected. He won't be elected; he can't be elected. No lawyer can vote for him because he ran once before when he was on the court and that's against the canons of judicial ethics. . . . I don't want to be any part of nominating or certainly not of drafting a man on the Supreme Court to run for a non-judicial office." Lawrence thought Blatt was just being "lawyerly." Blatt finally said, "If nobody runs against him I'll have to. He cannot have a draft out of this party; no one like that can have a draft out of this party who has embarrassed us before. No, sir, no way."[28] At the time, Lawrence did not reply, and he never did tell Blatt directly not to run. Joe Barr told her Lawrence thought she should not run.[29] Blatt ran and the scene for a party split was set.

Early in January 1964, Lawrence told Matthew McCloskey, in Ireland at the time, of turmoil among Philadelphia Democrats, although Tate and Frank Smith were talking and meeting. In addition, Milton Shapp, Pennsylvania industralist, was carrying on an extensive campaign with literature and propaganda, "but, up to now, there is no evidence that he has picked up any potential leaders in the state." Lawrence suggested Blatt was not pressing her campaign "and might fall by the wayside." Further, Lawrence sensed an attitude around the state that the Democrats should not run a woman against Scott "because of his aggressiveness." Finally, "I do think Genevieve has more strength than anyone mentioned, but I am not pleased with the lack of enthusiasm."[30] Before the Democratic state policy committee met, Shapp, who could have easily run, dropped out after a discussion with his good friend Walter Jenkins. According to Jenkins, the White House saw Pennsylvania as a critical state for Johnson and wanted to avoid a three-way split there and would appreciate Shapp's dropping out, which he did.[31]

In the meantime, Lawrence and Frank Smith met in Philadelphia, where they agreed to endorse Musmanno. When the state policy committee met, Blatt received seventeen votes on the first ballot, including those of Lawrence, Dilworth, Clark, and Barr. Still, Lawrence had made his committment to Musmanno, and on the second ballot Musmanno garnered the necessary votes. Lawrence reported the committee's actions, saying, "We could not get any general agreement on Miss Blatt. The two primary reasons advanced were that the Democrats would lose the office in which she is now incumbent and that she would not have the vote-getting power in the industrial counties that Justice Musmanno would have."[32]

As it turned out, those suppositions were incorrect. Blatt won sixty-six out of sixty-seven counties, but the margin was narrow and the results contested by a contentious Musmanno. Blatt was ahead by about 3,500 votes, but while absentee ballots were being counted, Frank Smith claimed there were 3,000 votes for Musmanno in Philadelphia that he had not received because the lower line of the voting machine had not been counted. This claim was thrown out. Still Musmanno and Smith contested the election all the way to the Supreme Court of the United States, although Lawrence was satisfied Blatt had won. After the primary, Lawrence said, "I just tried to do everything I could to avert the Primary clash which the Party in Pennsylvania had just been through. Over the years I have always counseled against these Primary clashes, which I have always found disastrous to the Party."[33]

With the primary outcomes tied up in the Supreme Court, Blatt's nomination was delayed and her campaign crippled. Lawrence thought Blatt would win the court test and hoped for her election. "I honestly believe she has an excellent chance by reason of what looks like a Johnson landslide." However, the court case carried over to mid-October and Blatt lost much of her momentum. Despite Johnson's commendable showing in Pennsylvania, Blatt lost to Scott. Lawrence observed, "She was no match for Scott, particularly in the Jewish districts throughout the state, and she was cut badly by the ethnic groups. I am fearful she will get practically all the blame for insisting on running."[34] In this wistful, seemingly nonsupportive statement, the term "ethnic groups" really means the Italians, who were upset by comments made by Senator Clark, one of Blatt's strongest backers during the campaign. Moreover, Lawrence tries to lay to rest the claim, particularly by Clark, that since Lawrence thought neither candidate could win over Scott, "he had better keep his fences mended with Frank Smith" by selecting Musmanno.[35] Giesey, on the other hand, remembered that it was a sad time for Lawrence, because it brought him into conflict with Blatt, McCloskey, and "other liberal party friends." Also, Giesey claims Lawrence was convinced Leader or Blatt could have beaten Scott, while Musmanno was a question mark. Judge Conaboy recalls Lawrence saying both Blatt and Musmanno neglected his advice in not avoiding the fight they had, nor was Lawrence necessarily convinced Scott was a sure winner. Finally, Jim Tate felt a lot of people remembered Blatt was for Stevenson in '60 and this hurt her.[36] What is puzzling in all this is that Lawrence seemed not to act forcefully. It was as if Lawrence gave his suggestion to Blatt and Musmanno and then sat back and watched. The fact that Lawrence was off the scene in Washington had somewhat to do with it, and Lawrence was even more convinced that his opposition to primary fights was the correct policy, a factor that became important in the 1966 Pennsylvania gubernatorial candidate contest.

Early in the considerations for Pennsylvania Democrats' candidate for governor, Lawrence complained of the difficulties involved in selecting a candidate, because, to his way of thinking, all the aspirants were known only in their immediate areas. At the same time, Lawrence said, "We are trying to avoid a bitter primary fight such as we went through in 1964."[37] In order to solve his problem, Lawrence, McCloskey, and several other leaders met at Joe Barr's home with George Leader and asked the latter to be the candidate. Leader declined, because "I would not have felt comfortable at that point putting my future in their hands." Leader saw his refusal disappointed the party leaders, since "they certainly didn't want Shapp." Leader felt they had Shapp pegged a maverick, "which indeed he is."[38] Bradley believed Lawrence questioned the depth of Shapp's sincerity and dedication, whereas Moorhead suggested Lawrence suspected Shapp was not a team player and, although Lawrence admired Shapp's business expertise, clearly he did not see Shapp as a candidate.[39] In a White House memo, Lawrence stated: "I think it would be a mistake to send a telegram to Mr. Shapp, as he is just using the White House to promote his candidacy. He has been waving your letter in meetings throughout the State. He would only use any further reply for the same purposes."[40]

Shapp was aware of Lawrence's negative attitude toward his candidacy and told Lawrence he did not seek the endorsement of the state policy committee. Shapp did not think the committee represented the full Democratic party and called for open primaries. Lawrence was unimpressed. At the same time, Shapp wrote Lawrence complaining about the appointment of John Rice as Democratic state chairman, suggesting it was not a position for a retired man. Lawrence resented this, but Shapp did not care, since the theme of his primary campaign was the defeat of the Lawrence machine.[41]

Eventually, Robert Casey, from Lackawana County, was selected as the organization's candidate. Casey was never really accepted by the Lackawana County Democrats. Some felt he was too standoffish. But, he was the protégé of Edward Lynett, publisher of the *Scranton Times*, a good friend of Lawrence. And although Lawrence felt Casey's religion and youth militated against his being a good candidate, he went along with Lynett and accepted Casey.[42]

Shapp won the primary with little difficulty. He then went to Washington to talk with Lawrence, who pledged to support him in the '66 campaign. Lawrence worked hard for Shapp, but he had great difficulty putting together independent groups and party groups in the various counties. This was one of the factors that led to Shapp's defeat by Raymond Shafer.[43] The night before the election, Lawrence collapsed while urging Democrats to unite behind Shapp and defeat the Republicans. To the very end of his political career, Lawrence played the role of leader.

In 1963, Lawrence had told President Truman the party in Pennsylvania hit rock bottom with the defeat of Dilworth, but a special congressional election that year gave the Democrats "a rous-

231

ing victory which was very heartening." Fred Rooney was elected despite his Catholic background. Lawrence suggested this augured well for the '64 presidential campaign.[44] Even Milton Shapp admitted Lawrence was still the power in the Democratic party when he left the governor's office. "And his affirmation of a policy or appointment was it, and his negative response was also it."[45] During the early sixties, Lawrence saw the party finances drained—mostly, he felt, because of Chairman Otis Morse's tenure. "He installed a Univac machine in the State Headquarters at great expense, and it was of absolutely no use to the Party." As a result, Lawrence asked John Rice to take over as chairman at no salary. With Rice in control, Lawrence said, "we are moving to get our finances back in shape." So we see Lawrence exercising his leadership in Pennsylvania to the very close of his life. George Leader viewed Lawrence's leadership as more of a "presiding over than directing." Leader felt Lawrence was not "in command" on many occasions. Moreover, he suggested Lawrence was very slow in making decisions, while not taking strong initiatives. " . . . Basically he hoped that things would fall into place; many times they did for him." It was, said Leader, "a type leadership not to be criticized, and maybe it's the best type politics" for a strong personality.[46]

Loyal Democrat that he was, David Lawrence, despite his misgivings about Milton Shapp's fitness for the governorship of Pennsylvania, was hard on the campaign trail in 1966, at the age of seventy-seven. On Sunday, October 23, he spoke informally at the Tri-State United Jewish Appeal luncheon at the Penn-Sheraton in Pittsburgh. In commenting on his long political career, he indicated that he would continue on "until the man with the spade pats me on the cheek." Some there felt this suggests Lawrence's premonition of the end. After the luncheon, while speaking with Kaspar Monahan of the *Pittsburgh Press*, Lawrence stressed, "Don't retire; don't even think of it. Keep at your work and when your time comes, why not die in harness? I intend to do just that."[47]

It may well have been that if Lawrence had had some indications that something was amiss, he stuck by his conviction to work right up to the end. He did not confide in any of his friends about the little signs that others noticed, or, at least, it appears as though

232

those around him would not suggest that he slow down a bit. If they had it in mind, they certainly would not come forward until the campaign was complete. They knew their man too well.

In October 1966, a gentleman from the Y who used to help Lawrence told Frank Ambrose that after taking some sunlamp, Lawrence had keeled over while putting on his shoes and socks. He was a little faint and lay on a training table for awhile. Twenty minutes later, he got up and left.[48] Art Rooney remembered being out of town when Lawrence was stricken. A few days before Lawrence's collapse, Rooney called his son from New York. Jim Rooney told his father that he had driven Lawrence to a political appearance in Clairton. Jim said he didn't think Lawrence was too well. Rooney continued, "I said, 'Why?' He said, 'I just don't know. I noticed that he repeated himself, something that he rarely ever did before. I just don't know if he's as well as he was.'"[49] A few days later, Lawrence suffered a fatal heart attack.

It is difficult to say whether or not Lawrence did anything about these seeming inconsistencies in his physical condition. Apparently, they did not seem to Lawrence to call for a lessening of his active participation in the 1966 campaign. On November 4, Allegheny County Democrats held a big rally in the Syria Mosque in the Oakland section of Pittsburgh. Lawrence and his grandson David were joined at dinner in a downtown restaurant that night by several political colleagues. When Lawrence arrived at the mosque, he was, according to Huck Fenrich, carrying on business as usual. He was seated in a back room receiving colleagues and arranging his schedule for the following day.[50]

The rally at the mosque was different in the sense that the major leaders of the party were seated in the audience. The stage was not utilized at all. A podium was set in the center of the mosque at the foot of the stage. City and county party leaders were seated in the first two rows.

When Lawrence went into the hall, all was not in readiness, and he bided his time in usual fashion by resorting to his proverbial jokes. He said to City Councilman Pat Fagan, "Pat, I got an Irish story for you." He pulled a paper out of his pocket and started reading it, and Fagan laughed heartily. "The meeting was supposed

233

to be at 7:30 and it was then twenty minutes to eight. He said to me, 'Tell that damn Jim Knox to get this thing started, will you!' Then he [Lawrence] said to me, 'I got to go to the men's room, take me up, will you?' "[51] Shortly thereafter the meeting was in order and Lawrence was called to the podium to speak. True to expectations of the party faithful, Lawrence filled the great hall with a rousing political speech, calling Milton Shapp the greatest candidate for governor of Pennsylvania the Democrats had ever nominated. In the process of calling for party unity and a major victory at the polls, Lawrence, in his inimitable style, blistered the Republicans. And then he fell. James Helbert of the *Pittsburgh Press* reported: "I heard a crash. Looking toward Mr. Lawrence I saw him fall back across the front of the stage. . . . Fighting every inch of the way, Mr. Lawrence struggled to his feet and tried to resume the speech. . . . Then he fell again. He didn't get up this time, lying on his back gasping for breath."[52] Congressman Fenrich, who gave Lawrence artificial respiration, remembers a doctor giving instructions and a young girl giving mouth-to-mouth resuscitation. "We spent an awful night that night at the hospital . . . waiting, waiting, waiting. And then it carried on so long, you know."[53]

Dr. Thomas Piemme, of Presbyterian-University Hospital, stated, "Upon his arrival we could not find any pulse or heart action. Our medical team began resuscitation measures and successfully returned him to his normal blood pressure and normal electro-cardiogram readings within twenty-five minutes. He was also taking oxygen. The heart stopped for a second time for ten minutes and later for a period of five minutes."[54]

As Lawrence's family rushed to the hospital from various points around the state, President Johnson wired Gerald Lawrence: "Mrs. Johnson and I are praying for the Governor. Please let us know if there is anything we can do to help." Ironically, less than forty-eight hours earlier Lawrence had wired the Johnson family, "We are thinking and praying for the President."

David Leo Lawrence never regained consciousness. He was indeed in harness when he spoke his last words. Death came to Mr. Democrat on November 21, 1966, at 2:50 P.M.

234

Notes

1. Giesey, p. 39.
2. Lawrence (JFK), pp. 34–36.
3. Hughes, p. 2.
4. Williams, pp. 2–3.
5. Moorhead, p. 2.
6. Giesey, p. 21.
7. *New York Times*, March 8, 1963, p. 11.
8. Bradley, p. 13.
9. Sloan, p. 6; Blatt, p. 11; Lawrence to Eli Covak, December 3, 1963, PSA, Lawrence Papers.
10. Lawrence (JFK), pp. 36–38.
11. Humphrey, pp. 3, 4–5.
12. Knox, p. 11.
13. DeSapio, p. 9.
14. Dent, pp. 6–7.
15. Brown, p. 2.
16. Arvey, pp. 5–6.
17. Lawrence (JFK), pp. 46–47, 52–53, 99–100.
18. David Donahue, p. 5.
19. Lawrence (JFK), pp. 101–104.
20. *New York Times*, November 27, 1963, p. 1; Dent, p. 7; Bradley, p. 14; Rooney, p. 4; David Donahue, p. 5; Humphrey, pp. 3, 4–5.
21. Lawrence to Honorable John S. Rice, PSA, Lawrence Papers, General File 18.
22. Saxe, p. 13.
23. Lawrence (JFK), pp. 44–45.
24. Speech, May 26, 1962, Sloan Collection.
25. Ibid., PSA, Lawrence Papers, press release, October 19, 1962.
26. Lawrence to Matthew McCloskey, December 11, 1962, PSA, Lawrence Papers, General File 60.
27. Clark, pp. 13–15.
28. Blatt, pp. 13–14.
29. Barr, p. 6.
30. Lawrence to Matthew McCloskey, January 12, 1964.
31. *The Reminiscences of Milton Shapp*, (1974), p. 2, in the Oral History Collection of La Salle University, hereinafter Shapp.
32. Lawrence to Mr. and Mrs. Charles Hamilton, February 5, 1964, PSA, Lawrence Papers.
33. Ibid., Lawrence to Robert W. Valimont, May 14, 1964.
34. Ibid., Lawrence to John Robin, September 21, 1964.

35. Clark, p. 15.
36. Giesey, pp. 34–35; Conaboy, pp. 4–5; Tate, p. 18.
37. Lawrence to Ralph A. Dungan, 1966, PSA, Lawrence Papers.
38. Leader, pp. 13–14.
39. Bradley, p. 16; Moorhead, p. 3; Plesset, p. 10.
40. Memo for Lee C. White, February 4, 1966, PSA, Lawrence papers.
41. Shapp, p. 3.
42. Conaboy, p. 3; Saxe, p. 12.
43. Shapp, p. 5.
44. Lawrence to President Truman, August 21, 1963, PSA, Lawrence Papers.
45. Shapp, p. 5.
46. Leader, p. 17.
47. *Pittsburgh Press,* November 22, 1966, p. 1.
48. Ambrose, pp. 9, 14.
49. Rooney, p. 8.
50. Fenrich, pp. 8–9.
51. Ambrose, pp. 9, 14.
52. The *Pittsburgh Press,* November 5, 1966, p. 1.
53. Fenrich, pp. 8–9.
54. *Pittsburgh Post Gazette,* November 5, 1966, p. 1.

Select Bibliography

I. Books

Alderfer, Harold F. *American Local Government and Administration*. New York: Macmillan, 1956.

Banfield, Edward. *Big City Politics*. New York: Random House, 1966.

Burton, Hal, ed. *The City Fights Back*. New York: The Citadel Press, 1954.

Cooke, Edward F., and G. E. Janesik. *Guide to Pennsylvania Politics*. Holt Rinehart and Winston, 1960.

De Tocqueville, Alexis. *Democracy in America*. Edited by Richard D. Heffner. New York: New American Library, 1966.

Duverger, Maurice. *Political Parties*. New York: Science Editions, 1963.

Dye, Thomas R., and Brett W. Hawkins. *Politics in the Metropolis*. Columbus, Ohio: Charles E. Merrill, Inc., 1967.

Flynn, Edward. *You're the Boss*. New York: Whittlesey House, 1935.

Griffith, Ernest S. *City Government*, vols. 1 and 2. London: Oxford University Press, 1927.

Hinderaker, Ivan. *Party Politics*. New York: Henry Holt and Co., 1956.

Kent, Frank R. *The Great Game of Politics*. Garden City, New York: Doubleday, Page and Co., 1923.

Key, V. O. *Politics Parties, and Pressure Groups*. New York: Thomas Crowell Co., 1955.

Klein, Philip. *A Social Study of Pittsburgh*. New York: Columbia University Press, 1938.

Lipset, Seymor M. *Political Man*. New York: Doubleday, 1963.

Lorant, Stephen. *Pittsburgh: The Story of an American City*. Garden City, New York: Doubleday, 1964.

Lubell, Samuel. *Future of American Politics*. New York: Harper, 1952.

Lubove, Roy. *Twentieth Century Pittsburgh: Government, Business and Environmental Change*. New York: Random House, 1969.

Munro, William B. *Municipal Government and Administration*, vol. 1. New York: Macmillan, 1921.

Ostrogorski, I. M. *Democracy and the Party System in the United States*. New York, 1921.

Reichley, James. *The Art of Government*. New York: Fund of the Republic, Inc., 1959.

Salter, J. T. *Boss Rule*. New York: Whittlesey House, 1935.

Stave, Bruce M. *The New Deal and the Last Hurrah*. Pittsburgh, Pennsylvania: University of Pittsburgh Press, 1970.

Talbott, Allan R. *The Mayor's Game*. New York: Harper, 1967.

Van Devander, Charles. *The Big Bosses*. New York: Howell Soskin Publishers, 1944.

Williams, Oliver, and Charles R. Adrian. *Four Cities*. Philadelphia, Pennsylvania University Press, 1963.

Zink, Harold. *City Bosses in the United States*. Durham, North Carolina: Duke University Press, 1930.

II. Dissertations, Manuals, and Pamphlets

Gillis, William. *The Pittsburgh Manual*. Pittsburgh, Pennsylvania University of Pittsburgh Press, 1950.

Gow, Steele J. "Metro Politics in Pittsburgh." Unpublished Ph.D. dissertation, University of Pittsburgh, 1952.

Manual of Pennsylvania Local and State Government. Associated Institute of Government of Pennsylvania Universities, Philadelphia, Pennsylvania.

Manual of the New York Bureau of Municipal Research. New York, 1963.

Pamphlet of the League of Women Voters, Pittsburgh, 1966.

Shames, Sally O. "David Lawrence." Unpublished Ph.D. dissertation, Division of Social Sciences, University of Pittsburgh, 1958.

III. Newspapers

Pittsburgh Catholic.
Pittsburgh Post-Gazette.
Pittsburgh Press.
Pittsburgh Sun-Telegraph.
New York Times.

IV. Periodicals and Articles

Beachler, Edwin H. "How Pittsburgh Did the Job." Pittsburgh Press, December 13, 1953.

"Big Time Community Planning in Pittsburgh." *Commonweal* 47 (January 2, 1948).

"Boss Was Drafted." *Newsweek* 51 (March 17, 1958).

Brunner, Jerome S. "The Boss and the Vote." *Public Quarterly* (Spring 1946).

"City Politics: Free Style." *National Municipal Review* 38 (November 1949).

Coulter, Philip, and Gordon Glen. "Urbanization and Party Competition." *Western Political Quarterly* 21 (1960).

"Decline of Big City Bosses." *U.S. News and World Report* 25 (September 3, 1948).

"Democrat's Decisive Dozen," *Time* 67 (June 18, 1956).

Evans, Burtt and Botsford. "Pennsylvania After the New Deal." *New Republic*, May 6, 1940.

Flinn, Thomas A., and Frederick M. Wirt. "Local Party Leaders: Groups of Like Minded Men," *Midwest Journal of Political Sciences* (February 1965).

Frost, Richard. "Stability and Change in Local Party Politics." *Midwest Journal of Political Science* 25 (Spring-Winter 1961).

Fuller, H. "Men to Watch at the Democratic Convention." *Harper's*, August 1964.

Gilbert, Charles E. "National Political Alignments and the Politics of the Large Cities." *Political Science Quarterly* 79 (1964).

Goldstein, Sidney, and Kurt Mayer. "Population Decline and the Social and Demographic Structure of an American City." *American Sociological Review* 29 (1964).

Greene, L. S., ed. "City Bosses and Political Machines: Symposium." *Annual American Academy* 353 (May 1964).

Greer, S., and D. W. Minal. "Political Side of Urban Development and Redevelopment." *American City Magazine* 352 (March 1964).

Grove, John T. "Pittsburgh's Renaissance." *U.S.A. Tomorrow,* October 1954.

Hawkins, Frank. "Lawrence of Pittsburgh: Boss of the Mellon Patch." *Harper's,* August 1965.

"Help Plant Your Community." *American City* 60 (April 1951).

Herbert, Jacob, and Michael Lipsky. "Outputs, Structures and Power: An Assessment of Changes in the Study of State and Local Politics." *Journal of Politics* 30 (1968).

Hicks, Granville. "How We Live Now in America: Some Unpropheticesized Fruits of the Machine." *Commentary,* December 1953.

Hine, Al. "Pittsburgh." *Holiday* magazine, October 1949.

Hirsch, W. A. "Administrative and Fiscal Consideration in Urban Development." *Annual American Academy* 352 (May 1964).

"Inexorable Trend." *Newsweek* 55 (May 2, 1960).

Knaft, J. "Pennsylvania's New Breed of Politicians." *Harper's*, October 1958.

Kubly, Herbert. "Pittsburgh." *Holiday* magazine, March 1959.

Lawrence, David Leo. "Balancing Good Politics and Good Administration." Excerpts from a paper presented at the meeting of the Pittsburgh meeting of the ASPA, reprinted in *Public Administration Review* (Spring 1954).

Lineberry, Robert, and Edmund P. Fowler. "Reformation and Public Policies in American Cities." *American Political Science Review* 3 (September 1967).

Lowe, J. R. "Rebuilding Cities and Politics." *The Nation* 186 (February 8, 1959).

Lowe, Theodore J. "Machine Politics—Old and New." *Public Interest* 9 (Fall 1967).

"Mighty Boss." *Time* 70 (November 4, 1957).

Miller, Guy V. "Pennsylvania's Scrambled Politics." *The Nation*, May 14, 1938.

Miller, T. "Pittsburgh Rushes Off in All Directions." *Nation*, 176 (April 4, 1953).

Moscow, Warren. "Exit the Boss: Enter the Leader." *New York Times Magazine*, June 22, 1947.

"New Faces." *New Republic*, November 3, 1959.

"New Fronts." *Life* magazine, July 13, 1953.

"New Strength in City Hall." *Fortune*, November 1957.

"Old Class." *Time*, December 2, 1966.

Patterson, Samuel. "Characteristics of Party Leaders." *Western Political Quarterly* 16 (1963).

Peel, Roy V. "New Machines for Old." *Nation*, September 5, 1953.

Phillips, Cabell. "Exit the Boss: Enter the Leader." *New York Times Magazine*, April 15, 1956.

"Pittsburgh Rebuilds." *Fortune*, June 1952.

"Pittsburgh Rebuilds from the Bottom Up." *Business Week*, June 21, 1952.

"Pittsburgh's Mayor Acclaims Research and Citizen Aid." *American City*, October 1949.

"Pittsburgh Rebuilds." *Fortune*, June 1952.

"Problems of Metropolitan Leadership." *Western Journal of Political Science* (February 1961).

Putnam, Robert D. "Political Attitudes and the Local Community." *American Political Science Review* 60 (1966).

Reese, Leslie, J. "Debits and Credits." *American City*, October 1953.

Rose, Irwin. "Big City Machines and Liberal Voters." *Commentary*, October 1950.

"Round Two in Pittsburgh's Redevelopment." *Business Week*, April 2, 1955.

Salter, J. T. "American Government and Politics." *American Political Science Review* (February 1940).

———. "Personal Attention in Politics." *American Political Science Review* (February 1940).

Schriftgiesser, K. L. "The Pittsburgh Story." *Atlantic*, May 1951.

Segel, Roberta, and Paul Friesma. "Urban Community Leaders' Knowledge of Public Opinion." *Western Political Quarterly* (December 1965).

Selby, Early and Ann. "The Democrats' Tough Old Pro." *Saturday Evening Post*, March 1959.

Shaffer, S. "So Pennsylvania Goes." *Newsweek* 52 (October 20, 1959).

"Some November Election Results." *American City* 60 (December 1945).

Sourauf, Frank. "Patronage and Party." *Midwest Journal of Political Science* 3 (1959).

———. "The Silent Revolution in Patronage." *Public Administration Review* 20 (1960).

Stein, Rose M. "The Pennsylvania Primary." *New Republic*, June 1, 1938.

Steinberg, Alfred. "Pittsburgh, a New City." *National Municipal Review* (March 1955).

"The Remodeling of Pittsburgh." *Business Week*, March 12, 1949.

"Strike That Didn't End." *Business Week*, October 23, 1954.

"The Great Steel Strike Begins." *Life* magazine, February 4, 1946.

"We Don't Want to Wait for Bombs to Clear Our City Slums." *American City* (April 1951).

"Welding Job." *Time*, August 25, 1947.

White, William S. "Consensus American—a Portrait." *New York Times Magazine*, November 25, 1956.

Williams, Richard L. "Politician Without a Future." *Life* magazine, May 1, 1950.

Wilson, James Q. "The Economy of Patronage." *Journal of Political Economy* (August 1961).

V. Unpublished Materials

Knox, John. Public Statement on the occasion of Lawrence's death, November 23, 1966.

Lawrence, David Leo. Public speeches delivered from 1945 until 1966. (Taken from public and private collections.)

Letter of Conveyance from the Democratic National Committee to the Lawrence Family, March 1966.

Moorhead, Congressman William S. "David Leo Lawrence—Creative Politician." Speech delivered in The House of Representatives, February 9, 1967.

Resolution of the Democratic National Committee, March 14, 1967.

VI. Other Sources

Files of the Pittsburgh Democratic Party, Democratic Party Headquarters, Pittsburgh, Pennsylvania.

Interviews with personal friends and associates of David Leo Lawrence.

Lawrence, David Leo. Papers on record with the Museum Commission of Harrisburg, Harrisburg, Pennsylvania.

———. Personal papers obtained from Lawrence family members.

S0-AYO-592

COUNTRY  PROFILES

INDIA

BY EMILY ROSE OACHS

BLASTOFF!
DISCOVERY

BELLWETHER MEDIA • MINNEAPOLIS, MN

Blastoff! Discovery launches a new mission: reading to learn. Filled with facts and features, each book offers you an exciting new world to explore!

This edition first published in 2018 by Bellwether Media, Inc.

Library of Congress Cataloging-in-Publication Data

Names: Oachs, Emily Rose, author.
Title: India / by Emily Rose Oachs.
Description: Minneapolis, MN : Bellwether Media, Inc., 2018.
  | Series: Blastoff! Discovery: Country Profiles | Includes
  bibliographical references and index. | Audience: Grades
  3-8. | Audience: Ages 7-13.
Identifiers: LCCN 2016055086 (print)|LCCN 2016057126
  (ebook) | ISBN 9781626176812 (hardcover : alkaline
  paper) | ISBN 9781681034119 (ebook)
Subjects: LCSH: India–Juvenile literature.
Classification: LCC DS407 .O23 2018 (print) | LCC DS407
  (ebook) | DDC 954–dc23
LC record available at https://lccn.loc.gov/20160550867

Editor: Christina Leaf   Designer: Brittany McIntosh

Printed in the United States of America, North Mankato, MN.

TABLE OF CONTENTS

THE TAJ MAHAL

A pair of **tourists** walks toward a large gateway in the early morning light. They pass through a long, arched passageway. At first, all they can see is a low mist before them. But soon, the beautiful white dome of the Taj Mahal appears above the mist. **Minarets** reach toward the sky.

4

MINARET

OTHER TOP SITES

GATEWAY OF INDIA

GOLDEN TEMPLE

QUTUB MINAR

RED FORT

Slowly, the rising sun clears the mist. The marble building's archways and magnificent details become visible. A long, narrow pool stretches between the tourists and the Taj Mahal. Its still waters reflect the majestic **landmark**. This is India!

5

LOCATION

CHINA

PAKISTAN

NEW DELHI

NEPAL

INDIA

KOLKATA

HYDERABAD

MUMBAI

ARABIAN SEA

BAY OF BENGAL

BENGALURU

CHENNAI

N
W E
S

SRI LANKA

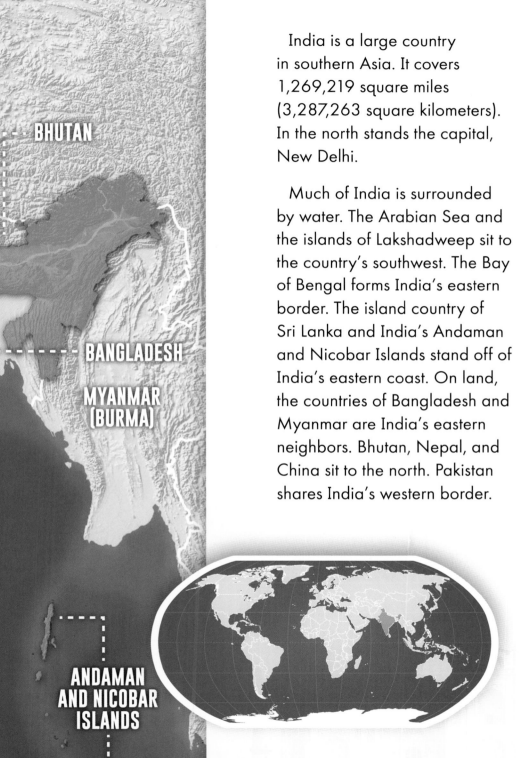

BHUTAN

BANGLADESH

MYANMAR
(BURMA)

ANDAMAN
AND NICOBAR
ISLANDS

India is a large country in southern Asia. It covers 1,269,219 square miles (3,287,263 square kilometers). In the north stands the capital, New Delhi.

Much of India is surrounded by water. The Arabian Sea and the islands of Lakshadweep sit to the country's southwest. The Bay of Bengal forms India's eastern border. The island country of Sri Lanka and India's Andaman and Nicobar Islands stand off of India's eastern coast. On land, the countries of Bangladesh and Myanmar are India's eastern neighbors. Bhutan, Nepal, and China sit to the north. Pakistan shares India's western border.

7

LANDSCAPE AND CLIMATE

The towering Himalayas follow India's northern border. The Ganges River starts high in these mountains. It then flows southeast across low **plains**. The Vindhyas and other mountains and hills separate the plains from the southern Deccan

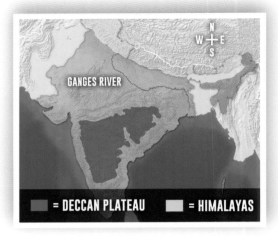

GANGES RIVER

= DECCAN PLATEAU   = HIMALAYAS

Plateau. Along the edges of the plateau are the Ghats Mountains. They follow India's eastern and western coasts. In northwestern India, sand dunes cross the Thar Desert's dry landscape.

GANGES RIVER
RISHIKESH, UTTARAKHAND

8

HIMALAYAS
JAMMU AND KASHMIR

NEW DELHI
Average monthly highs and lows

JANUARY
HIGH: 68 °F (20 °C)
LOW: 46 °F (8 °C)

APRIL
HIGH: 99 °F (37 °C)
LOW: 70 °F (21 °C)

JULY
HIGH: 95 °F (35 °C)
LOW: 81 °F (27 °C)

OCTOBER
HIGH: 91 °F (33 °C)
LOW: 66 °F (19 °C)

°F = degrees Fahrenheit
°C = degrees Celsius

Three main seasons exist in India. **Monsoons** bring heavy rains from late June to September. The cool, dry season lasts from October to February. Between March and early June is the hot season.

9

India's national animal is the powerful Bengal tiger. This predator hunts buffalo, antelope, and other animals in India's forests. Woodlands are often home to peafowl, the national bird. The males, called peacocks, impress females with their bright, fanned tails.

Crocodiles hide in India's rivers, while Indian pythons slither through **marshes**. In the northeast, small groups of Indian rhinoceroses live in grasslands and swamps. Asian elephants march through the dense **tropical** forests of the Ghats. Climbing through the Ghats' treetops are monkeys, such as lion-tailed macaques and Nilgiri langurs.

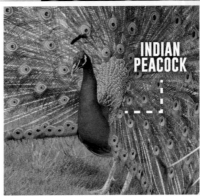

INDIAN PEACOCK

INDIAN PYTHON

ASIAN LIONS

Not all lions live in Africa! About 500 wild Asiatic lions live in India's northwestern Gir National Park. They are smaller in size and have thinner manes than their African cousins.

ASIAN ELEPHANT

10

BENGAL TIGER

BENGAL TIGER

Life Span: 11 years
Red List Status: endangered

Bengal tiger range = ▪

| LEAST CONCERN | NEAR THREATENED | VULNERABLE | ENDANGERED | CRITICALLY ENDANGERED | EXTINCT IN THE WILD | EXTINCT |

11

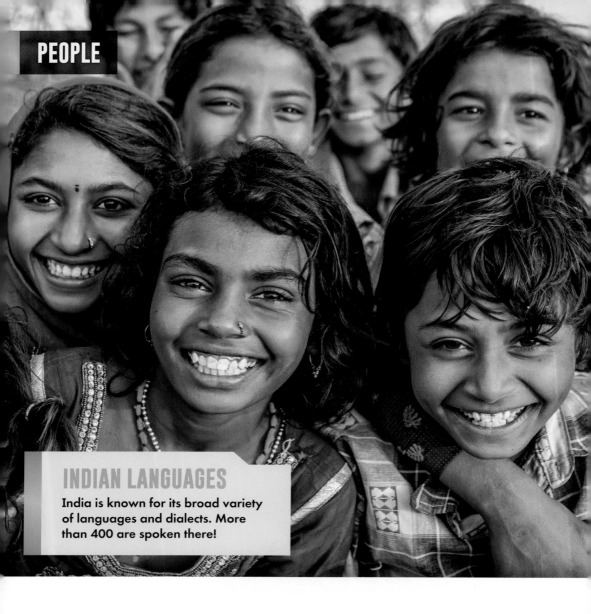

PEOPLE

INDIAN LANGUAGES
India is known for its broad variety of languages and dialects. More than 400 are spoken there!

India has the second-largest population in the world, with nearly 1.3 billion people. Two main groups make up India's population, the Indo-Aryans and Dravidians. Many small tribes also live there. India's most common language is Hindi. Many Indians also speak a local language or **dialect**, such as Bengali or Marathi. English is often used in universities and for the government's official business.

12

The Hindu religion was born in India. It is the country's most popular religion. About four of every five Indians practice it. Other Indians may be Muslim, Christian, or **Sikh**.

FAMOUS FACE
Name: Priyanka Chopra
Birthday: July 18, 1982
Hometown: Jamshedpur, India
Famous for: Winner of Miss World 2000, pop singer, star of many Bollywood movies, and a star in American television

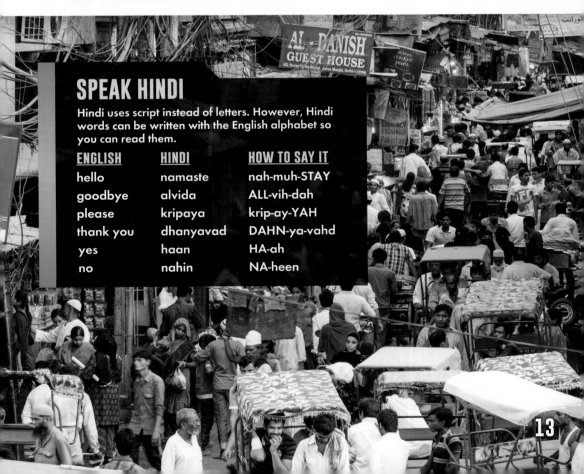

SPEAK HINDI
Hindi uses script instead of letters. However, Hindi words can be written with the English alphabet so you can read them.

ENGLISH	HINDI	HOW TO SAY IT
hello	namaste	nah-muh-STAY
goodbye	alvida	ALL-vih-dah
please	kripaya	krip-ay-YAH
thank you	dhanyavad	DAHN-ya-vahd
yes	haan	HA-ah
no	nahin	NA-heen

COMMUNITIES

About two out of three Indians call **rural** villages home. Their small houses are usually built of mud, brick, or concrete. Major cities, such as New Delhi and Mumbai, are crowded. Wealthier Indians may have houses or apartments, while poorer Indians often live in **slums**.

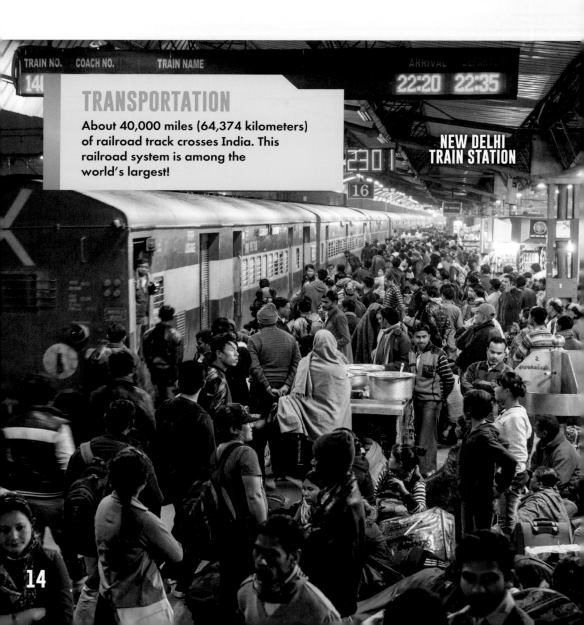

TRANSPORTATION

About 40,000 miles (64,374 kilometers) of railroad track crosses India. This railroad system is among the world's largest!

NEW DELHI TRAIN STATION

14

Family is a very important part of Indian life. In cities, **nuclear families** are becoming common living situations. Still, multiple generations of Indians may share a home. After getting married, a bride often moves in with her husband and his relatives.

15

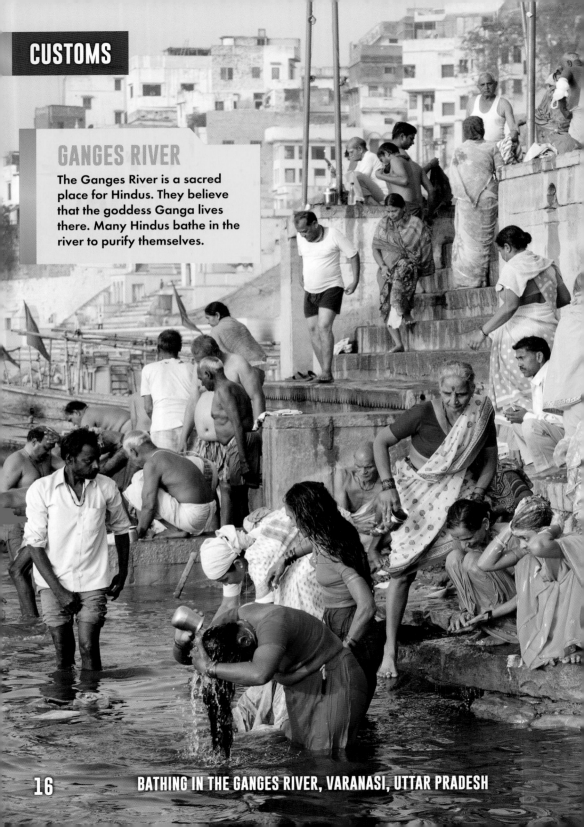

CUSTOMS

GANGES RIVER

The Ganges River is a sacred place for Hindus. They believe that the goddess Ganga lives there. Many Hindus bathe in the river to purify themselves.

16   BATHING IN THE GANGES RIVER, VARANASI, UTTAR PRADESH

For thousands of years, Indian society has been strictly divided into **castes**. These castes determine a person's social rank and career. The system still exists today, but has lost some influence. Indians are now more likely to mix with people from other castes. People are also working to end the system. Laws prevent **discrimination** against castes.

Often, Indian parents plan marriages for their children. Hindu wedding celebrations can last for several days. Everyone dresses in bright colors and bold jewelry. Brides wrap themselves in long cloths called *saris*. Grooms wear buttoned jackets called *sherwanis* for the celebration.

HINDU WEDDING CELEBRATION

SCHOOL AND WORK

Education is very important to Indians. Children must attend school from ages 6 to 14. Public schools offer free education to these students. Some students then complete four years of secondary school and enter university.

18

About half of India's people work in farming. They raise cattle and tend to crops of rice, cotton, and chickpeas. Many others work in **service jobs**. Some Indians mine iron ore, coal, gems, and other **natural resources** from the earth. The country then **exports** some of these to other countries. Clothes, jewelry, and leather are other top exports.

HARVESTING TEA LEAVES

BOLLYWOOD

India has a booming film industry called Bollywood. More than one thousand movies come out of Bollywood each year. These films are famous for their songs, dancing, and bright colors!

19

PLAY

CRICKET

Indians are passionate about cricket, field hockey, and soccer. These sports were brought to India by the British. Each draws many millions of fans. People love to cheer on their favorite players from the stands or while watching on television.

FIELD HOCKEY

Over the years, India's field hockey team has seen great Olympic success. It won six gold medals in a row and two more in later years!

20

Traditional sports are also popular in India. A game called *kabaddi* features elements of wrestling, rugby, and tag. In *Gilli Danda*, players use sticks to play a game similar to cricket. In their free time, Indians may also gather with friends to play chess or see movies.

KABADDI

MANDALA

Mandalas are circular designs of repeating shapes. They are important in Hinduism. They have many uses, including helping people to meditate.

What You Need:
- white paper
- drawing compass
- ruler
- pencil
- colored pencils or markers

Instructions:
1. Use the compass to draw a few circles of different sizes in the center of a piece of paper. Make sure each circle has the same center point.

2. Use the ruler to draw a "+" through the center point. Then draw an "X" through the center point. This should divide each circle into eight equal pieces, like a pie.

3. Draw a design in one of the "pie pieces." Repeat that same pattern in the other similar pieces.

4. Continue to do this until all of the circles have been filled in. The result should be a repeating design.

5. Use a black marker to trace over your pencil lines. Then, color in the designs on your mandala!

21

FOOD

RELIGION AND DIET
Many Indians rarely eat meat. This may depend on their religion. The Hindu religion forbids its followers from eating beef, and Muslims do not eat pork.

In cities, families often dine together. Traditionally, Indians eat with their right hands. Sometimes they may use banana leaves instead of utensils to eat.

22

Rice is a **staple** food in most of India. Popular rice dishes include *biryani*, which is rice mixed with meat and vegetables, and steamed rice cakes called *idlis*. Indians often serve rice with vegetables or fish in spicy sauces called curries. Northern Indians may eat a dinner of *chapati* bread with *dal*, a porridge made of lentils, beans, or peas. Throughout India, yogurts and fresh fruits like guavas and mangos are favorite foods.

BIRYANI

IDLIS

CURRY

KHEER (RICE PUDDING) RECIPE

Ingredients:
2 cups milk
2 cups coconut milk
3 tablespoons granulated sugar
1/2 cup Basmati rice
1/4 cup raisins
1/4 teaspoon ground cardamom
1/4 cup sliced almonds

Steps:

1. Combine the milk, coconut milk, and sugar in a saucepan. With an adult present, bring the mixture to a boil.

2. Once boiling, add the Basmati rice.

3. Lower the heat until the liquid is simmering. Cook for about 20 minutes, uncovered. The rice should be soft, and the liquid should have thickened.

4. Add the raisins and cardamom. Stir until well mixed. Continue to cook for about 3-5 minutes. Serve in a bowl and enjoy!

23

CELEBRATIONS

Indians observe Republic Day on January 26 each year. Huge parades with talented performers honor the country's formation. Independence Day falls on August 15. It brings flag ceremonies, political speeches, and kite flying. On October 2, Indians honor the life of Mahatma Gandhi with the celebration *Gandhi Jayanti*. They sing, pray, and decorate statues of the political leader.

With the fall comes *Diwali*, the Festival of Lights. People decorate with thousands of lights and lamps to honor Lakshmi, the Hindu goddess of wealth. Regardless of religion, Indians come together to celebrate this festival!

REPUBLIC DAY

24

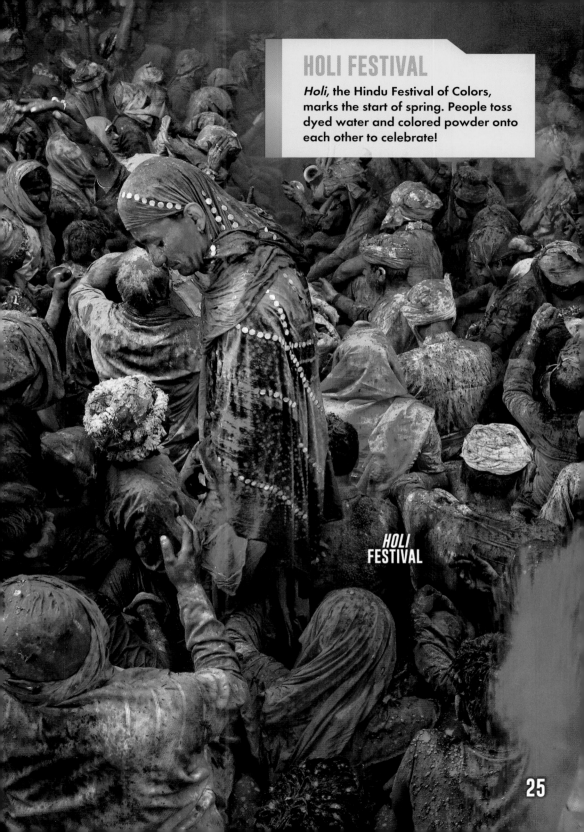

HOLI FESTIVAL

Holi, the Hindu Festival of Colors, marks the start of spring. People toss dyed water and colored powder onto each other to celebrate!

HOLI FESTIVAL

25

TIMELINE

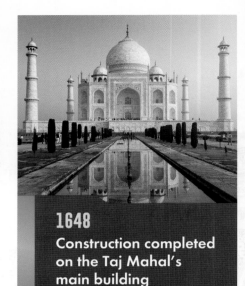

320 CE
Start of the Gupta dynasty, a prosperous time for India

1648
Construction completed on the Taj Mahal's main building

324 BCE
Mauryan Empire unites all of India for first time

AROUND 2500 BCE
Indus Valley civilization thrives in western India

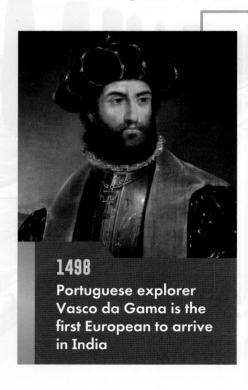

1498
Portuguese explorer Vasco da Gama is the first European to arrive in India

26

1950
Republic of India established

1920
Mahatma Gandhi becomes a leader in India's independence movement

1858
Britain begins direct rule over India

1947
India wins independence from Britain and separates from Pakistan

2007
Pratibha Patil elected as India's first female president

27

INDIA FACTS

Official Name: Republic of India

Flag of India: Three horizontal bands of color stretch across India's flag. On top, the orange stripe stands for courage and sacrifice. On the bottom is a green band. It represents faith. The white stripe in the middle is a symbol for purity. A blue wheel stands in the middle of the white band. It represents the cycle of life. India adopted the flag in 1947.

Area: 1,269,219 square miles (3,287,263 square kilometers)

Capital City: New Delhi

Important Cities: Mumbai, Chennai, Bengaluru, Hyderabad, Kolkata

Population: 1,266,883,598 (July 2016)

WHERE PEOPLE LIVE

CITY 32.7%

COUNTRYSIDE 67.3%

28

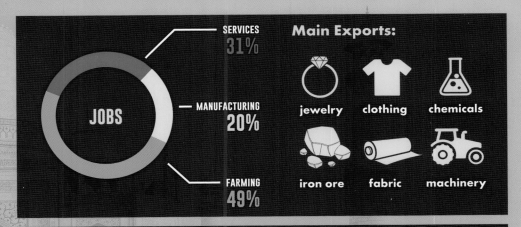

JOBS

SERVICES
31%

MANUFACTURING
20%

FARMING
49%

Main Exports:

jewelry clothing chemicals

iron ore fabric machinery

National Holiday:
Republic Day (January 26)

Main Languages:
Hindi, English

Form of Government:
federal parliamentary republic

Title for Country Leader:
president

RELIGION

OTHER
3.7%

CHRISTIAN
2.3%

MUSLIM
14.2%

HINDU
79.8%

Unit of Money:
Rupee; one hundred *paise* are in one rupee.

29

GLOSSARY

castes—social groups that divide Indians; people are born into their castes.

dialect—a local way of speaking a particular language

discrimination—the treatment of people in an unequal or unfair manner

exports—sells to a different country

landmark—an important structure or place

marshes—wetlands that are filled with grasses

minarets—tall towers used to call Muslims to prayer

monsoons—winds that shift direction each season; monsoons bring heavy rain.

natural resources—materials in the earth that are taken out and used to make products or fuel

nuclear families—families that include only the parents and children

plains—large areas of flat land

plateau—an area of flat, raised land

rural—related to the countryside

service jobs—jobs that perform tasks for people or businesses

Sikh—a follower of a religion that began in India and believes in one God

slums—parts of cities that are crowded and have poor housing

staple—a widely used food or other item

tourists—people who travel to visit another place

traditional—related to customs, ideas, or beliefs handed down from one generation to the next

tropical—part of the tropics; the tropics is a hot, rainy region near the equator.

TO LEARN MORE

AT THE LIBRARY
Hoobler, Dorothy and Thomas. *Where Is the Taj Mahal?* New York, N.Y.: Grosset & Dunlap, 2017.

Lee, Michelle. *Holi*. Minneapolis, Minn.: Scobre Press, 2016.

Sen Gupta, Subhadra. *A Children's History of India*. New Delhi, India: Rupa Publications, 2015.

ON THE WEB
Learning more about India is as easy as 1, 2, 3.

1. Go to www.factsurfer.com.

2. Enter "India" into the search box.

3. Click the "Surf" button and you will see a list of related web sites.

With factsurfer.com, finding more information is just a click away.

31

INDEX

activities, 20, 21
Bollywood, 13, 19
capital (see New Delhi)
castes, 17
celebrations, 17, 24-25
Chopra, Priyanka, 13
climate, 9
communities, 14-15
customs, 15, 16-17, 22
Diwali, 24
education, 18
fast facts, 28-29
food, 22-23
Gandhi Jayanti, 24
Gandhi, Mahatma, 24
Ganges River, 8, 16
Holi, 25
housing, 14, 15
Independence Day, 24
landmarks, 4, 5
landscape, 8-9, 10
language, 12, 13
location, 6-7

mandala (activity), 21
New Delhi, 6, 7, 9, 14
people, 12-13
recipe, 23
religion, 13, 16, 17, 21, 22, 24, 25
Republic Day, 24
size, 7
sports, 20, 21
Taj Mahal, 4-5
timeline, 26-27
transportation, 14
wildlife, 10-11
work, 19